Stage Fright

Martin Puchner

Stage Fright: *Modernism, Anti-Theatricality, and Drama*

The Johns Hopkins University Press

BALTIMORE

© 2002 The Johns Hopkins University Press
All rights reserved. Published 2002
Printed in the United States of America
on acid-free paper

Johns Hopkins Paperback edition, 2011
9 8 7 6 5 4 3 2 1

The Johns Hopkins University Press
2715 North Charles Street
Baltimore, Maryland 21218-4363
www.press.jhu.edu

*The Library of Congress has catalogued the hardcover edition
of this book as follows:*
Puchner, Martin, 1969–
Stage fright : modernism, anti-theatricality, and drama /
Martin Puchner.
    p.   cm.
Includes bibliographical references and index.
ISBN 0-8018-6855-6 (alk. paper)
1. Drama — 20th century — History and criticism.   2. Drama — 19th
century — History and criticism.   3. Modernism (Literature)
I. Title.
PN1851 .P83   2002
809.2′9112′0904 — dc21

2001006622

A catalog record for this book is available from the British Library.

ISBN 13: 978-1-4214-0399-1
ISBN 10: 1-4214-0399-4

For my mother,
my brothers,
and in memory
of my father

Contents

Acknowledgments

My first thanks go to those who advised this project in its dissertation phase: James Engell, Barbara Johnson, and Judith Ryan. Particularly generous in helping me to turn the dissertation into a manuscript were David Damrosch, James Engell, Barbara Johnson, Martin Meisel, and Joseph Roach, as well as Alan Ackerman, Ivan Asher, Ursula Heise, Jean Howard, Noah Heringman, Klaus Mladek, Larson Powell, and Matthew Smith. And I am much indebted to Barbara Johnson and Joseph Roach for their assistance in turning the manuscript into a book.

I would also like to thank those colleagues who have created an intellectual community at Columbia and Barnard in which work on drama and theater can thrive: Arnold Aronson, Patricia Denison, Helene Foley, Steve Friedman, Shawn Marie Garrett, David Kastan, Denny Partridge, Julie Stone Peters, Austin Quigley, James Shapiro, Amy Tompetter, and the members of the theater colloquium. I am also indebted to all my students, in particular those who helped me directly with my manuscript: Jeannie Im, David Kurnick, Matt Laufer, Sun-Young Park, Matt Rebhorn, Akiko Takeuchi, and the students in my seminar on modernism and theatricality. A separate round of thanks goes to my friends Nicholas Dames, Amy King, Sascha Lehnartz, Caroline Levine, Jon McKenzie, Dan Sherer, Henry Turner, and Rebecca L. Walkowitz.

I would like to thank former Johns Hopkins University Press humanities editor Maura Burnett for being an ideal editor and Joanne Allen for her fabulous copyediting.

My brothers, Stephan and Elias, were unwavering in their interest and support, and my mother, Annelore, was instrumental to this project in founding and directing a diegetic theater, the shadow theater Imago.

I don't know how to thank Amanda Claybaugh for thinking and reading through this project innumerable times, commenting on its broadest theoretical conception and its smallest details. She is present in every argument and in every word of this book.

A portion of chapter 1 appeared in *Criticism* 32 (1999): 25–39 as "Polyphonous Gestures: Wagnerian Modernism from Mallarmé to Stravinsky," and I gratefully acknowledge permission to use it here.

Stage Fright

Introduction

The Invention of Theatricality

Alfred Hitchcock's *Stage Fright* (1950) is a murder mystery set in the demi-monde of the theater. Marlene Dietrich plays a diva whose mourning for her murdered husband is so obviously theatrical that she immediately becomes the film's primary suspect. She is trailed by a young acting student, who sets up a trap to reveal her guilt. Eagerly awaiting the diva's exposure, the audience walks into another kind of trap, one baited by the neat contrast between the immoral actress, whom we cannot trust because acting has become her second nature, and the novice, whom we can trust because of her inexperience on the stage. The murderer, however, is not the diva but a psychopathic man who has killed before. It turns out that the stage fright to which Hitchcock's film refers is not the actor's fear of the audience but the audience's fear of the actor.[1]

This fear or suspicion, which Hitchcock evokes in order to expose it to our critical appraisal, is part of a seemingly ineradicable and moralizing anti-theatricalism, what Jonas Barish has called the "antitheatrical prejudice." This prejudice is diverse in its philosophical, religious, and moral underpinnings, if not in its conclusions, for it keeps coming back to a limited number of obsessions: the immorality of public display, of arousing the audience, and, most importantly, of those who professionally practice the art of deception.[2] And so we lovers of the theater might be tempted to regard all forms of anti-theatricalism as symptoms of a prejudice from which culture must be cured in order for the theater to thrive. The impulse to protect the theater against all anti-theatrical enemies has its polemical merits, and the effectiveness of Hitchcock's bait demonstrates the continued necessity of such protection. But at the same time the defensive attitude that is the result of such protectiveness also has its price: the attempt to undo or exorcise anti-theatricalism obscures the fact that a suspicion of the theater plays a constitutive role in the period of modernism, especially in modernist theater and drama.[3] Instead of simply discrediting the modernist critique of the theater as unfounded prejudice, blindness, or ideology, we must therefore ask why it is that a substantial tradition within modernism would find it necessary to define itself against the theater.

The best way to characterize this constitutive anti-theatrical dynamic within modernism is as a form of resistance. One does not need to turn to Freud in order to understand how much the act of resistance remains determined by that which is being resisted. The negation and rejection inherent in the term *anti-theatricalism* is therefore not to be understood as a doing away with the theater, but as a process that is dependent on that which it negates and to which it therefore remains calibrated. Even the most adamant forms of modernist anti-theatricalism feed off the theater and keep it close at hand. The resistance registered in the prefix *anti* thus does not describe a place outside the horizon of the theater, but a variety of attitudes through which the theater is being kept at arm's length and, in the process of resistance, utterly transformed.

By analyzing an anti-theatrical impulse within the period of modernism, I do not wish to come up with one more monolithic theory of modernism. As Richard Scheppard has argued recently, such attempts have failed ever since the term *modernism* was first used.[4] At the same time, I do not content myself with announcing an undifferentiated plurality of modernisms, a stance that is not an argument about modernism but only the refusal to make one.[5] Navigating between a monolithic modernism and a happy plurality of modernisms, I argue that there exists a tradition within modernism that can be described in terms of its various forms of resisting the theater, but I readily acknowledge that there are modernisms that do not fall into the category of anti-theatricalism. In fact I argue that the modernist anti-theatricalism finds its counterpart in a second tradition, which I call (pro)*theatricalism*. The difference between anti-theatricalism and (pro)theatricalism is not so much a stable dichotomy but rather a tool for analyzing a variety of positions and phenomena that will turn out to be variously intertwined and interconnected.

In order to fathom the features of the resistance to the theater within the period of modernism, one may turn to those theorists who explicitly define the values of modernism through an attack on the theater: Friedrich Nietzsche, Walter Benjamin, and Michael Fried. In 1888 Nietzsche claimed that the theater was incapable of achieving organic coherence and must therefore be kept from exerting its deplorable influence over the other arts: "Theatrocracy [*Theatrokratie*]—, the craziness of believing in the primacy of the theater, in the right of the theater to rule over the arts, to rule over art."[6] Nietzsche here takes the theater to be a force that imposes its "rule" over the other arts, leading to a "theatrocracy," a form of theatrical government. According to Nietzsche, this theatrocracy is particularly evident in

Wagner, who subjects every art, even music, to the primacy of theatrical representation and in particular of actors; the result is a music that has acquired attributes of the theater and of acting, what Nietzsche polemically calls scenic or gestural music. If one is surprised to find the author of *The Birth of Tragedy* (1871) denouncing the theater with such vehemence, it may be helpful to remember that Nietzsche's analysis of Greek tragedy contained the impossible projection of a theater without script, without an audience, and, most importantly, without individual and individualized actors. We can begin to recognize here that behind Nietzsche's derogatory use of the term *theater* is a specific objection to actors and their gestures.

Nietzsche's anti-theatrical position is echoed, sometimes verbatim, by Michael Fried, who likewise considers the theater, or theatricality, to be the enemy of art *tout court*.[7] Like Nietzsche's, Fried's dismissive understanding of the theater concerns primarily the influence of the theater on the other arts, in his case not on music but on painting and sculpture. And again we find a particular critique of the actor motivating this anti-theatrical stance. In Fried's often metaphorical formulations, "theatrical" paintings or sculptures are described as if they were actors; these sculptures are "aware" of the audience and thus lose their self-sufficient unity and integrity, in the process of which they start to resemble vain human actors pandering to the audience. Indeed, Fried ascribes to such theatrical works an "anthropomorphic" quality leading to a form of personalized "naturalism."[8] The suspicion of the live actor that speaks through Fried's figurative language becomes apparent when he reveals that the one art form safe from such deplorable anthropomorphic effects is film. In contrast to the endlessly personalizing theater, film not only removes the actors from the presence of the audience but also cuts them into pieces through close-ups and montage.[9]

It was Walter Benjamin who turned this difference between the theater's and the cinema's attitude toward actors into a general theory of modernist art. For him, the theater, more than any other art form, retains from ritual its investment in the intense live presence that binds the actor to the audience.[10] This experiential presence and hence uniqueness means that the theater is singularly invested in what Benjamin calls the "aura," which turns this live character into an absolute value. For Benjamin, this use of the term *aura* is itself a back projection, for his essay is mainly concerned with the manner in which film escapes this auratic quality by turning the performing human actor into nothing but one material among others, a material that is endlessly manipulated, fragmented, and depersonalized by an apparatus that now mediates the relation between actor and audience. Since "The Work of Art in the Age of Mechanical Reproducibility" thus derives all its "negative" terms from the theater, it must be understood less as a pro-film than as an anti-theatrical tract in which the living actor becomes the obstacle for a truly modernist art.

The extreme and polemical nature of these statements might in part be explained by their respective contexts: Nietzsche's break with Wagner (roughly between 1876 and 1878); Fried's attack on minimalism in 1967; and Benjamin's attempt to come to terms with the implications of film in 1934. Considering these contexts also means acknowledging that these theorists' attacks on the theater do not indicate a simple rejection of it. Nietzsche, for example, sought to introduce a form of theatricality into his philosophy; Benjamin was drawn to the allegorical drama of the German *Trauerspiel;* and Fried's polemic is directed not against the theater per se but against certain types of painting and sculpture; he even admires Brecht for turning the theater against itself. Nevertheless, the anti-theatrical articulations of these diverse theorists point beyond their polemical contexts and toward a larger, if also more diffuse, anti-theatrical tendency operative within the period of modernism.

Traces of such theoretical forms of anti-theatricalism can be found, for example, in the work of Theodor W. Adorno. Adorno inherits from Nietzsche a critique of theatrical and gestural music, which he then directs not only against Wagner but also against Stravinsky, whom he accuses of letting the ballet influence his music, thus causing it to regress to the level of children's "play gestures." [11] For all of Adorno's differentiated theory of mimesis —and his defense of mimesis against its formalist detractors—what stands behind his critique of Wagner and Stravinsky is a critique of a primitive form of mimesis that reminds Adorno of the acts "android apes perform in the zoos." [12] This apish or "clownish" mimesis must not be simply repressed; it must be internalized and "remembered in consolation [*tröstlich*]" (181) for the express purpose of avoiding the type of regression of which Stravinsky is guilty. Only once it has successfully sublated this aping mimesis can art integrate mimesis into a properly modernist form.

Contemplating these scattered formulations, one begins to suspect that the apes and clowns that stand for an atavistic form of mimesis are figures for the debased actor. When we read Adorno's essays on Brecht and Beckett in this light, it becomes clear that for him the success of modernism in the theater depends on the theater's ability to resist the personal, the individual, the human, and the mimetic—all of which are tied to impersonating actors. In fact, Adorno claims that the dependence of the theater on individuation is an "unbearable burden" (54) from which even Brecht suffered but against which he also successfully rebelled. Beckett, however, is the dramatist who dealt with this burden most convincingly, by relentlessly attacking the presence of "reality and persons" in the theater and by turning these persons into "empty personae."[13] Living human actors are permissible only when they are utterly depersonalized.[14] What is striking about Adorno, Fried, and Benjamin is that their various anti-theatricalisms are based, not on an external attack on the theater, but on the modernist theater itself. That Brecht and Beckett keep coming up in these polemics not as examples of what is wrong with the theater but as solutions to these theorists' objections to the theater can serve as a first indication of the formative and productive role anti-theatricalism played for modern drama and theater.

What stands behind the anti-theatricalist attacks on actors is not the more traditional, moralizing suspicion that actors are whores (or, as in the case of Marlene Dietrich, prone to murder their husbands), nor the other seemingly ineradicable topoi of the traditional anti-theatrical prejudice (that they subvert the social order; that they teach deceit and lies), but a set of specifically modernist values that it is one of the purposes of my study to detail. Not that the modernist forms of anti-theatricalism never draw on the older, moralizing prejudice. But no matter how much modernist critics of the theater are still infused with this "prejudice," they integrate it into a new and specifically modernist set of concerns. What they tend to object to is a particular form of mimesis at work in the theater, a mimesis caused by the theater's uneasy position between the performing and the mimetic arts. As a performing art like music or ballet, the theater depends on the artistry of live human performers on stage. As a mimetic art like painting or cinema, however, it must utilize these human performers as signifying material in the service of a mimetic project. Once the nature of mimesis is subject to scrutiny and attacks, as it is in modernism, this double affiliation of the theater becomes a problem because, unlike painting or cinema, the theater remains tied to human performers, no matter how estranged their acting might be. The theater thus comes to be fundamentally at odds with a more widespread critique, or complication, of mimesis because this critique requires that the material used in the artwork be capable of abstraction and estrangement. Directors may try to estrange or depersonalize these performing humans, training and controlling their movements and gestures, and Joseph Roach's analysis of the "science of acting" traces the history of these attempts.[15] But the actor's impersonation remains nonetheless fundamentally stuck in an unmediated type of mimesis that keeps the work of art from achieving complex internal structures, distanced reflectivity, and formal constructedness.[16]

The troubling presence of the human actor on the stage has been obscured by most branches of theater semiotics, which tend to assume that as soon as a human body is framed by a stage, it automatically becomes a sign, as if by definition.[17] However, simply declaring actors to be "homo-material" signs — a human (rather than paint or ink) signifying another human — tends to erase the particular tensions and problems caused by the continuing presence of human actors in the production of these signs.[18] One pressing problem is that no full control over the emission of these signs will ever be possible. From the point of view of reception, this fact causes a crisis of the theatrical signs: we will never quite know which gestures and movements are part of the artwork and which ones are the result of accidents on the stage. While this uncertainty may not be a problem for the formal apparatus of semiotics, it is a problem for the audience, which continues to be faced with what it cannot help but see as contingencies, accidents, individual mannerisms, and idiosyncrasies. The same problem appears on the side of production. Theater reformers such as Edward Gordon Craig insist on retaining total control over their material and therefore try to replace living actors with marionettes, while others, such as Oskar Schlemmer, Nicolai Foregger, and Vsevolod Emilievich Meyerhold, attempt to turn the human actor into a machine. Even D. H. Lawrence wrote that "drama is enacted by symbolic creatures formed out of human consciousness: puppets if you like: but not human individuals. Our stage is all wrong, so boring in its personality."[19] These diverse writers seem to agree on one thing: the theater's reliance on human actors is its greatest liability, and a modernist theater can arise only out of an attack on them. This assault on the actor can also be said to have caused what Elinor Fuchs calls the "death of character": once the figure of the actor comes under attack it can no longer promise to impersonate what was previously known as a character.[20]

In order to understand the emergence of a modernist resistance to the theater, it is necessary to examine the tradition against which this anti-theatricalism reacts and by which it is therefore also shaped: the rise, in the later nineteenth century, of an unprecedented celebration of the theater and of theatricality that one could call theatricalism.[21] It is hard not to be affected by the nervous energy of those turn-of-the-century reformers and revolutionaries of the theater who made it their business to rescue the theater from what they thought of as its accelerating decline. While the symptoms of this decline — the greed of theater managers, the vanity of star actors, the hackwork of dramatists, and the vulgar tastes of audiences — may strike us as familiar topoi in the history of the theater, the conclusions these theater utopians drew from them are not. Their critique of contemporary theater was undertaken not so much to improve management, actors, dramatists, and audiences as to rescue and promote the theater, or theatricality, as such.[22] The tautological rhetoric of these reformers was captured in a phrase Georg Fuchs coined in 1904: "the re-theatricalization of the theater."[23] This slogan was echoed by the new class of star directors and theorists, who tried to wrest the theater from the hands of actors and producers; it can be found, for instance, in Edward Gordon Craig's *On the Art of the Theatre* (1911), Adolphe Appia's *La mise-en-scène du drame Wagnérien* (1895), Jacques Copeau's *Rejuvenation of the Theatre* (1913), and Nikolai Evreinov's *The Theater as Such* (1913).[24] These positions were subsequently taken to an extreme by the emerging avant-garde: F. T. Marinetti declared in 1915 that "everything of any value is theatrical";[25] the dadaists did their utmost to drag all the arts onto the stage of the Cabaret Voltaire; and Antonin Artaud called for a merging of life and theater.[26] What we begin to see here is that the polarization between anti-theatricalism and theatricalism corresponds to some extent to the distinction made by a number of theorists between high modernism and avant-garde. We may thus speak of a modernist anti-theatricalism and an avant-garde theatricalism.[27]

However, I am less interested in maintaining the old distinction between high modernism and the avant-garde than in recasting it in terms of anti-theatricalism and theatricalism. In fact, modernist anti-theatricalism and avant-garde theatricalism sometimes come to similar conclusions, for example, a critique of the actual theater. The desire to go beyond the circumscribed spaces of the theater made some of the theatricalists dissatisfied not only with the stage and its mimetic actors but with almost all forms of existing theater, an attitude visible, for example, in Marinetti's call for a "teatralitá senza teatro" (theatricality without theater) (1086). The more radical forms of theatricalism thus arrive at some of the same conclusions as those reached by anti-theatricalism, and at times a particular critic of the theater seems to belong to both camps (one example is Craig, another, perhaps, Nietzsche). This does not mean, however, that a division cannot be drawn between attacks on the theater motivated by a celebration of the value of theatricality and those motivated by a resistance to it. What the partial agreement of pro-theatricalists and anti-theatricalists demonstrates is an irreversible dissociation of the value of theatricality from the realities of the actual theater. This dissociation has wide-reaching implications, the most important being, not that pro-theatricalism may turn against the actual theater, but, conversely, that anti-theatricalism may return to the theater. If there exists, as Marinetti suggests, a "theatricality without theater," then there also exists a "theater without theatricality." Modernist drama and theater might be considered to be just that, a theater at odds with the value of theatricality. An analysis of anti-theatrical theater demands, not a descriptive history of the theater, but a history of the value of theater or theatricality, what one might call, borrowing from Nietzsche, a "genealogy" of the theater.

Not surprisingly, contemporary discourses on the theater have not been sympathetic to the modernist resistance to the theater. Innumerable articles in the field of theater and performance studies start with an attack on alleged "enemies" of the theater, such as Michael Fried.[28] These attacks are of limited value, not so much because they do not do justice to Fried's theory, but because they perpetuate the unwillingness or inability of theater studies to take anti-theatricalism to be anything but an evil force. At the same time, most theoretical practices that helped institutionalize literary modernism—New Criticism, formalism, structuralism, and deconstruction—have tended to neglect the category of the theater. Yvor Winters and Helen Vendler, for example, openly reduce Yeats's plays to poetic literature that has nothing to do with the theater.[29] Jacques Derrida is too invested in subsuming the theater under a general *écriture* to recognize in Mallarmé's textual theater a resistance to the theater.[30] Even semioticians explicitly devoted to analyzing the plurality of sign systems in the theater, such as Patrice Pavis, routinely rely on the notion of a "performance text," while others, such as Anne Ubersfeld, use the act of reading to describe the activity of watching a play, as if they simply were not able to come up with a theory of emitting and receiving signs that was not at least metaphorically modeled on writing.[31] The problem with such readings is not, as scholars in the field of theater studies sometimes argue, that they fail to celebrate writers such as Yeats or Mallarmé as neglected geniuses of the theater. Rather, the complete erasure of the category of theater makes them incapable of analyzing these writers' resistance to the theater, which is the central feature of their work. One might say, then, that just as contemporary theater studies tends to continue avant-garde theatricalism by virtue of its largely uncritical dedication to the value of theater, studies on literary modernism tend to perpetuate the modernist anti-theatricalism through an uncritical erasure of the category of theater. In this book I try to relate these two traditions critically to one another, not with the pretension of stepping outside this history of value entirely but with the hope that a reflection on this history might lead to the genealogy of the value of theatricality that modernist theater demands.

In order to understand the avant-garde's triumphant theatricalism and thus the modernist resistance to it, it is necessary not only to look forward, toward contemporary theater studies, but also to look back, for the figure to which many partisans of the theater continue to refer in one way or another, and from whom they derive their central slogans, is Richard Wagner. It is for this reason that my study begins by attributing to Wagner, who was also the first modern star director, the "invention" of what subsequently became avant-garde theatricalism. In this sense, it was due to Wagner that theatricality became charged with all the reformist, revolutionary, and utopian fervor that characterizes his own manifestoes and manifesto-like writings and those of the historical avant-garde. However, rather than envisioning some form of abstracted, theoretical theatricality, Wagner insisted that his notion of theatricality must be realized on a real stage in the form of the *Gesamtkunstwerk*. Wagner's significance for modernism resides, then, in the fact that he took the theater to be an absolute value and, at the same time, aspired to realize this value in the theater. It is precisely because Wagner turned the theater into a value that he was celebrated by the avant-garde, and for the same reason he became the object of modernism's most polemical anti-theatrical attacks.[32] This can be called the Wagner effect: forcing the arts to take a definite stance toward the theatricalized theater. The first section of this book, therefore, locates the emergence of a modernist ambivalence about the theater in the writings of Wagner's critics, for whom he, almost like a stage diva himself, continues to stand for everything that may be grandiose and compelling, but also dangerous and objectionable, about the theater and theatricality.

Once we recognize that central aesthetic values dominant in the period of modernism stem from a resistance to the theater, we can ask why these values arose in the first place. What were the conditions under which a tradition within modernism began to adopt precisely those values that put it at odds with the theater? In order to answer this question, it is necessary to turn to the historical and social conditions that gave rise to high modernism. It has become a critical commonplace to observe that much of modernist art deliberately cut itself off from all direct engagement with the public sphere and the modes of representation necessitated by it, in particular the idea that the public sphere would inevitably lead to a popular art, an art for the masses.[33] Modernist anti-theatricalism can be seen as one reaction to this fear of the masses and the public sphere. By the same token, the avant-garde's embrace of the theater and of theatricalism can be taken as a sign of the avant-garde's greater affinity to populism and the masses, what Andreas Huyssen calls the "hidden dialectic" of avant-garde and mass culture.

The theater has always been the most public art form, and it continued to depend on collaboration and collectivity even at a time when modernism celebrated the figure of the individual artist who withdraws from the public sphere and the allegedly undifferentiated masses. Intersecting more directly with the raw constraints of business, the theater depends on a process of collaborative production that includes business-minded managers, actors dreaming of stardom, and playwrights ready to gratify a pleasure-seeking audience. This collaborative process was anathema to the anti-theatrical modernists, but it also bothered reformers of the stage more generally. The rise of the so-called director's theater in the late nineteenth century can be seen as an attempt to reduce collaboration in the theater and to concentrate the act of creation in the hand of one super director. This motivation is particularly evident in the case of Craig, whose polemical attacks on theater were in the service of gaining full control over the production process and thus of eliminating all the contingencies associated with collaboration.[34]

The process of collaborative production is, however, only one side of the problem; the other side is the collective reception of theatrical performances. For many modernists, collective reception proved to be even more disturbing than collaborative production, and it was for this reason that they began to celebrate aggressively the virtues of solitary reading as the model for watching a play. Fried gave a name to this preference, shared by many modernists, for reading over watching and for text over theater, namely, *absorption*.[35] Fried is troubled by living actors on stage, but he is at least as disturbed by people in the audience, whose presence disrupts what has become the sine qua non of modernism: an intense concentration on works that conform to the modernist ideal of difficulty.[36] This ideal requires a control over the external circumstances of reception that is impossible to implement in the theater. A number of modernist writers were willing to draw a radical conclusion from the inherent collaborative and collective nature of the theater: led by Mallarmé, they withdrew into their private studies and closets, which thus became the birthplaces of modernist drama.

Both the friends and the detractors of the theater have always suspected that along with its collaborative production and collective reception came a more direct relation to the social and the public spheres. Anecdotes and histories about uprisings and revolutions caused by theater performances occupy a prominent place in the imagination of theater enthusiasts. And indeed, the communal gathering of a public in the theater has been used as a recurring model for the public at large. This affinity helps explain why sociological studies such as Habermas's *Strukturwandel der Öffentlichkeit* (1962) would consider the people assembled in the theater to be a "training ground" for the formation of a proper political public.[37] And what for Habermas is only a prefiguration becomes the organizing model in Richard Sennett's *Fall of Public Man* (1977), which uses the history of the theater and its audience as, alternatively, a local instance of, a cause of, and an objective correlative to the changing nature of the public sphere in the eighteenth, nineteenth, and twentieth centuries.[38] Sennett's study itself continues a long tradition of political thought that considers the public sphere to be some form of a *theatrum mundi*. The force of this tradition is registered most clearly, perhaps, by its greatest critic, Jean-Jacques Rousseau, whose fear that the theater would corrupt the public sphere presumes that the two are homologous enough for the former to have such a detrimental effect on the latter.[39]

The perceived affinity between the theater and the public sphere is a key factor in the formation of a specifically modernist anti-theatricalism. Due to this affinity the theater, or the act of theatricalizing other art forms such as music or sculpture, threatens to restore art to the public sphere. The investment in shielding recipients from the public is not only meant to allow them to apprehend, with maximum concentration, the complexity of the work of art. Both the insistence on complexity and the types of reception necessitated by it are responses to the fear that the theater would actually provide a forum in which the constitution of public opinion might take place. The modernist critique of realism, mimesis, and literalism and its fixation on silent and solitary absorption are thus not independent values that happen to be at odds with what the theater represents; they are barriers erected against the possibility of the public role of art suggested by the theater.

Here too we can see to what extent the polarization between anti-theatricalism and pro-theatricalism corresponds to that between modernism and the avant-garde. While modernist anti-theatricalism attacked the theater to foreclose direct political engagement, the avant-garde recognized that the theater was the Archimedian point from which it could attack modernism's most central values. The avant-garde did not simply celebrate theatricality out of an innocent love for the theater; it chose theatricality—as well as everything associated with it, such as collaborative production, collective reception, distraction, and riotous audiences—as its slogan precisely because theatricality promised to lead art back to the public sphere from which modernism had so eagerly distanced itself. This theatrical commitment to the public sphere is already visible in the work of Richard Wagner. For him the theater of Bayreuth becomes an ideal political arena epitomizing Germany and the German *Volk*. However, taking the theater as a privileged political place did not originate with Wagner. The theater has been the art form of choice for projects seeking to fuse aesthetics and politics as is visible, for example, in the arguments put forth across Europe in favor of establishing national theaters. The instrumentalization of the theater for politics also stands behind Walter Benjamin's anti-theatrical diagnosis of the fascist "aestheticization of politics," for this aestheticization is most drastically achieved in the theatrical rituals fabricated by fascism, from mass spectacles and parades to the carefully orchestrated Nuremberg rallies.[40] Benjamin's anti-theatrical critique of auratic art is thus motivated by his experience of the politico-theatrical rituals of fascism.

Benjamin's thesis about fascism, however, must be extended to include a wider range of phenomena, for the conjunction between aesthetics and theatrical politics can be found also in revolutionary projects such as Berlin dada, as well as in Evreinov's agitprop spectacle *The Storming of the Winter Palace* (1920). Both are extreme forms of what Raymond Williams has called "theater as a political forum."[41] Without creating a false parallelism between the theatrical politics of fascism and those of the early Soviet Union, which would, for example, erase the difference between a passive mass audience overwhelmed by a spectacle and a politicized mass that participates in the re-creation of a collective revolutionary action, it is nevertheless central to recognize that both pinned their hopes for the creation of a political public on the theater. Indeed, the rise in the early twentieth century of what is now known as mass politics, which was greeted by some theatricalists, such as Marinetti, as the realization of a new theatricality, gave the late-nineteenth-century distrust of the masses a new, overtly political dimension. Even though this association of the mass public with the theater may appear to be based on a limited understanding of both the theater and the public sphere—and I will indicate some alternative ways of thinking about this relation—it is important to recognize that this association is one of the driving forces behind (avant-garde) theatricalism and (modernist) anti-theatricalism alike.

But where does this account leave the modernist theater? Caught, so to speak, between the hammer of modernism's critique of the theater and the anvil of avant-garde theatricalism, how could a modernist drama and theater—rather than avant-garde spectacles—emerge from this battle over theatricality? Must not the very term *modernist theater* strike us now as an oxymoron? I argue that modern drama and theater, perhaps surprisingly, did not so much suffer from their modernist enemies and avant-garde enthusiasts; instead, they internalized both their critique and their enthusiasm for the purpose of a far-reaching reform of the dramatic form and of theatrical representation. Drama, like Hitchcock's film, has always recorded and responded to the arguments of its detractors. Euripides' *The Bacchae,* for example, personifies the dangerous actor in the Asiatic Dionysus and anti-theatrical stage fright in the moralist Pentheus. Modern drama continues to record anti-theatricalism—nowhere more obsessively than in the oeuvre of Luigi Pirandello—but it allows itself to be shaped by anti-theatricalism as well. Brecht's mistrust of the theater, Yeats's tirades against actors, Stein's nervousness in the presence of live actors, and Mallarmé's rejection of the theater are varieties of a resistance to the theater that are structural and fundamentally formative, shaping these writers' use of the dramatic text, of *dramatis personae,* and of actors. No longer interested in banishing actors or closing down theaters, modernist anti-theatricalism does not remain external to the theater but instead becomes a productive force responsible for the theater's most glorious achievements.

The Modernist Closet Drama

Part II constructs and analyzes a group of texts that are directly marked by the modernist resistance to the theater, what I call the *modernist closet drama.* Predictably, the closet drama was scorned by promoters of theatricalism such as Wagner, who called it an "outrageous" aberration,[42] for its stubborn refusal to acknowledge the value of total theatricality. But Wagner was far from the only one to have contempt for the genre. The closet drama interests neither a theater (and performance) studies hostile to the literary text nor a literary studies with no interest in the theatrical (even when the value of theater is being questioned). The result of this double neglect is that the closet drama is one of the most underexamined and least understood genres. And yet, as I argue, it is only through the closet drama that we can begin to understand how modern drama relates to the theater.[43]

The only theorist to recognize the importance of the closet drama was Georg Lukács, who saw it as a symptom of a central dilemma in modern drama at large. Now seen primarily as a critic of the novel, Lukács actually started out as a scholar of drama, and his earliest critical study describes nineteenth-century theater as suffering from an increasing loss of the audience, a process that ultimately led to a scission between drama and theater.[44] Lukács views this loss of the audience as the result of the theater's failure to express the modern condition. "Life is no longer dramatic" (115), he exclaims, concluding that drama is no longer capable of speaking to a mass audience. The symptom of this dilemma, if not its solution, is the emergence of the closet drama, or *Buchdrama,* which has given up on the audience entirely. Without subscribing to Lukács's pessimistic diagnosis and its underlying assumptions about the relation between life and the dramatic form, I hold onto the observation that the closet drama expresses something critical about the condition of modern drama. But where Lukács takes the closet drama to mark the failure of modern drama, I see it as the clearest expression of a modernist resistance to the theater.

One reason for the relative neglect of the closet drama is the particularly unstable nature of this category. The closet drama seems to depend on the whims of theater managers and on the hurt pride of dramatists, from Seneca through Milton to Byron, who "officially" refused to write for the stage as soon as they felt rejected by it. But what happens when theatrical fashion (and censorship) changes and these closet dramas end up being performed after all, against the declared will of the pouting dramatist? Today, our understanding of the relation between text and theater has changed so much that almost every type of text can be and has been brought into the theater. Moreover, while many intended closet dramas are retroactively put on stage, Greek tragedy, at least since Aristotle, has long been considered to be a branch of literature and consequently integrated into the pedagogical canon. This means that it is read, studied, circulated, copied, transcribed, translated, and finally printed as literature rather than as scripts meant for performance. A similar reception history has occurred with Shakespeare.[45] Coleridge's observation that Shakespeare had his "proper place in the heart and in the closet" can be taken as a representative sentiment for a whole tradition of anti-theatrical admirers of Shakespeare.[46] The consequence of this conviction was that any drama ready to compete with Shakespeare would have to aspire to the condition of Coleridge's closet.[47]

Intentionality and reception history are, however, only the external markers of what I take to be intrinsic to the closet drama as a genre: its resistance to the theater. This resistance is manifest throughout the history of the closet drama, especially at its origin in the Greco-Roman tradition, namely, Plato's dialogues. (One might consider the largely dialogic Book of Job to be the first closet drama in the Judeo-Christian tradition; it also served as the framing model for Goethe's *Faust,* which was the most influential closet drama of the nineteenth century.) Calling Plato's dialogues closet dramas is itself a retrospective attribution since they are neither tragedies nor comedies and thus would not have been recognized by the Greeks as drama at all, despite their mimesis of movement, interaction, and gesture.[48] Aristotle, however, did have an eye for what is sometimes, and awkwardly, called the "literary form" of these Socratic dialogues, and he slyly related them to the prose comedies of Xenarchus and Sophron.[49] The connection he thus draws is an underhanded critique of his teacher, who would not have wanted to be remembered as the author of comic sketches, let alone be categorized as the creator of pieces of mimesis in prose. That Plato, the founder of anti-theatricalism, would turn to the dramatic form certainly complicates his anti-theatrical stance, but it bespeaks a tension that marks the closet drama throughout its history, for it remains attached to the theater it struggles to resist.[50]

The resistance to the theater in Plato's dialogues manifests itself in two traditions of the closet drama, which one might call the *restrained* closet drama and the *exuberant* closet drama. The restrained closet drama, ranging from Plato through Milton and Swinburne to Hofmannsthal, consists of philosophical or poetic speeches and monologues, a theater characterized by a withdrawal from and resistance to scenic action. In fact, Hofmannsthal drew an explicit connection between his lyrical closet drama *Der Tod des Tizian* and Plato, observing that perhaps "one shouldn't call it a play for the theater [*Theaterstück*], but a dialogue in the manner of Plato of Athens."[51] The exuberant closet drama also resists the stage, but it does so through an excess of theatrical action. Goethe's *Faust II,* Flaubert's *La Tentation de Saint-Antoine,* and Wyndham Lewis's *Enemy of the Stars* are examples of such free-floating, often allegorical theatricality, whose constant changes of scenes, large casts of characters, sudden appearances and disappearances, and strategic mixture of hallucination and reality willfully exceed the limits of theatrical representation.

I emphasize the closet drama's resistance to the theater because the modernist closet drama takes this resistance to an extreme. And like any form of resistance, the closet drama constantly refers to and thus keeps in touch with what it resists. Whether it tends toward the restrained or the exuberant tradition, the modernist closet drama never leaves the theater alone and systematically transforms its spaces, actors, and objects. For this reason it would be wrong to consider the closet drama a negation of the theater. On the contrary, we must ask what the closet drama wants from the theater, how it feeds off its critique of the theater, and how this necessary relation leads the closet drama, not to do away with the theater, but to transform it.

Such transformations take on particularly compelling and wide-ranging forms in the closet dramas of Mallarmé, Joyce, and Stein, which therefore stand at the center of my analysis. In the hands of these writers projected *dramatis personae* are turned into isolated assemblages of gestures and poses that are infused with symbolist significance (Mallarmé), or used for the construction of a theatrical montage (Stein), or made to oscillate between hallucination and stage reality (Joyce). It has become common to attribute to turn-of-the-century theatrical culture a return of the body, what Harold Segel called "the body ascendant," and the rise of this body is often taken to be a reaction against not only the dramatic text but also a more widespread "crisis of language," as Erika Fischer-Lichte has argued.[52] The closet drama can be seen as the underside of this polarization: here it is language, in the form of a closet drama, that responds to and even "solves" what then might be called the crisis of the living actor. What is more remarkable, perhaps, than this reversal is the fact that theatricalism and anti-theatricalism here meet once more in their shared attack on the individual and human nature of the actor. While Craig demanded that the actor be replaced by a marionette, many writers of lyrical dramas either wrote plays for marionettes, as did Maeterlinck, or fantasized about having their plays performed by marionettes, as did Hofmannsthal.[53] In the case of Mallarmé, Joyce, and Stein, however, no reference to an actual replacement of the human actor is necessary to bring about a complete depersonalization of the human figure, for they employ modes of textual representation that explicitly foreclose any act of impersonation.

Given that the closet drama's resistance to the theater is a particular instance of the modernist resistance to the public sphere, it is tempting to direct against it the type of critique Lukács and Bürger leveled at high modernism more generally. From such a perspective, the genre of the closet drama would appear to be indicative of a deplorable retreat from artistic responsibility and a narcissistic embrace of some variant of *l'art pour l'art;* indeed, the first modernist closet dramas, from Mallarmé to Hofmannsthal, are undeniably part of aestheticism. And since the closet is what is defined by its separation from the public sphere of the audience, it is tempting to regard it as the very figure of a retreat into the private space. However, this view is itself caught in the undifferentiated equation of theater, the public sphere, and politics on which the political theatricalism of Wagner, Marinetti, and Meyerhold is premised. As soon as we suspend this assumption, we can see that the closet dramas of Mallarmé, Stein, and Joyce withdraw from the public not so much to celebrate narcissistically their own autonomy but to resist the particular forms of normativity they associate with theatrical representation.[54]

The most visible aspects of the theater's normativity are the greater vigilance of the censor, the (perceived) conservatism of theater managers and public taste, and forms of internalized censorship. Drama has tended to function as a privileged genre for moral reflection and instruction by virtue of representing the actions of participants in a socialized world. Even though this moral role has led to forms of theatrical opposition to the status quo, more fundamentally it has led to a greater policing of theatrical representation. That the theater is entangled in the normative tends to come as a surprise for those theater and performance scholars and practitioners who think of the theater as a place where systems of value and social norms are invariably on shaky ground, subject to displacement and critique, due to the primacy in the theater of performance over ontology and of masks over essence.[55] If we are performing socialized actions in the theater, does that not mean that we are implicitly declaring these actions to be "mere performances" and thus social constructs that can be changed? Is not theater history full of attempts to destabilize the status quo?

Questions about the subversive nature of theater and performance have recently led to a debate between theorists of performance and theorists of performativity. While performance studies tends to consider performance art to be subversive, critics such as Judith Butler have emphasized that theater and performance also produce the social normativity that they may intend to subvert in particular performances.[56] We can thus turn to Butler's theory of performativity to explain the theater's inherent normativity. Every act of parodying a scripted, normative act is also a repetition of that normative act and thus participates in forming, rather than abolishing or overcoming, the norm that governs it. Theatrical estrangements of norms are dependent upon and therefore involved in producing the norms they might seek to subvert. In her introduction to *Bodies That Matter* (1993) Butler makes this consequence of her theory explicit, insisting that theatrical performances are scripted by normative behavior and public rituals outside the theater (12). To the extent that the theater, more than any other art form, replicates the social world and in particular human interaction through real humans on stage, it can therefore be considered the art form that is most directly tied to social normativity.

Another way to approach the normativity of the theater is to analyze the manner in which the closet drama seeks to evade theatrical representation. The closet drama creates a space that allows Mallarmé to claim that a female dancer is no longer a female dancer, a space where he, the male poet, can assume various female pseudonyms; it is the condition that allows Leopold Bloom to turn into a woman (and this means to turn actually and really into a woman rather than just cross-dressing); and it is the condition under which it will never be possible to reduce Stein's St. Therese to any particular shape, body, or character. At this point we may also remember that the history of the closet drama is in fact filled with various forms of deviance, from Plato's *Symposium* and Seneca's *Medea* through Shelley's *Cenci* to Flaubert's *Temptation of Saint Anthony,* not to mention the text that has shown, once and for all and with all its possible and impossible implications, that the closet of the closet drama is also a boudoir: the Marquis de Sade's closet drama *Philosophy in the Bedroom.* Because closet dramas use their freedom from the normativity of the theater to create worlds characterized by various forms of ambiguity and deviance, it is possible to adopt Eve Kosofsky Sedgwick's project of an epistemology of the closet for the closet drama.[57]

The resistance to the normativities of the theater at work in deviant closet dramas becomes clearly visible when these closet dramas are brought back to the stage. In the stage versions of the *Livre,* "Circe," and *Four Saints in Three Acts* Mallarmé's dancer becomes female once more; Leopold Bloom never becomes a woman; and St. Therese perhaps even dallies with St. Ignatius. When one contemplates these changes, it becomes clear that what Mallarmé, Stein, and Joyce are concerned about is not so much a simple retreat from the public sphere as a bracketing or estrangement of full theatrical representation, in particular of the human actor. The structure of resistance suggests that the closet drama does not manage to escape from theatrical normativity entirely; that what looks like freedom from the theater is but an effect of the resistance to it. This is true, but it does not mean that these effects are not significant. What it means is that the closet drama's resistance to the theater also produces a theater, one that breaks apart the human figure and rebels against the mimetic confines of a stage and theatrical action. It is in the gesture of rebellion that the closet drama is still calibrated to the theater and derives from it the material whose decomposition is the process through which it constitutes itself.

The modernist closet dramas seek to undo the theater and its human actors through programs that are best described by terms such as *literariness, écriture*, and *writerliness*. It is important to recognize that in the context of the closet drama these terms do not simply describe the condition of literature but signify a choice of literature over theater. From the perspective of the closet drama the valorization of literariness can be understood to be a reaction against theatrical representation. And just as *literaturnost* and *écriture* are terms directed against the theater, so theatricality is often directed against the dramatic text and thus literature at large. (Evreinov, for example, coined the term *teatralnost* roughly at the same time as Roman Jakobson coined the term *literaturnost*.) Perhaps the study of the closet drama is a privileged place for thinking about the contentious relation between text and stage and thus, by extension, between literary culture and the theater. Recognizing the essential relation to the theater at work in the closet dramas of Mallarmé, Joyce, and Stein, who achieved prominence through other literary genres, may be a good way to introduce the category of the theater, including the resistance to it, into the study of literary modernism at large.

Modernist Drama and Theater

It is only by way of the closet drama and its construction of the audience as reader that we can begin to understand why Beckett deems stage directions to be as important as dialogue or why Brecht wants to teach the audience to adopt the attitude of a reader. In the last section of this book I argue that Yeats, Brecht, Beckett, and in less developed ways the entire canon of modern drama adopt from the modernist closet drama strategies for incorporating anti-theatricalism not only into the dramatic form but also into theatrical representation.

This claim may seem counterintuitive given that these three dramatists were active in the theater. Yeats's use of dance, Brecht's epic theater, and

Beckett's meticulous stagings bespeak the fact that rather than rejecting the theater altogether, these writers took a keen interest in theatrical matters. Although this is certainly true, I show that Yeats, Brecht, and Beckett were nevertheless engaged in an explicitly anti-theatrical discourse at various moments in their lives: Yeats in his earliest phase of writing symbolist plays, Brecht in his polemics against Wagner, and Beckett in his crusade against actors. More important, however, than their at times categorical denunciations of the theater and of theatricality (denunciations that echo verbatim the anti-theatricalism of the closet drama and of modernism's anti-theatrical theorists) is the fact that these figures channeled their resistance to the theater back into the theater itself. Brecht's explicit "mistrust of the theater" led him to turn actors into witnesses,[58] and Yeats's early control fantasy of confining actors to barrels was slyly put into practice in Beckett's ploys of arresting actors in urns, ashcans, and mounds. Yeats's theater is traditionally labeled as symbolism, Brecht's as political drama, and Beckett's as theater of the absurd. Despite these differences, they constitute three manifestations of a shared modernist resistance to the theater. In fact, I argue that it was their resistance to the theater that proved to be the driving force behind the reforms and revolutions in the theater for which they are now most well known.

One way in which the latent anti-theatricalism of these writers and directors registers is in their objection to the theatrical politics propagated by Wagner and avant-garde theatricalism. Like Mallarmé and Joyce, Yeats and Brecht view the affinity between the audience and the public sphere with the greatest suspicion and seek to build into their political theaters as many anti-theatrical elements as possible, the most important being an obsessive limiting of the audience. It is for this reason that the most programmatic plays of these authors are chamber plays, plays infused with a deep distrust of the audience and a theatrical politics. The small audiences envisioned by these writers are explicitly nonpublic, their selection is always an exclusive affair, and even their behavior is meticulously prescribed so as to keep the collectivity from developing any dynamic of its own, in particular anything resembling the riots so willfully and strategically provoked by the avant-garde theatricalists.

The limiting and control of the audience is something modern drama learned from the closet drama, which often accepted, as a kind of compromise, a small coterie audience attending a dramatic reading or even a chamber staging: the closet of the closet drama, in other words, can be a place for an intimate audience as much as for solitary reading. That small theaters are the driving force behind most turn-of-the-century reforms thus not only reflects economic pressures but also registers a deliberate retreat from a mass public into an intimate and private space. The attempt to create a private counterpublic purged of everything associated with political theatricality is visible even in Mallarmé, the most radical of the closet dramatists, who envisioned perfectly scripted readings of his plays for a select group of friends, an intimate audience resembling perhaps that of a salon. By the same token, some closet dramas do not reject altogether, but qualify, the idea of the *theatrum mundi,* as did Hofmannsthal, who reduced Calderón's *Great World Theatre* (ca. 1641) to *Das kleine Welttheater* (The small world theater) (1897). It is this attempt to create a "small" and therefore ideal public that we can see at work in such chamber plays as Yeats's "Plays for Dancers" and Brecht's *Lehrstücke.*

The persistence of anti-theatricalism in modern drama means that it, like the closet drama, plays its own literariness off against its theatricality. In fact it is this reliance on the dramatic text as a strategy against the theater that registers most clearly the affinity between modern drama and the closet drama. Most importantly, however, modern drama, more so than any previous drama, becomes a literary genre directed at a reader as well as at an audience. Here my project intersects with the history of the book. Through a long process, one that Julie Stone Peters has reconstructed in *The Theatre of the Book,* print culture and performance have had a contentiously intertwined history. Drama had been printed since before the Elizabethan period, and individual playwrights such as Ben Jonson devoted considerable energy and explanatory notes to the printed version of their plays, which they sometimes preferred to theatrical performances.[59] Over the course of the eighteenth and nineteenth centuries contemporary drama (as opposed to Greek tragedy, Shakespeare, or "the classics") gradually constructed its "implied reader," to borrow from Wolfgang Iser, not only as a theater professional responsible for realizing it on stage but as a general reader: every dramatic text, then, is also, if not exclusively, a reading or closet drama.[60]

One of the few contemporary observers to recognize the importance of print for modern drama was the American critic Archibald Henderson, who attributed the rising significance of printed editions to the international character of modern drama, which had circulated in the form of translations and translated anthologies, a trend epitomized in the singular influence across Europe of Ibsen's plays.[61] This mode of publication encouraged the practice of reading contemporary drama, a practice enforced, Henderson noted in 1914, by the increasing study of dramatic literature at Harvard, Yale, and Columbia. Additional causes Henderson could have added to his list were of a legal nature. Censorship has always been more restrictive with respect to theatrical performance than with respect to printed plays, an imbalance that is itself the product of an ingrained and moralizing anti-theatricalism.[62] And changes in national and international royalty laws on the eve of the nineteenth century abolished some of the disincentives for playwrights to publish their work prior to its performance.[63] The integration of drama into the general publishing markets thus involves a number of practical, legal, and economic factors, through which drama becomes akin to, if not coextensive with, the closet drama.[64]

The quantitative data available about the publication of plays are often insufficient.[65] What makes quantitative research on print and publication especially precarious in the case of drama is the fact that plays were frequently pirated by theater managers trying to avoid royalty payments or printed in cheap editions intended for actors and producers.[66] The lack of precise data marking the evolving publication practice of drama, however, does not matter all that much for my argument, which is concerned less with quantitative causes than with their qualitative effects on the generic form of the rather small canon of modern drama. Again, it was Henderson who noticed one particular effect, namely, that not only did Shaw spend an unusual amount of time selecting print, typeset, and format for the publication of his *Plays Pleasant and Unpleasant* but the manner of publication actually altered the dramatic form: Shaw added lengthy prefaces and narrative passages and thus changed the form and function of his stage directions.

What Henderson observed in Shaw can be taken as an indication that modern drama more generally realized itself as reading drama, primarily through the integration of stage directions into the primary dramatic text. This change in the function of stage directions is one consequence of the history of printed drama, and one that only materialized fully in the later nineteenth century. No longer the technical "l. exit, r. exit," stage directions were now devoted to elaborate descriptions of character, setting, and movement, descriptions directed at the general reader. Stage directions thus became a privileged place for formal innovation. The emergence within modern drama of elaborately descriptive and narrative stage directions is an instance of a more general reliance on the part of modern drama on language that mediates, describes, prescribes, and interrupts the mimetic space of the theater. Pointing to these strategies does not mean taking sides in the endless struggle between text and performance. However, it means recognizing, on the one hand, that theatrical performance is part of the horizon of any dramatic text—even the closet drama is concerned with the mimesis of the stage, if largely in a negative manner—and, on the other hand, that a theatrical performance often inserts textual mediations between the viewer and theatrical mimesis. I propose a term to designate the descriptive and narrative strategies through which modern drama tries to channel, frame, control, and even interrupt what it perceives to be the unmediated theatricality of the stage and its actors. This term is *diegesis*.

Mimesis, Diegesis, and Gestures

Diegesis is not a neutral term in the debate between text and theater, for it stems from the anti-theatrical writings of Plato, where it is used in the midst of what might be seen as the original quarrel between verbal diegesis and theatrical mimesis. At the center of this quarrel stands the figure of the actor. Plato arrives at his critique of the actor only by way of a circuitous route, via the Homeric rhapsode, who narrates the action occurring in the past, the present, or the future in a mode that Plato calls "diêgêsis" [διήγησις].[67] However, once the poet, or rhapsode, switches from the third person to the first, he no longer reports a character's speech but "likens" (ὁμοιεῖν) his voice and gesture to those of the character; the rhapsode no longer is a narrator but is on his way to becoming an actor. At this moment rhapsodic diegesis turns into the mimesis performed by an actor. For Plato this performance would thus become a "diegesis through mimesis" [διὰ μιμήσεως τὴν διήγησιν] (393c), as opposed to the pure or simple diegesis, which would be defined through its difference to mimesis as a "diegesis without mimesis" [ἄνευ μιμήσεως . . . διήγησις] (393c–d). In the eyes of Plato this switch from rhapsode to actor is fateful because it means that the poet "hides" [ἀποκρύπτειν] (393c) himself under the mask of the character, a mask made out of a false voice and false gestures.

The diligent interlocutor of this dialogue—or closet drama—immediately recognizes that what Socrates is really talking about here is not the performing rhapsode but the dramatic actor. It is possible, in principle, to imagine an epic poem without any direct speech and thus a rhapsode who never tries to imitate the voice and gestures of characters, though such an abstinent recitation never really occurred, for the recitation of epic poetry was a staged event drawing large crowds. In order to demonstrate this possibility, Plato offers a translation into the third person and thus into diegesis of Chryses' speech in the first book of the *Iliad*. This type of translation is in theory possible for epic poetry, but it would change everything if it were applied to drama, for drama depends generically on actors speaking in their own voice as a way of imitating the voices of the characters they are impersonating. While in theory the rhapsode and epic poetry could be saved (if they were properly transformed into pure narrative without dialogue), the actors and the dramatic form are hopelessly lost because they must imitate the voices and gestures of other persons, especially, Plato remarks, the voices and gestures of women and cowards (395a). It is therefore not surprising that when speaking about actors, Plato uses the standard Greek term, namely, ὑποκριτής, or *hypokrites,* a word whose very meaning was increasingly infiltrated by Plato's own anti-theatricalism until it took the derogatory meanings it has today.

Aristotle's *Poetics* presents itself as a defense of mimesis against Plato, using such concepts as catharsis and the human drive to imitate. What is often overlooked, however, is that Aristotle too feels ambivalent about the figure of the actor. Aristotle's largest concession to Plato is the claim that drama should be able to do without acting altogether and content itself with being read (ἀναγινώσκειν) (1462a), and Aristotle probably envisions here a silent reading. But Aristotle, as always, strives for a compromise position, which means that he also wants to defend, at least to some extent, the spectacular and visual aspects of the theater (ὄψις). For this purpose, he points out that all performing arts, including rhapsody and music, for better or worse participate in some form of visuality. This visuality, like the actor, is a mixed blessing, and Aristotle recounts a negative example, namely, the ridiculous gestures (σχημάτων) of flutists who try to imitate Scylla instead of sublating these external imitations into their music (1461b)—Aristotle here sounds almost like Adorno. This desire for a compromise becomes particularly acute when it comes to actors, for Aristotle's desire to save good actors from Plato's critique leads to symptomatic shifts in his terminology. Frequently he evades Plato's standard term for *actor,* namely, *hypocrites,* using instead the word πράττοντες, or *prattontes,* which is derived from the word *praxis* and thus suggests the execution of a real action, in contrast to deceitful make-believe. Aristotle's decision to use *praxis* and *prattontes* to denote an action presented by a dramatic text on the stage is meant to defend the theater from the accusation that it features hypocrites who feign emotions. And once Aristotle has constructed a nonhypocritical agent-actor, he can proceed to save the visuality of the theater, what he calls *opsis:* ἐπεὶ δὲ πράττοντες ποιοῦνται τὴς μίμησιν, πρῶτον μὲν ἐξ ἀνάγκης ἂν εἴν τι μόριον τραγῳδίας ὁ τῆς ὄψεως κόσμος [since the characters/actors produce mimesis, it follows that in the first place tragedy will consist of visual spectacle] (1449b30–32). This distinction between *hypocrites* and *prattontes* mirrors the difference between the theatrical and the non-theatrical. On the one hand, words such as *acts, agents, actions,* and *actors* denote actions and their consequences in the world. At the same time, however, these concepts also mean the representation of action on a stage. Aristotle recognizes both of these meanings and strategically conflates them by using the word *praxis* to denote the theatrical actor: now the theater ceases to feign and engages instead in real action. Aristotle then goes one step further, shifting the emphasis from actors to actions. We can imagine tragedy without characters, Aristotle says, and thus, one might conclude, without actors impersonating them (1450a24). But there could be no tragedy without action or praxis. In the last analysis, then, Aristotle may save actors by associating them with nondeceitful action, but eventually it is action, and not the actors, that stands at the center of tragedy.

Because Aristotle wants to salvage the good actor, he takes care to evade the term with which Plato conducted his attack on the theater: *diegesis.* This evasion is overlooked by even such a rigorous narratologist as Gérard Genette, who wrongly claims that Aristotle "accepts" Plato's notion of diegesis when he in fact conspicuously avoids it.[68] Instead, when Aristotle talks about narrative he often uses alternative terms such as ἀπαγγελία, or *apaggelia,* which means "report" or "story." This change in terminology is strategic because it is geared toward circumventing Plato's categorical opposition between diegesis and mimesis, just as the term *prattontes* was geared toward circumventing the deceptive make-believe of the *hypocrites.* Instead, Aristotle hopes to categorize epic poetry, lyrical choral poetry, and drama as different forms of mimesis so that what Plato referred to as diegesis without mimesis is now a subform of mimesis.[69] The term *diegesis,* Plato's anti-theatrical weapon, thus has been effectively discharged.

Aristotle's strategy for saving an expanded notion of mimesis and for suppressing Plato's term *diegesis* has been so successful that the term *diegesis,* with its implied anti-theatrical thrust, has by and large dropped out of the analysis of drama and theater and is used only in the study of narrative. One must certainly applaud Aristotle's attempt to outmaneuver Plato's critique of actors and its hypothetical consequence, the closing of the theaters and the banishment of actors. But this sympathy for Aristotle's cause should not keep us from using the term *diegesis,* because it registers precisely the anti-theatrical forces at work in modern drama and modern theater. In order to examine these forces, it is necessary to insist with Plato and against Aristotle on the distinction, and therefore the struggle, between diegesis and theatrical mimesis. This means that we must distinguish between the indirect, descriptive or narrative representation of objects, persons, spaces, and events through language (either spoken by a rhapsode, narrator, chorus, or author or represented in the dramatic text for the reader) and the direct presentation of such objects, persons, speeches, spaces, and events on a stage. Only a terminology that recognizes this distinction can capture the strategies through which modern drama and theater try to resist theatrical mimesis.

Greek tragedy and comedy, and in fact much Western and non-Western drama, have always included various forms of diegesis. Narrative passages about the past can be spoken by actors, and present-tense commentary by the chorus. Actions happening offstage, for example, are often reported by messengers or by actors pretending to "see them on the other side of a wall" *(teichoscopia)*. The regular function of such forms of diegesis in Greek drama, and in Western drama more generally, is to expand the realm of representation beyond the stage. When messengers report what has gone on or what is going on elsewhere, offstage or behind a wall, they add to the mimetic space on stage what Michael Issacharoff calls a diegetic space offstage.[70] This is not, however, the sense of diegesis that is specifically connected with modern drama, although it is the basis for it. For modern drama introduces an important change into the function of these diegetic strategies. Instead of importing onto the mimetic space of the stage something that happens offstage, modernist diegesis refers to the mimetic space of the stage itself.[71] Characters, objects, and events that are already mimetically present are suddenly confronted with modes of diegesis that project onto the mimetic space their own version of it.

What stands behind this tactic of directing diegesis toward and against theatrical mimesis is the desire on the part of modern drama to frame, control, and interrupt the theatrical space of the stage. Theatrical representation is not left to designers, actors, and the director but is placed, once again, into the hands of the dramatic author. Instead of visual representation, such as stage props, lighting, and the organization of the space of the stage, as well as movement, choreography, and acting, we now have descriptive language. Most forms of modernist diegesis, however, are not the result of the power battles between directors, actors, and authors; as is characteristic of the debate about theatricality, this anti-mimetic stance turns into an attack on theatricality as such. Diegesis redefines what we see and thus conditions our perception and reception of the theater. In doing so, it mediates the theater through an art form much more acceptable to modernism, namely, literature. Plato's diegesis, on which all his anti-theatrical energy was concentrated, is thus taken up by the modern drama for the purpose of keeping under control and mediating the theatrical mimesis of actors and objects on the stage. Aristotle's strategy of recategorizing diegesis as a form of mimesis may have once saved the theater, but it does not help us understand the subtle interconnections between modernism, anti-theatricality, and the dramatic text. My book therefore examines modern drama through the lens of Plato's term *diegesis,* and in this sense it might be considered a study not so much of non-Aristotelian theater, as Brecht calls it, as of a theater indebted to Plato. Modernist drama and theater is a Platonist theater, by which I mean not a theater of abstract ideas but a theater infused with types of anti-theatricality first developed in Plato's closet dramas.[72]

In order to map out the various diegetic mechanisms at work in modern drama and theater, it is necessary to differentiate between written or printed diegesis (stage directions, descriptive and diegetic speech in closet drama) and performed diegesis (diegetic speech spoken by a chorus, choruslike commentators or narrating or descriptive characters). All stage directions are descriptions or prescriptions of the mimetic space on the stage, but traditionally the doubling inherent in this projection disappears because stage directions are considered dispensable technical appendixes that do not appear in the end product, the performance. But when drama realizes itself as reading drama, its stage directions no longer disappear and thus suddenly take on new significance; they constitute a narrative or third-person discourse that takes over, for the reader, the mimetic space of the stage. While some commentators, most notably Marvin Carlson, have observed the rise and changing significance of stage directions, few have recognized in this phenomenon the most central shift taking place in modern drama.[73] The growing importance of stage directions reaches one climax in Beckett's stage directions, not because they are particularly long, for in this respect they are trumped by those of Shaw and O'Neill, but because they enfold a universe parallel to, and thus at all times competing with, the drama of speech.[74] Reading the plays of Beckett requires a double reading of direct speech and stage directions, and his plays are therefore split between a theater of dialogue and a theater of objects and gestures, the latter captured by the descriptive diegesis of stage directions.

The textual diegesis of modern drama appears in distilled from in the modern closet drama, whose implicit and explicit stage directions conjure a mimetic theatrical space only in order to disassemble it entirely. This may be the place to point out that the modernist closet drama does not constitute an "imaginary" theater in the sense that the reader is simply to "imagine" a "virtual" performance while reading. Such an imaginary stage is produced in the act of reading any traditional dramatic text; it is an effect of a dramatic form that is geared toward the theater. The modernist closet drama, by contrast, does not leave the theater intact, not even in the form of an imaginary theater, but seeks to interrupt and break apart any possibility for either an actual or an imaginary stage. In this sense the modernist closet drama is an instance of what Evlyn Gould has called "virtual theater," but it also turns against this tradition by seeking to de-imagine, de-visualize, and de-theatricalize the act of reading drama.

The diegetic disassemblage of even an imaginary theatrical space is the most specific instance of the more general way in which the modernist closet drama resists the stage. The diegetic function of stage directions and descriptive speeches emerges most conspicuously in the awkward attempts to bring closet dramas onto the stage, against the force, so to speak, of their most anti-theatrical, diegetic strategies. Such adaptations—of Mallarmé's *Livre,* of Joyce's "Circe" chapter, of Virgil Thomson's authorized libretto version of Stein's *Four Saints in Three Acts*—introduce perforce the figure of a narrator or commentator in order to accommodate these texts' diegetic stage directions. These awkward narrators nevertheless register the fact that the stage directions of closet dramas are located at the heart of the genre and can no longer simply disappear in the process of staging.

Narrators or commentators presenting the closet drama's diegetic stage directions belong to a larger class of diegetic characters populating the modern stage. Derived from the Greek chorus or the Nôh chorus, diegetic figures project speech that conditions the mimetic space that is simultaneously present to the audience's eyes. Yeats's Nôh plays, for example, use a chorus that does not participate in the action of the play but rather comments on it and, more particularly, controls its reception through descriptive, diegetic speech. Diegesis is not, however, always reduced to such a chorus, located at the margin of the stage. Brecht's entire acting reform can be seen as an attempt to turn actors into diegetic narrators, speaking as if they were reporting their own speech and condition. The confrontation between mimesis and diegesis here happens with each and every actor/character.

The central function of such seemingly diverse phenomena as increasingly long stage directions, the use of a chorus or choruslike figures, commentators, and finally characters who become their own observers can only be understood if we recognize that they have one thing in common: they superimpose onto the mimetic space of the stage layers of description whose purpose is not to replicate the stage, as if to preserve its particular theatrical and mimetic character, but to adapt, transform, and interrupt it. It is in this process of transformation or adaptation that we can see the mark of a productive resistance to the theater, a resistance singular in its anti-theatrical motivation but diverse in its effects. Mallarmé's operator, Joyce's dramatic narrator, Stein's descriptive and narrative passages, Yeats's chorus, Brecht's epic actors, and Beckett's stage directions thus can be gathered under the term *diegesis* because all are directed, in Plato's sense, against the unmediated presence of theatrical mimesis.

While *diegesis* can be used to describe the resistance to the theater, it nevertheless also contains that which it resists; stage directions and diegetic narrators do not leave theatrical mimesis alone but fold it back into the literary either as text or as diegetic speech. This means that diegesis not only effects the filtering of theater through literature but also creates, in the process, a new form of theater. This dynamic becomes particularly visible through the recurrent use of the term *gesture*. Time and again, the manner in which writers of closet dramas as well as modern dramatists speak about their texts is by way of the gestural, from Wagner's notion of gestural language and Joyce's flirtation with Marcel Jousse's theory of gestures to Brecht's notion of *gestus*. While drawing on the longstanding debate about the gestural origin of language and the hope that an excavation of that origin might lead to a rejuvenation of literary language, the particular investment in gestural writing signals literature's desire for the theater. This tradition ranges from Richard Blackmur's analysis of poetry in *Language as Gesture,* itself indebted to Kenneth Burke's so-called dramatism, to Derrida's notion of Mallarmé's *écriture gestuelle,* a tradition invested in the theatricality of that literature. At the same time, there is a second tradition, ranging from Wagner and Artaud to Pavis, devoted to developing theories of gesture in the hope of creating specifically theatrical signs that would nevertheless function like writing. Both traditions draw on theories of the gestural origin of language to stabilize the term *gesture* right at the border between literature and theater.

Gestures are never simply text or writing, but they infuse the text with remnants of the theatrical even as they suggest that a theatrical performance resembles the signifying practice of texts. Julia Kristeva comes close to such an understanding of gesture in her study Σημειωτική (1969), in which she detaches the term *gesture* from its usual role as an origin of language and uses it for a Marxist-inspired analysis of the production of linguistic signs.[75] Gesture here becomes a word for the praxis and labor that go into the production of language and linguistic communication, the labor that is more or less erased in the finished, linguistic product. An analysis of the gestural in literary texts then becomes an inquiry into this hidden praxis, a domain that for Kristeva is characterized by two attributes: the impersonal and the spatial. One could add a third attribute, which she does not mention perhaps because of her exclusive attention in this study to the novel, and that is the theatrical. A "gestural" analysis of modernism leads directly to the contentious relation between text and theater, or to be more precise, the respective values placed on them.

The analysis of the gestural, then, reveals the underside of resistance, the fact that the theater the closet drama and anti-theatrical theater more generally also produce a form of theater within their very act of resistance.[76] It is this complicity of rejection and production that stands behind the various forms of modern drama. Their analysis is the subject matter of this book.

Part I
The Invention of Theatricality

Richard Wagner:
The Theatrocracy of the Mime

Wagner's Anti-Theatrical Critics

> Through Wagner, modernity arrives at its most intimate language:
> it hides neither its good side nor its evil side. . . . one has almost
> passed judgement on the value of modernity when one comes to
> terms with the good and the evil in Wagner.[1]

It would be rash to accept Nietzsche's remark, made in 1888, when modernism as we understand it had barely begun, if it were not for Theodor Adorno, who almost sixty years later continued to speak of a specifically "Wagnerian modernism" haunting late-nineteenth- and early-twentieth-century art.[2] Indeed, the modernist opera and theater, from Arnold Schönberg to Kurt Weill, define themselves in relation to Wagner; pathbreaking directors from Adolphe Appia to E. G. Craig were profoundly influenced by Wagner; and no theatrical space inspired more praise and ridicule than Wagner's Festspielhaus at Bayreuth. Moreover, poets and novelists such as Charles Baudelaire, Stéphane Mallarmé, Marcel Proust, James Joyce, T. S. Eliot, and Robert Musil kept returning to Wagner, who had unified the function of composer, director, and poet.

Upon closer examination, however, it becomes clear that Mallarmé did not admire Wagner as a poet, that Appia did not admire Wagner as a director, and that Kurt Weill had at best an ambivalent admiration for Wagner as a composer. It turns out that Wagner's singular impact on modernism is not due to the particular contributions he made to the different branches of art, although his music might be singled out as an exception. Rather his works derive their impact from the fact that they changed the way we talk and think about the theater and the notion of theatricality; they present an entirely new understanding of music, poetry, and acting in the state of total theatricality. The argument I advance here is that Wagner's pivotal role with respect to modernism was transforming the concept of theatricality from a description of the theater as an art form — defining what happens onstage — into a value that must be either rejected or embraced. With slight exaggeration one could claim that after Wagner it was no longer possible to take a neutral position with respect to the theater; after Wagner one had to declare one's allegiance to the theater or come forward with a critique of its value. Thus Wagner can be said to have polarized the cultural field of the later nineteenth and early twentieth centuries in Europe, and even outside Europe, around theatricality. What Wagner demands therefore is a reflection not only on the theater but on theatricality, what Nietzsche would call a "genealogy" of the theater as value. Only such a genealogy of the theater and of theatricality can help us understand what drew late-nineteenth- and early-twentieth-century theater to embrace or reject Wagner. In this sense, one might agree with Nietzsche that understanding modernism means coming to terms with Wagner.

A genealogy of theater as value should begin with those who oppose it, for Wagner's detractors are more keenly aware of the consequences of turning theatricality into a value than his admirers. For this reason I begin this chapter with two of Wagner's modernist critics, Nietzsche and Adorno, whose attacks on Wagner have proven to be both symptomatic of and constitutive for modernism's ambivalent relation to Wagner. Reservations about the theater and mimesis may not define the entire gamut of modernist art and thought, but they constitute one of its dominant characteristics, even for a large number of modernist playwrights. Mallarmé and Henry James turn away from the theater in disgust; Yeats, Stein, and Hofmannsthal approach it with great hesitation; and the ambivalence of these and many other writers is enforced by a whole tradition of theorists, ranging from Yvor Winters to Michael Fried, who define the canon of high modernist art through its opposition to the theater and theatricality. Their values are matched by those theorists, such as Adorno, who see in modernism's formal and innovative strategies a crusade against art's reliance on those simple forms of mimesis that are often associated with the theater.

The most symptomatic feature of Nietzsche's and Adorno's critiques is the linkage of, or slippage between, two terms: *theatricality* and *mimesis*. This slippage, perhaps surprising to us today, is due to the essential reliance of the theater on the actor or the mime. Openly or covertly, critics of mimesis agree that there is no mimesis more vulgar than the mimesis of actors and that if we must have some kind of mimesis—for an art entirely without mimesis would be unthinkable—it should be one as far removed as possible from actors, who practice the most basic and mindless kind of mimesis with their hands and postures, grimaces and mannerisms. Nietzsche praises Wagner sarcastically as "the greatest Mime [*größte Mime*], the most astonishing genius of the theater . . . our *scenic creator par excellence*" ("Fall," 105), and Adorno repeats this attack on Wagner's theatrical imagination diligently, saying that "It is as if the aversion to mimic art [*Scheu vor der Mimik*] did not have full power over him" and calling this reliance on mimesis "Wagnerian acting" [Schauspielerei].[3] Nietzsche's anti-theatricalism becomes compatible with Adorno's reservations about some primitive form of mimesis, so that what for Nietzsche is a sign of Wagner's pathetically theatrical imagination for Adorno becomes an example of his unreflected mimesis. Thus the actor becomes the scapegoat of modernism.

As a performing art, alas, the theater continues to depend on such actors, and for this reason a critique of the actor's mimesis frequently leads to a critique of theatricality. Nietzsche sees in Wagner's operas a "theatrocracy [*Theatrokratie*] — , the craziness of believing in the primacy of the theater, in the right of the theater to role over the arts, to rule over art" ("Fall," 117), and he not only criticizes the dominance of the theater over the other arts but also places the theater almost outside the arts altogether. What makes Nietzsche an interesting case in the history of the anti-theatrical prejudice as detailed by Barish and others is that unlike so many critics of the theater, from Plato to the Puritans, Nietzsche does not attack art as such, even though the term *theatrocracy* comes from Plato, who grounded his attack on all forms of art in his own aversion to the vulgar μιμος, or *mimos*. Nor does Nietzsche attack the theater itself; what he attacks is what the theater does to the other arts, the particular quality it imposes on the other arts. It is in this fear that the theater might have a bad influence on the other arts that we can see the workings of theatricality, not as a description of the theater, but as an aesthetic value, and more particularly one that must be opposed.

Although Nietzsche's anti-theatrical turn is most conspicuous in his later writings against Wagner, his suspicion of mimetic theater is at work even in what is commonly seen as his most theatrical or pro-theatrical text: *The Birth of Tragedy from the Spirit of Music*.[4] Even when Nietzsche celebrates Wagner as the return of Greek tragedy in a different form, this celebration is based on an implied critique of the actor embedded in the opposition between a participatory, Dionysiac experience and its Apollinian representation on the stage. Before Apollo's intervention there were neither spectators nor actors, only the collective, participatory experience of Dionysiac dance to the rhythms of archaic music. For Nietzsche, as for Plato, the "emotionless coolness of the true actor" (112) becomes the theater's greatest liability because the calculating actor deceives the audience with fake passions; it is the same dichotomy between coolness and passion that Denis Diderot foregrounds in his famous paradox, according to which the representation of passions on the stage can only be performed by a dispassionate actor. Nietzsche develops a more general critique of theatrical representation, according to which the actor inserts between the Dionysiac chorus and the audience a visual and scenic "middle world" (184), which keeps the two from merging into a participatory Dionysiac ritual. Nietzsche's historical speculations anticipate those emphatic believers in the return to ritualistic practices, such as Victor Turner, Richard Schechner, and Eugenio Barba, who have long turned to anthropology to find rituals to fulfill the Dionysiac promise of overcoming the representational theater of the actor's mimetic art. (The discipline of performance studies, in its practice of analyzing social ritual in the everyday world through the expanded terms of the theater, extends this trajectory into our critical practice.)[5] As far as Nietzsche is concerned, we can detect the birth of his aversion to the mime in a genealogy that attributes the invention of the actor to Apollo, who sought to diminish the role of the tragic chorus, that last and already nostalgic bastion of collective and tragic experience.

If there is one recurrent theme in the anti-theatrical attacks on Wagner, it is the fear that the theater is not just one art form among others but a condition that potentially affects the other arts. And if theatricality is a problem for art in general, it is particularly contaminating when it exerts its influence over music, which is the purest of all arts, at least according to the romantic and more particularly Schopenhauerian hierarchy of the arts, which Nietzsche never abandons. Nietzsche's harshest judgment, therefore, holds that Wagner is "probably the most passionate mimomaniac [*begeistertste Mimomane*] who ever lived, *even as musician*" ("Fall," 132, Nietzsche's emphasis). In fact, the suspicion that Wagner's mimic theatricality would intrude even into his music is the most frequently recurring trope in Wagner criticism, whose terms of abjection — *mimomaniacal* music, *theatrical* music — circumscribe a music that is born from the figure of the mime. But how are we to define, how do critics of (Wagnerian) theatricality define, this dangerous influence of the theater on the other arts and in particular on music?

It is a fortunate circumstance that the theoretical alliance between Nietzsche's anti-theatricality and Adorno's concern about mimesis not only has a common source — the unacknowledged aversion to the mime — but also a common term through which this aversion operates: *gesture*. Nietzsche and Adorno agree that Wagner's art suffers from being too gestural and that his fixation on gestures, even and especially in music, is an effect of both his theatricality and his excessive reliance on vulgar mimesis. Following this debate about gestures and gestural art in Wagner helps us understand what is at stake in modernism's ambivalence about the theater and why gestures increasingly become a central concern for a critique of the theater.

Wagner himself admits to placing music in the service of the theater. Indeed, it is one of the central formulations in his theoretical opus, *Oper und Drama:* "The mistake of the artistic genre of opera consists in the fact that a means of expression (music) became the end, the end of expression (drama) however, became a means."[6] While it remains to be specified what Wagner means by this form of subjection, Nietzsche sees in it a thinly concealed acknowledgment that what really dominates music is not the drama nor theater in general but more specifically the gesticulating actor. Hence Nietzsche's polemical translation of Wagner's formula: "Even if it was Wagner's theory that 'drama is the end, music only its means' —, his practice really was . . . 'attitude is the end, drama, even music, is only its means.' Music as a means of highlighting, amplifying, interiorizing dramatic gestures and actor-sensibility [*dramatische Gebärde und Schauspieler-Sinnfälligkeit*]; and the Wagnerian drama becomes merely an occasion for many interesting attitudes" ("Fall," 132). Wagner's program of seeing in music the means and in drama (theater) the end is here reduced to the gestures and attitudes of actors and singers. "Interesting" attitudes and dramatic gestures are the true stuff of which Wagner's music dramas are made. The total work of art, the epic drama, the elaborate music are nothing but means to an end: the gestures and, even more abjectly, the "attitudes" of actors and opera singers, whose overly "dramatic" movements have been a common object of critique and ridicule through the centuries. Wagner thus exemplifies the "emergence of the actor in music" (113), and the result of such acting is a labored "gestural hocus-pocus" (131), through which actors seek to endow their banal mimesis with mystique and depth.[7] In this way the full force of the anti-theatrical polemic is applied to the value — or lack thereof — seen in an aesthetics of gesture. Gesture becomes a shorthand for the mimetic actor lingering at the heart of the theater and, due to the general slippage between anti-mimesis and anti-theatricality, for the theatrical effects the theater imposes on the other arts.

Because theatrical acting is nothing more than an imitation of art, it relies on pretense, which threatens to become a lie.[8] Adorno, who devotes a whole chapter of his essay "Versuch über Wagner" to the notion of *gestus,* launches this charge with his usual emphasis on its relation to mimesis: "Through repetition and gestural representation, the mimetic drive [*mimetische Regung*] degenerates to mere imitation and ultimately to lying" (35). While putatively defending some proper kind of mimesis, Adorno dismisses theatrical mimesis and therefore considers a work of art based on gestures to be nothing but a false imitation of mimesis. Here Nietzsche and Adorno align themselves with the most sweeping of the Platonist anti-art positions, which Oscar Wilde would provocatively reverse and thus leave intact in his celebration of the art of lying.[9] That Adorno would accept Nietzsche's terminology even though the two were separated by the very experience of high modernism, from Schönberg to Beckett, testifies to the energy behind the entanglement of anti-theatricalist and anti-mimetic positions as they are expressed, here and elsewhere, in the common critique of gestural art.[10]

But what does a gestural artwork look like, and how are we to tell it apart from a nongestural and therefore nontheatrical one? Nietzsche's polemical but discerning description of Wagner's oeuvre gives us a first hint: "Wagner begins with hallucinations: not of notes but of gestures. And then he searches for a semiotics of music [*Ton-Semiotik*] to go along with them. If you want to admire him, watch how he works here: how he separates, how he creates small entities, how he exposes them, makes them vivid and visible . . . how pitiful his attempt to develop them, to insert into one another [*durcheinander zu stecken*] that which did not grow into anything [*auseinandergewachsen*] in the first place" ("Fall," 103). This passage catalogs the effects of an artwork that is born from the spirit of gesture: gestures cannot be developed into continuous forms and shapes nor, as Nietzsche details a little later, be used to create "organic works of art" [organische Gestalten] (103); rather, they lead to small and isolated entities that can only be amplified and exaggerated. Instead of developing themes, motives, and (musical or dramatic) lines, all Wagner can do with his disjointed gestural entities, which have never "grown" into anything [auseinandergewachsen], is to put them all together, to amass them in an aggregate within which they are not organically connected but only mechanically "inserted into one another" [durcheinandergesteckt]. Thus the Wagnerian artwork devotes its energy to creating small units, or details, into which everything must be "compressed" [gedrängt] (104), leading Nietzsche to the seemingly paradoxical statement that Wagner's megalomaniac works represent a "miniaturism" in music because they are aesthetically based on single, isolated gestures.

In this line of critique, Nietzsche no longer thinks explicitly of the origin of gestural art in the vulgar mime but explores the effects of these gestures once they are removed from the mime and applied to shape and structure whole works of art, such as the *Ring*. In this context gestures are not simply mimetic remnants but have begun to denote an atavistic form of art. What the gestural work of art retains from the actor is the inability to arrive at a constructive principle that could organically unify those gestures disjointed by nature.[11] All that mimes can do is perform different kinds of gestures, one after the other, without being able to indicate that one gesture modifies or comments on other gestures. Gestures can only be performed one at a time, and they all have the same status.[12]

This critique of an aesthetics of gesture remains unchanged for an antitheatrical modernism eager to point to the dangerous influence of the theater on the other arts. Adorno, for example, repeats verbatim Nietzsche's observation about the disjointed quality of Wagner's "gestural" work of art: "Gestures can only be repeated and amplified, but they cannot really be developed" ("Versuch," 34). In addition, however, he adds specificity to Nietzsche's critique in that he sees Wagner's gestural composition at work particularly in the orchestra, thus echoing, intentionally or unintentionally, Wagner's own theory of the gestural orchestra. When Adorno speaks of a "gesticulating theater music " [gestikulierende Bühnenmusik] (32), he refers to the gestural quality of Wagner's orchestra, which destroys every attempt to achieve a constructive and self-sufficient musical composition: "The interventions of the orchestra . . . fulfill a gestural function [*gestische Funktion*]. They interrupt . . . the fabric of the composition and redraw [*nachzeichnen*] the figures on the stage. In this sense they have an intermittent character" (33). It is impossible for an aesthetics of gesture, even if it is musical, to detach itself from the gestures of mimes on the stage. Because they "redraw" [nachzeichnen] the gestures performed onstage, the interventions of the orchestra are inextricably tied to the mimetic and disjointed quality of theatrical gestures, interrupting every competing compositional principle that the opera might have developed; anchored in crude, literal gestures, the orchestra imposes onto the composition its interruptive and interrupted gestural quality. It is true that theater music can never entirely ignore the stage and must therefore find some kind of relation to gestural and scenic action. What turns Wagner, for better or worse, into an example of an aesthetics of gesture is that these gestures become the compositional principle on which the entire oeuvre relies: "For Wagner, the intermittent gesture [*die intermittierende Geste*] becomes the principle of composition" (33). Rather than arriving at a composition that could balance the intermittent and interruptive quality of gestures, Wagner bases his entire opera on them. In fact most aesthetic theories of gesture, from Benjamin and Brecht to Giorgio Agamben, will follow Nietzsche in that they foreground the interrupted, nonorganic, repetitive, and theatrical nature of an aesthetics based on gesture.[13]

It is Adorno who finally develops a differentiated terminology of gestures in music, one centered on the term *leitmotif*. For him, leitmotifs are interrupted pieces of melody that are attached directly to objects, themes, and actions on the stage. Because of its direct relation to the theater, the leitmotif can, and has been, cataloged according to theatrical, or dramatic, entities: the fire motif, the Siegfried motif, the fate motif, the Valhalla motif, the Valkyries motif, among others.[14] Such names, Adorno perceptively observes, turn these motifs into allegories for which these names function as a *subscriptio,* the explanatory name underneath a pictorial allegory: "Like an illness, the motifs fall prey to an allegorical rigidity. Gesture freezes and becomes an expressive image [*Bild des Ausdrucks*]" ("Versuch," 44). This allegorical quality in turn is nothing but a pictorial derivative of an interrupted and frozen gesture. Because of their orientation toward the theater, leitmotifs are tied to actors and are thus subjected to the same sequential and paratactic organization as actual gestures; the composition "disintegrates into sequences of reified allegorical leitmotifs" (44). These short motifs are never really developed but instead lead to precisely those repetitions that Nietzsche and Adorno see as the effects of Wagner's "mimomaniacal" determination to have gestures, paired with musical motifs, structure the composition of the opera. Because they remain too close to their mimetic origin, and thus to mimetic content, gestures can never be transformed into a pure and formal principle of composition. If, as in Wagner, they nevertheless are endowed with such a function, so contrary to their nature, the result is an incoherent patchwork of intermittent gestures, halfway between the compositional form they are meant to fulfill and the mimetic content to which they must remain attached.

It is important to point out that Adorno's position on mimesis is not one of simple rejection. Mimesis assures that the work of art will not be totally rationalized and that the desire for constructive form will be counterbalanced by the specific material introduced by mimetic operations. However differentiated Adorno's understanding of mimesis may be, he keeps his distance from the theater and its gestural form of mimesis, and it is in this distancing that we can perceive the ever powerful symbiosis of antitheatricalism and a critique of mimesis. In a characteristic fusion of a residual Hegelianism and a vaguely psychoanalytic vocabulary, Adorno denounces Wagner's gestural theatricality as a regression to an earlier state of mimesis: "Musical logic is replaced by a kind of gesticulating. . . . Certainly, all music points back towards this gestural quality [*das Gestische*] and retains it within itself. In the Western world, though, music has spiritualized and interiorized [*vergeistigt und verinnerlicht*] this quality to become expression, while, at the same time, musical lines have to be synthesized logically by means of construction. . . . Wagner is at odds with this development" (32). Western music must overcome its gestural origin by "sublating it" [bewahrt es in sich auf] and by making this corporeal origin more ideal or cerebral *(vergeistigen)*. By insisting on his gestural art Wagner eclipses history, or psychoanalytically speaking, he regresses into an earlier state of development. This schema of musical history as an increasing sublation of mimesis proved paradigmatic for Adorno's subsequent work on music. After writing his critique of Wagner, Adorno added an essay on Stravinsky to his already existing piece on Schönberg to form his *Philosophy of Modern Music*. Here Adorno recycles the anti-mimetic, anti-theatrical, and antigestural terminology from his Wagner essay and directs it against Stravinsky.[15] According to Adorno, Stravinsky regresses into archaic mimesis, in part caused by his fixation on theatrical ballet gestures, and thus into an "infantilism" reminiscent of "children's play gestures" (150). The combination of archaic regression and infantile imitation of children's gestures shows Adorno's anti-theatrical stance, and it shows that childlike behavior, imitative gestures, and phylogenetic regressions form the negative underpinnings of Adorno's paradigm. What Adorno's anti-theatricalism also indicates is that Wagner and Stravinsky are part of a tradition of music that does not shy away from the external gestures of music, even their visual appearance. The dichotomy between Nietzsche and Adorno on the one hand and Wagner and Stravinsky on the other is part of a split between those who deem the visual appearance of gestures to be an external distraction and those who see in them something that is intimately related to the music itself. As Edward Said and Lydia Goehr have pointed out, this debate ultimately leads to the question whether music should remain a performing art or whether it should be rescued by the aural purity of audio recording.[16]

Even Adorno's *Ästhetische Theorie* relates mimesis to the theater, and here the *agon* between gestures and construction is more visibly tied to an aversion to the mimesis of "primitive" actors. Now the type of regression identified in Wagner's gestural leitmotif appears as an atavism of the most primitive types of mimesis imaginable: that of the clown and the ape. The mimetic remnants, which modern art must not suppress but which it must sublate and spiritualize, are described in terms of their clownish-apish quality: "Art remembers, with comfort [*erinnert Kunst tröstlich*], its prehistory in the animalistic world. What android apes perform in the zoo collectively resembles acts of clowns" (181). While the reassuring memory of its phylogenetic past is necessary if art wants to avoid a dangerous "suppression" [Verdrängung] (181), it must never begin to sacrifice its constructive distance from this apish mimesis. The clown and the ape lurk in Adorno's brief history of art, which is driven by an irreversible Hegelian progress through which the ape's, the clown's, and also the mime's mimesis must be increasingly sublated and interiorized precisely so that they can be remembered, with comfort, as origin but not as form. Adorno is concerned that we might no longer remember these primitive origins of mimesis and that, forgetting them, we might blindly stumble back in the history of the world, or at least of the West. Adorno may have cherished mimesis because it preserved an irreducible particularity in the work of art, but this appreciation of mimesis did not keep him from despising the vulgar mime, in whose gestures he never ceased to detect those of the ape. While Nietzsche places theatricality outside of art, because it is a mere imitation of art, Adorno's ape functions as the icon of a prehistoric mimesis, not just outside art but before art even began.

The Theatricality of Gestures

How is it that Wagner managed to turn theatricality into a value that would make critics such as Nietzsche and Adorno, who were not in any simple sense "enemies" of the theater, express their critique in anti-theatrical terms? This question has not received the attention it deserves because of a terminological confusion in Wagner's writings. Wagner's formula that "music" should henceforth serve the "drama" has led to many stimulating discussions of Wagner's conception of the dramatic as opposed to the epic form, from which he nevertheless continued to borrow most of his material. The scope of the *Ring,* for example, has led commentators such as Thomas Mann to conclude that Wagner's operas are epic rather than dramatic because they violate so starkly Aristotle's rules.[17] David Levin pointed out in detail the extent to which Wotan, Mime, Siegfried, and Alberich are all obsessive narrators and therefore register a tension between the dramatic and the epic forms. And as Herbert Lindenberger has shown, Wagner's dramaturgy rests uneasily between epic and drama, trying to enfold the one into the other.

However, the reading I advance here rests on the assumption, also made by Nietzsche, that when Wagner uses the term *drama* what he really means is *theater.* Wagner's formula that music should serve the drama does not mean primarily that music should serve the plot of the libretto, but that it should be intimately tied to theatrical action (which includes, but is not limited to, dramaturgy). Indeed, Wagner's theory and practice of the *Gesamtkunstwerk,* as well as the anti-theatrical critiques leveled against it, cannot be fully understood from within the opposition between epic and drama. Rather, it is necessary to introduce a third term, namely, *theatricality.* Wagner's scenes of narration, and the epic construction that makes them necessary, do not diminish his commitment to total theatricality; they testify to it, because they attempt to drag onto stage that which exceeds the spatial and temporal boundaries of a given scene.[18] Even the very acts of narration are theatricalized as thoroughly as possible by gestural music, layers of leitmotifs, and melodramatic acting.[19] It is central, therefore, to keep separate the question of a dramatic versus an epic construction of plot and the question of theatrical representation, and it is also important not to assume that scenes of narration always signify an ambivalence about theatricality.[20] Wagner, more than anyone, wanted to force everything into total theatrical representation; that he did not abandon the project of staging an increasingly epic work such as the *Ring* demonstrates that he operated with an expanded notion of theatricality.[21]

While Wagner himself does not use the term *theatricality*, he does use the term used by his anti-theatrical critics, namely, *gesture (Gebärde)*. *Gebärde* is not as well known as some of Wagner's other terms, and while it is quite clear that Adorno clandestinely takes his notion of gesture, along with most of its critical implications, from Nietzsche, it is much less certain whether either of them knew, or was interested in, Wagner's own understanding of gestures. Nevertheless, it is through this term that Wagner articulates the main tenets of his theory. In fact, one might speculate that it was due to Wagner's theory and practice of gestural theatricality that Nietzsche and Adorno were provoked into their anti-gestural and anti-theatrical critiques.

In contrast to Nietzsche and Adorno, Wagner was first and foremost a practitioner of the theater, as extreme in his criticism of the average singer, composer, and actor as in his praise of his idols such as Schröder-Devrient.[22] His reform of opera therefore begins with a critique of the imbalance in the distribution of power in Europe's opera houses: the dominance of music over drama, of the aria over the orchestra, and of the singer's voice over the art of acting. Music overshadows the diminished dramatic action, and the orchestra merely accompanies the singers' aria, which the singers' acting only serves to emphasize. In his essay "Über Schauspieler und Sänger" (1873), for example, Wagner attacks the Italian *canto* style as being centered exclusively on the voice and demands a "German" style that includes actor's training and theatrical mimesis (9:234ff.). Wagner's solution to this imbalance—music must serve the drama—is not just a new version of Monteverdi's controversial claim that music must be subservient to the text of the opera (a dogma Monteverdi himself frequently violated), even though Wagner, like Gluck before him, sought to endow the libretto with a renewed dignity. The real provocation of Wagner's claim, however, lies in the fact that he transformed the most neglected and debased element of the opera, namely, the awkward acting of those divas who attended exclusively to their celestial voices, into the central component of the theatrical work of art.

Beginning with his early manifesto-like essay "The Artwork of the Future" (1849), Wagner leaves no doubt that the central part of the total work of art is neither music nor the libretto, but the theatrical performance of singers, whose gestures constitute the foundation of the *Gesamtkunstwerk*. *Dance,* which for Wagner is the term that designates all movements of the human body, "is the condition for the other arts" (3:87); the moving body, therefore, becomes the central agent of the "one artwork of the future," which must find its "ground" [Boden] in the "plastic movement of the body" [plastische Leibesbewegung] (3:108). The one unified artwork of the future rests on the physical, literal gestures of bodies on stage; their theatricality is, therefore, the point of departure for the whole artwork. In addition, the actor also embodies the unity of the arts, for it is in the actor that "the three sister arts come together in order to find a new expressivity" (3:85). For the same reason, Wagner admired Wilhemine Schröder-Devrient, not for her singing, but rather for her "breathing" and, most importantly, for her acting.[23] In his essay on actors and singers Wagner reiterates the central importance of actors, arguing that the theatrical work of art rests first and foremost on the shoulders of actors, whom he now calls "Darsteller," a word derived from the term for theatrical representation, *Darstellung,* to which the *Gesamtkunstwerk* aspires (9:193). It speaks to the boldness, but also the precariousness, of Wagner's aesthetics that the embarrassing gestures of divas and singers should be the future of the opera and the foundation of its theatricality.

Wagner's overdetermined investment in a theatrical notion of gesture makes extreme demands on the actors and singers, "the creators of the *Gesamtkunstwerk*" (3:129). It thus comes as no surprise that Wagner was engaged in a lifelong project of reforming and controlling acting, in particular operatic acting.[24] Together with his ample staging instructions, Wagner turned out a large number of pamphlets, several of them about acting and gesture, phrased in a nationalist manner against the so-called French style.[25] Wagner keeps telling actors to train by improvisation and to trust their natural "drive to imitate" [Nachahmungstrieb] to be the basis for a genuinely "German" type of acting. This call for imitative acting was grounded in the reform movement of the theater in the early nineteenth century, as represented by, among others, Eduard Devrient from the Dresden Theater, where *Tannhäuser* premiered in 1845. Devrient, in his *Geschichte der deutschen Schauspielkunst,* had condemned exaggerated and exalted acting, and Wagner, in his essay on acting, praises Devrient's production of *King Lear* as an instance of a more natural staging (9:194). Both Wagner and Devrient argue against the use of the preestablished, fixed gestures and poses that were available in manuals such as the ones composed by François Delsarte (1811–71).[26] Delsarte, a trained opera singer steeped in the opera's melodramatic style of acting, was forced to give up his career when his voice failed him, and he turned to codifying the gestures of operatic performance. That Wagner and Devrient attacked preestablished gestures does not necessarily mean that either of them was a protonaturalist, but it does demonstrate a renewed interest in gesture and a gestural theater in the nineteenth-century theater, whose contours have been detailed by Martin Meisel.[27]

The actor's gestures are more than the physical center of the work of art:

Wagner also derives from them the material for the theatrical aesthetics of the *Gesamtkunstwerk*. To integrate the actor's gestures into such a general aesthetics, Wagner develops a somewhat forced theory according to which the total work of art must be neatly divided into different regions and their corresponding modes and media of expression. In order for the libretto and the aria to complement one another, there is—must be—something that language cannot say and that melody cannot express. That which language cannot say is expressed through gestures, for they are, as Wagner claims time and again, the "language" of the unsayable: "Gesture [*Gebärde*] . . . expressed to the eye only that which verbal language [*Wortsprache*] could not express—if verbal language could express it, gesture would have become superfluous and disturbing" (*Oper,* 331). Carefully ensuring that gestures do more than merely imitate language, Wagner reserves for them the particular mode of expressing only that which verbal language cannot express, the "unsayable" of verbal language. This idea that gestures can supplement language grows out of a tradition of thinking of gestures as both like and unlike language. Historically, this understanding of gestures derives from the debate about the origin of language—Condillac, Herder, Rousseau, and Warburton—in which gestures regularly occupy the gray area between nature and culture, between pure expression and conventional articulation, between the unsayable and the sayable. Even Nietzsche wrote a small treatise on the gestural origin of language, which may well have laid the ground for his critique of gesture in Wagner, denouncing the visual and mimic qualities of gestural poetry and praising its allegiance to music.[28] Wagner, like Nietzsche, recognizes that this theory of the gestural origin of language is based on a theatrical category, but in contrast to Nietzsche, he uses the theatrical nature of these original gestures as the foundation of the artwork: tied to music and libretto from the beginning, gestures infuse them both with an irreducible theatricality that can be exploited on the stage. *Gesture*—now that it is a principle, Wagner uses the term in the singular—is therefore the term around which Wagner's theory and practice of theatricality revolve.

The gestures on the stage do not express the whole range of the unsayable, for they are addressed only to the eye. In Wagner's division of the total work of art, there is a related unsayable for the ear, namely, that which melody cannot express, and for this reason there must be an auditory form of the unsayable as well as an analogous mode of expression for this "second" unsayable. Wagner takes this mode of expression to be the music of the orchestra, which he consequently describes as a complimentary, auditory gesture: "Just as gestures express to the eye something that only they can express, the orchestra expresses something correlating [*genau Entsprechende*] to this expression [*Kundgebung*] to the ear" (*Oper,* 333). In Wagner's view, the music of the orchestra should not accompany the melody sung by the singer; rather, it should follow a mode of expression akin to their gestures. The new opera is a unified work of art in which the orchestra and the actors overcome their old, imitative dependence on melodic arias and create a new form of gesturality that unifies the orchestra and the actors in a multiplicity, or "polyphony," of gestures on the stage and in the orchestra.

What enables orchestral music to express the "auditory unsayable" to the ear is its kinship to the "language" of gestures on the stage, and this kinship stems from the origin of the opera in a unified performance of dance and music: "The orchestra's ability to speak [*Sprachvermögen*] relies on its kinship with gesture, the way we know it from dance. It speaks in sound figures [*Tonfiguren*]" (336–37). In these sound figures, or sound gestures, which import gesture as an expressive principle from the stage to music, we can recognize Adorno's description of the gestural leitmotifs performed by the "gesticulating" orchestra.[29] Again, *gesture* becomes the term through which Wagner and Adorno articulate what we may otherwise call the *theatricalization* of music. For Wagner, basing an opera aesthetics on gesture means attacking the aria at the place of its production: the singer's voice is degraded, and the previously neglected gestures are moved to the center of the total work of art. Once the singer's gestures attain their new significance, the same operation can be repeated on the level of composition by creating a symphonic opera based on the gestures of the orchestra and not on the arias, whose usual purpose is only to show off the singer's voice. Orchestra and acting, orchestral gestures and literal gestures, are thus aligned in their common struggle against the overpowering melodic aria and the dominant position of the voice in the opera industry.[30] Wagner's obscure conception of the unsayable and the expressivity of gestures can be understood as a strategy for saving the opera from its fatal attraction to the singer's voice.[31]

One last step is needed to complete the gesturalization or theatricalization of the arts. In his theory of alliterative language, Wagner extends the theatrical notion of gesture from the stage to language and literature. In a highly metaphoric passage, often criticized for its lack of precision, Wagner associates the consonant with the rhythm of language and the vowel with the sound of the root, thus positing that the consonant is directed toward rhythmic dance and ultimately toward dramatic and visual gestures, while the vowel represents, in contrast, the purely auditory aspect of the word. Wagner calls the consonant, because of its relation to visual rhythm and gesture, "the eye of hearing" [Das Auge des Gehörs], and the vowel "the ear of hearing" [Das Ohr des Gehörs] (*Oper,* 286).[32] (It is due to such formulations that writers from Baudelaire to Kandinsky considered Wagner to be a promoter of synaesthesia.)[33] This alliterative concept of language introduces an expanded notion of gesture, the gesture of language. No longer reserved for the acting on stage or the music of the orchestra, *gesture* now also describes the alliterative poetics of the libretto.

Wagner embarks here on a project of formulating a theory—and also a practice—of a gestural poetics, an art of writing gestures. While this theory of gestural poetry may seem particularly obscure and far-fetched in its use of etymology and physiognomic metaphors, Wagner's own poetic practice can be understood as complementary to both the theatrical gestures of actors and the gestures in the orchestra: his endless alliterations imitate the irregular rhythm of actors as they try to re-create medieval, and Germanic, diction.[34] The naiveté of this conception lies in the hope that the return to a primitivist poetics would foster, at the same time, a poetry of the future, akin to gestural music and, of course, the acting and theatricality on the stage. Wagner's alliterations are nevertheless significant in their attempt to theatricalize poetry, a project continued, often under a similar name, by writers as diverse as Mallarmé, Joyce, and Brecht. We can generalize, then, and describe the *Gesamtkunstwerk* in terms of a theatrical aesthetics of gesture: it is only through their participation in the aesthetics of gesture that the different arts—dance, music, literature—can hope to come together functionally under one theatrical principle holding together Wagner's breathtaking construction of the total theatrical work of art.[35] For both promoters and critics, *gesture* is therefore the term that stands for the elevation of theatricality into a value.

The effects of Wagner's theatricalization of the theater can be seen everywhere in his operas. Everything Wagner touches is forced onto the stage, where nothing must be left unsaid or unexpressed. He was the first to hide the orchestra, to dim the lights in the audience, to calculate the overpowering impact of the interplay between mythos, music, and acting; he initiated a new architecture of the opera house and reconceived of opera as a festival event, removed from the banality of modern, everyday life. Despite Wagner's desire to make music visible, the visibility he imagined was not in the service of exposing the means of musical production, as Kurt Weill would demand, but an illusionist type of visibility. In his relentless illusionism Wagner was the precursor of those magicians of the stage, from Max Reinhardt to Robert Wilson, whose spectacular successes never cease to raise questions about the price extracted by an art that overwhelms the audience's rationality by unleashing a theatricality that collapses critical distances and disables analytic responses. In addition to being the creator of a whole apparatus of illusion, Wagner was, as Adorno and others have pointed out, a visionary of film and film music and also a predecessor of the twentieth century's totalizing media.[36] Consequently, Wagner calls the separation of the arts, as it is practiced in pantomime, absolute music, or the closet drama, "the shameless" [das Unerhörte] (3:132) and an "egotistical" obstruction to the unity of art. His scorn for both closet drama and pantomime bespeaks the gulf that separates him from his symbolist admirers, such as Baudelaire or Mallarmé, for whom Wagner's commitment to theatrical representation was a continuing source of irritation. Wagner almost called his operas *Schauspiel*—the regular German word for "play" but literally meaning "seeing play"—and adds that his definition of music drama is "the deeds of music become visible" [ersichtlich gewordene Thaten der Musik] (9:364). The lasting contribution of the *Gesamtkunstwerk* is, for better or worse, a theatricalization of art based on an aesthetics of theatrical, and therefore ultimately visible, gestures.

As important for Wagner's critics as this theory of gestural theatricality is the fact that this theory is part of a political project. Throughout the late eighteenth and early nineteenth centuries there was a strong tradition in the German states to bring about their unification by aesthetic means. Schiller's notion of the aesthetic education of mankind is perhaps the most well known, but by no means the only, attempt in this direction. And since the theater is the most social and therefore the most political of the arts, it has always occupied a privileged place in the minds of those, like Schiller, invested in the public use of art. Wagner continued this project and related it directly to the collaborative process of creating the total work of art.[37] When Wagner speaks about the political function of the theater's collaborative production and collective reception in essays such as "German Art and German Politics," it becomes clear that he thinks of his theater as internally forging the unity of the politically divided German *Volk:* the collaboration of the artists becomes a model for the collectivity of the people, the identity or at least structural similarity between musicians and audience on the one hand and *Volk* on the other. And now we can see the political program behind the total work of art. Just as the total work of art unifies the hitherto isolated and scattered "sister" arts, so it will unify the scattered *Volk.* Wagner even uses the term *communism* to describe this union, a term reminiscent of his days as a radical '48 revolutionary and admirer of Bakunin. By midcentury, however, Wagner's communism had turned into a nationalistic communitarianism that found its expression in the theater: pure politics, which in this case means class politics, is to be replaced, or sublated, by the theater. That Wagner ended up turning to King Ludwig II to have this theater funded is not a historical irony, but shows that by that time the theater was all that mattered to Wagner; it had become the better politics.

The specter of the analogy between theater and the public sphere has haunted the history of the theater across a wide spectrum of political thought and action. While Wagner attributes to the creators an active function and to the audience a passive one, Meyerhold, who never denied his debt to Wagner despite their political and aesthetic differences, in his staging of *The Storming of the Winter Palace* had the audience collaborate in the representation and repetition of a historical event in which they might have even actively participated themselves. What both Wagner and Meyerhold have in common is the idea that the audience is more than just a segment of the general public, that it could be seen to represent this diffuse public (or at least to be the politically advanced avant-garde of this public). It was the fear of this idea, what one could call the ideology of the theater audience, that motivated anti-theatrical theorists as diverse as Mallarmé and Brecht, both of whom feared the political implications of the enthralled audience. Wagner, however, did not have such scruples. After watching the failure of the 1848 revolution, in which he took an active part and which forced him into French exile, Wagner shifted his political ambition to the space of the theater, envisioning the theater as the better arena for the *Volk*.

This fear of a theatrical politics stands behind Benjamin's critique of the ritualistic and auratic theater (and his embrace of film), and it also motivates Adorno's aversion to gestural music and his critique of the aesthetics of Wagner's *Gesamtkunstwerk*. Interestingly enough, in Adorno's case this critique is only indirectly leveled at the figure of the actor and much more directly leveled at a figure that could be seen as the actor's double: the gesticulating conductor. Wagner's own essay on conducting faults conductors for their imprecision in rhythm and lack of sensibility to tempo. It is important to remember here that for Wagner the controlling conductor we know, who interprets the musical work and uses the orchestra to this end, constituted a relatively new phenomenon. Before the mid-nineteenth century, the harpsichordist or, later, the first violinist fulfilled the coordinating function of the conductor. And previously conductors had faced the audience, rather than the orchestra. Adorno recognizes in the emerging class of conductors something like the secret center of Wagner's gestural work of art. According to him, Wagner wrote the first "music for conductors" [Kapellmeistermusik], music geared exclusively toward the conductor's beating gestures: "His music is created in the gesture of beating [*Gestik des Schlagens*], is governed by images of beating. . . . As the one who beats, the conductor amplifies in a terrorist fashion what the audience demands" ("Versuch," 28). The dictatorial role of the gesturing conductor reflects the equally gestural "beat-quality" of the composition. The *Gesamtkunstwerk* is framed, then, by these two gesturing figures, the invisible conductor in the orchestra pit and the visible mime on the stage, and it is in the invisible conductor that Adorno senses the totalitarian secret of Wagner's theatrical politics.

The Costs of Theatricality

As much as Wagner relentlessly promoted theatricality as value, his absolute belief in this value did breed a repressed fear of his construction, one might say a form of stage fright. In particular, it was his encounter with Schopenhauer, who also stood behind Nietzsche's insistence on pure music and on the unique position of music among the arts, that left in Wagner's thinking anti-theatrical and anti-mimetic traces, even as the continuously deplorable state of operatic acting made the success of Wagner's acting reform questionable. These doubts are most pronounced in his essay "Beethoven," which is written entirely in a Schopenhauerian vocabulary.[38] Now Wagner claims that music is "entirely different from poetry or the visual arts" (9:89), and although he still speaks about the rhythmic connection between music and acting, everything that has to do with the visual arts is denounced with a quote from Goethe's *Faust* as "mere spectacle." Suddenly, the theater is nothing but deceptive appearance, which can only be saved by music. Music is geared too much toward the theater when it "loses the power to deliver [the theater] from its fallen appearance" (9:100). The gestural has not disappeared entirely, but it has been sublated by music (here Wagner sounds almost like Adorno): "Music expresses the innermost essence of gesture directly . . . so that we understand it without seeing it" (9:95). While in Wagner's original conception the theatrical visuality of gesture is the "ground" of the artwork, here this ground is fully absorbed and contained by pure music; we no longer need to see these gestures on the stage.

For a moment here we can perceive coming to the surface an anxiety about theatricality. Even though actors may still be the "backbone" of the theatrical work of art, their vulgar theatricality must be refined through music. A similar anxiety led Wagner to the vision of a theater in which actors would be as invisible as the orchestra.[39] More tangible is another moment of Wagner's doubts about actors, which led him to think of the mime as an imaginary figure, as he supposedly was for Shakespeare, whose texts Wagner praises as "fixed mimic improvisations" (9:172). The actor in the mind of the poet anticipates some of the poetic practices of Mallarmé's textual *Gesamtkunstwerk*.

These scattered remarks and speculations must be seen as moments of doubt in Wagner's theatricality of gestures; they do not, as is sometimes argued, constitute a complete revocation of Wagner's theory and practice of theatricality. It was Nietzsche who noted how much this rejection of the visible world coexisted and even depended on Wagner's insistence on theatricality. In his fourth "Untimely Meditation," which already exposes his growing rift with Wagner, Nietzsche notes laconically: "In Wagner the visible world wants to become auditory. . . . At the same time the auditory world wants to become visible for the eye . . . wants to obtain corporeality."[40] The Schopenhauerian moments in Wagner demonstrate a hesitation, not about the primacy of the theater, but about how literally this gestural and corporeal theatricality was to be understood, whether visible gestures were literally the material even of music or whether gestural music would be only metaphorically derived from them.

It is as part of this lingering ambivalence about literal and visible theatricality that Wagner places the figure of the false actor at the very center of his main opera, *Der Ring des Nibelungen,* in the figure of Mime. Mime is the scapegoat for everything that is suspect about theatrical mimesis, and for Wagner's anti-Semitic imagination the best figure to embody such false mimetic theatricality is the figure of the Jew. Adorno is the first to call attention to the clearly coded anti-Semitic features of Mime; what Adorno does not mention, however, is that the anti-Semitism exposed through the figure of Mime is in the service of expressing his ambivalence about theatrical mimesis.[41] Bearing in mind this association of false acting and the deceptive Jew, we can see that the association of these two topoi works both ways: actors become discredited because they are seen to be as false as Jews (because they both are vagabonds, outside the established social structure, etc.); and Jews are rejected because they are said only to imitate externally—as actors—the authentic culture that surrounds them.

By claiming that Wagner uses the figure of the Jew to express his anxiety about theatricality, I do not wish to diminish the anti-Semitic valence of this figure. On the contrary, that Wagner would use a Jewish figure to express his anti-theatrical and anti-mimetic anxiety is one more argument —if more arguments be needed—to confirm the claim that Mime is in fact part of an established anti-Semitic topology. In the *Ring,* however, Wagner's anti-Semitism merges with his denunciation of acting. Mime is the most skilled artisan of the Nibelung, the smith whom Alberich employs to manufacture the magic cap.[42] His artistry is useless, however, when it comes to creating, from its fragments, the sword Nothung; only Siegfried's naive but original power can achieve such a triumph of art. Mime's main fault, however, is not his limited artistry but his false theatricality. As foster father to Siegfried, Mime is reduced—another anti-Semitic topos—to being the effeminate housekeeper and cook who even claims that he is both father and mother of Siegfried.[43] A view in the mirror finally reveals to Siegfried's keen physiognomic eye that he cannot be related to this deformed and deceptive dwarf. But the final and cathartic exposure of Mime's deception is reserved for a scene that stages, for the benefit of Siegfried and the German audience, the breakdown of Mime's theatricality.

This scene takes place after Siegfried has killed Fafner, guardian of the ring, and returns to Mime. In a number of asides, Mime reveals to the audience that he intends to kill Siegfried in order to get the ring and that for this purpose he will use his art of acting and deception "to deceive the child through false familiar talk."[44] Consequently, the stage directions demand that when Siegfried approaches, Mime welcome him with "flattering gesture" (669). The ensuing interchange is one of Wagner's attempts to use a comic device in his operas—not exactly his *forte*—namely, the technique of dramatic irony: not only is Siegfried warned of Mime's scheme in advance by the birds, whose language he has learned to understand, but he, along with the audience, can hear the actual thoughts behind Mime's lies. Wagner puts the audience in the same position as Siegfried: like Siegfried, we hear what Mime thinks and not what he falsely says, and this means, for the purposes of theatrical representation, that Mime is saying what he thinks and not what he believes he is saying. Mime thinks he is flattering Siegfried, while he is in fact revealing his secret plan of killing him. Luckily enough, Siegfried and the audience have become resistant to Mime's deceptive theatricality; they only hear truth.

Mime's deceptive theatricality, as opposed to the truth that comes out of his mouth despite himself, is represented through his "flattering gestures" and his friendly tone of voice. While he is, unwittingly, revealing to Siegfried his true intentions, Mime talks, as the stage directions demand, "(as if he were promising him wonderful things)" or "(with friendly jesting)" (677). These gestures and intonations are paralleled by the "gestures" of the orchestra, which accentuate Mime's sweet and deceptive theatricality. Orchestral music and Mime's voice are thus played off against the grim content of his speech. The breakdown of Mime's theatricality is presented by creating a split within Mime between his true intentions and the theatrical masking of these intentions by means of gestures, intonations, and music, all of which are thus revealed as lies. Here Wagner seems to anticipate, or participate in, the anti-theatrical and anti-mimetic stance of his critics, for whom an aesthetics based on theatrical gestures—on a deceptive "gesture hocus-pocus" (Nietzsche), theatrical "lies," and a theatrical orchestra (Adorno)—was the very reason for their critique of Wagner's *Gesamtkunstwerk*.

Again, we should not understand this scene, or any of Wagner's other doubts, as a revocation of his total theatricalization of the work of art. Mime does not prove that Wagner envisions an essentially nonmimetic and nontheatrical art. What he shows instead is Wagner's anxiety about false mimesis and false theatricality, an anxiety that is deeply rooted precisely because Wagner's entire conception of the work of art is based on such theatrical and mimetic gestures.[45] Wagner and the audience can safely laugh about the dilemma in which Mime is caught without having to acknowledge that perhaps a similar kind of theatrical mimesis, theatrical gestures, and gestural music lies at the very center of Wagner's entire oeuvre. It is Wagner's nightmare that the association of actors *(Schauspielergenossenschaft),* which for him is the agent of the theatrical artwork of the future, would turn out to be a bunch of Mimes and that their theatricality and mimesis would never be anything but deception and lies. The orchestra based on gestures and the theatricality of actors define Wagner's entire music drama. That they are revealed as dangerous and false casts a shadow over his entire work, a shadow that Wagner tried to expel from his own art by calling it Jewish.

This conjunction of anti-Semitism and the notion of a false theatricality fulfills such a central function for Wagner's operas because Wagner trusted the theater, including the actors, with the task of modeling the *Volk.* And so just as he needed to assure the purity of this *Volk* by expelling the Jews, who would at best only imitate what it meant to be German, he also needed to expel false actors, who only imitated what the real *Schauspielergenossenschaft* was all about, namely, exemplifying and representing the *Volk.* In the scapegoat of Mime, therefore, Wagner reveals the underside of his fateful unification of theater and politics: the totalitarian politics of the total work of art.

The Notation of the *Gesamtkunstwerk*

Wagner's investment in acting created an intricate problem that has been largely disregarded but is intimately connected to the theatricality of actors and also their control: the notation of the total work of art. All the tensions within the *Gesamtkunstwerk* reappear, often in an intensified manner, in the question of how the different notation systems of the respective arts can be coordinated and unified. If the different performing arts are really akin to one another through their reliance on gesture, it is a source of immense irritation that they continue to make use of different and incompatible notation systems, different languages that may even defy any attempt at translation.[46]

In response to this difficulty, Wagner tried to tie the notation of gestures as closely to the score as possible. In a letter through which he was trying to control the staging of *Der Fliegende Holländer,* he writes:

> With the repetition of the words "This is the curse of damnation!" his head and his whole body is bent down; he remains in this position during the first four measures of the postlude; with the tremolo of the violins (E-flat), he raises his gaze toward the sky, while the rest of his body remains in the bent position; with the trills of the timpani in the ninth measure of the postlude, a gruesome shaking takes hold of his body, his fists clutch convulsively, his lips quiver, when he finally (still with his gaze directed toward the sky) begins the phrase "I ask you." (4:162)

Wagner here reads single gestures and poses into or out of the score, which thus begins to function as a new notation system for gestures: the beginning of the violins as well as the entry of the timpani concern not only the music but also the performance on stage.[47] The logic behind these translations from music to gestures operates on various levels. The relation between the timpani and the "gruesome quivering" is perhaps intuitive; the quality of the timpani trills translates into the movement of the body by means of imitation. The correspondence between the high E-flat of the violins and the upward-directed gaze is more abstract, as is the relation between the continued bent position and the passage as a whole. The gesture or posture of the elevated gaze also contributes to the transition to the next movement, a maestoso, which constitutes a new beginning; the violin trills and the gaze both are moments of anticipation and therefore can be said to fulfill similar functional roles. In addition to the possible correspondence between gestures and music, what is striking in this letter is the melodramatic nature of these gestures, which seem far removed from the desire to achieve the natural imitation Wagner mentions. Bernard Shaw, himself obsessed with stage directions, was among those who first recognized in Wagner's stage directions the "quaintly old-fashioned tradition of half rhetorical, half historical-pictorial attitude and gesture," revealing the affinities among the melodrama, the declamatory style of rhetoric, and the gestural repertoire of painting.[48] Wagner did not have available to him a language other than the melodrama for speaking about the gestures of actors.[49]

Relating gestures directly to the score can take even more literal forms than the retrospective translation in the passage above. In particular, as Dahlhaus and others have noted, the gestural form of the leitmotif at times resembles a literal inscription of gestures in the musical score, for a number of these leitmotifs almost function as pictorial representations of the

Fig. 1. Richard Wagner, *Der fliegende Holländer,* act. 1, aria.

objects with which they are associated: the motif of Siegfried's sword, for example, looks like the unsheathing of a sword; Wotan's spear motif, like a lowered spear.[50]

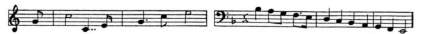

In these instances the musical score operates as a combination of a symbolic and a pictorial or iconic mode of representation. Wagner did not reflect on this pictorial quality of his score, perhaps because it presents too literal of a correspondence between music and gesture. Together with the angry tone of his letter, the ideal of the iconic score demonstrates Wagner's high hopes but also his ultimate failure to achieve a unified system of notation.

Instead, Wagner had to settle for the second-best solution, namely, descriptive and prescriptive stage directions. Because of his investment in gestures, Wagner, more than anyone else before Beckett, tried to force directors to conform to his stage directions, and the devotion of his followers can be measured by their willingness to obey his stage directions. Cosima Wagner was on of the few who carried out her master's fantasy, insisting that Wagner's stage directions were the ultimate authority as soon as she took over the Bayreuther Festspiele. Her endeavors were appreciated half a decade later by the composer Hans Pfitzner, who, in his reactionary worship of Wagner, considered the composer's stage directions and staging instructions as the absolute authority for any performance. Such devoted adepts, however, were in the minority, and even during his lifetime Wagner had to struggle to enforce his stage directions.

The limits of such control emerge clearly when one considers the case of Adolphe Appia, the most important Wagnerian director, whose attempt to continue Wagner's heritage led him to a direct confrontation with Wagner's notation of the *mise en scène,* in particular with his stage directions.[51] Appia's resistance to stage directions, however, made him embrace all the more Wagner's dream of reading the *mise en scène* directly out of the libretto and, more importantly, out of the musical score. For this purpose he began collaborating with the choreographer Émile Jacques-Dalcroze, whose system of movement—eurhythmics—and its curious notation system promised to facilitate the translation from the score to the stage.[52] Like Jacques-Dalcroze, Appia was convinced that all "dramatic action remains embedded in the score" (90). However, the dream of a unified notation system remained unfulfilled.[53] Appia's struggle against Wagner's stage directions, his attempt to continue Wagner's project of fusing gestures, theater, and music, and his commitment to the primacy of the *mise en scène* make him the first in a long line of directors, composers, and writers whose work is committed, in one way or another, to Wagner's total theatricality. In his failure to create a unified notation system Wagner anticipated all those who, like Appia, continued his dream of a specifically theatrical notation or language of gestures. The notebooks of Craig and the *Regiebücher* of Max Reinhardt, for example, all aspire to and fail to achieve such a unified notation.

More important than this failure to achieve a unified notation system is the fact that the emerging class of professional directors drew on Wagner's notion of the total work of art to legitimize the primacy of the *mise en scène* over the dramatic text. These directors' debt to Wagner testifies to the impact, not of Wagner's specific aesthetics, which some of them rejected, but of his invention of theatricality as a value. This value stands behind a larger shift within the field of late-nineteenth-century theater that is marked, as Pierre Bourdieu has argued, by an extraordinary differentiation among theaters based not so much on their dramatic repertoire or actors as on their *mise en scène*.[54] Paul Fort and Lugné-Poe opposed Antoine's Théâtre Libre, and Antoine in turn opposed the Théâtre-Français; Meyerhold differentiated himself from the work of his teacher Stanislavsky; Otto Brahm and Die Freie Bühne, Max Reinhardt, and Copeau and Artaud in various ways sought to further the value of theatricality against all established theaters. Not all of these directors were Wagnerians, but a significant number of them responded to Wagner's invention of theatricality to legitimate their cause.

As significant as this tradition devoted to the Wagnerian value of total theatricality is a second tradition, one that responds to the absolute value of theatricality with ambivalence and suspicion. The polarization around the value of the theater does not necessarily involve a struggle between theater and those who oppose it. Since theater and theatricality no longer describe, neutrally, the specific art form theater, but a value that also concerns the other arts, this value can be opposed even from within the theater. Once theatricality is a value, it is necessary to talk about not only theatrical and anti-theatrical music or poetry, but also theatrical and anti-theatrical theater. I argue that in reaction to Wagner's invention of theatricality as value there emerged a varied tradition of theater that must then be called anti-theatrical. This does not mean that this theater is self-destructive; it means that it is a theater that distrusts the (Wagnerian) belief in the value of a total theatricality. The rest of this book is devoted to developing an understanding of this tradition and its impact on modern drama.

Part II

The Modernist Closet Drama

Stéphane Mallarmé:
The Theater in the Closet

Hérodiade and *Igitur:* Drama against the Stage

The only theater in which Mallarmé ever played an active role, namely, that of *metteur en scène* and *souffleur,* was the amateur summer theater Théâtre de Valvins, instituted by his nephew Paul Margueritte and his daughter Geneviève. For all other purposes, Mallarmé's plans to succeed on the stage ended in the 1860s. By then he had written two short, fragmentary poetic plays, *Hérodiade* and *L'Après-midi d'un faune,* and submitted them to the Théâtre-Français. When Théodore de Banville and Constant Coquelin rejected both plays (even though they admired Mallarmé), Mallarmé made desperate plans for additional and more popular plays using elements of vaudeville and comedy that would allow him to gain the glorious floor of the Théâtre-Français. They too never amounted to anything.[1] Thus began Mallarmé's systematic retreat from the stage.

The Théâtre-Français's loss, if a loss it was, is our gain, for no writer profited more from such a retreat than Mallarmé. The process of turning *Hérodiade* into a closet drama, for example, prompted him to formulate the famous doctrine of symbolism: "To paint not the object, but the effect which it produces" (*Correspondance,* 1:137).[2] For drama, this doctrine requires that the object not be shown in the theater but rather be suggested through language. Consequently, *Hérodiade* was "no long tragedy, but poem" (*Correspondance,* 1:174), a text in alexandrine verse whose purpose resided only in being read; it finally published a few years later in the *Parnasse contemporain* (1871).[3] The clearest external marker for this change from play to closet drama is that Mallarmé erased all stage directions, as if to prove how little he was thinking of theatrical representation. Indeed, Mallarmé's judgment about Villiers's play *Elën* sums up his new attitude toward the theater; it is a work, he writes, "for which the theater would be too banal" (*Correspondance,* 1:153).[4] *Hérodiade* henceforth evokes a theater as withdrawn from reality as is the aestheticist protagonist in Huysmans's *A Rebours,* Des Esseintes, whose favorite activity resides in reading Mallarmé's poetic dramas in the solitude of his own closet.

This new *Hérodiade* seems to belong to the tradition of the poetic closet drama, which includes the plays of Swinburne and Tennyson, which are likewise characterized by a lack of external theatrical action and an abundance of long monologues and speeches. Mallarmé, however, introduces a significant change into the structure of the closet drama: rather than using the genre's minimal theatricality as a background for the presentation of more or less self-sufficient speeches, this play is fully bound up with its setting and characters, as well as with movement, gesture, mimicry, and costume. *Hérodiade* not only shows more interest in theatricality than the usual closet dramas do; it also projects theatricality in such a way that it forecloses whatever mimetic acts real actors might engage in. It would be technically possible to perform all of *Hérodiade,* but it would make relatively little sense to do so: Mallarmé fully transforms the actors and the setting into gestures and signs, so that an actual staging would seem to be not an enactment of the text but rather its vulgar and corporeal double. All this is to say that after being rejected by the Théâtre-Français, Mallarmé began not only to turn *away* from the theater but to turn *against* it. As he himself put it, "[*Hérodiade* is] absolutely scenic, not possible in the theater, but requiring the theater" (*Correspondance,* 1:166). There is perhaps no better formulation for the closet drama's resistance to the theater than this pairing of a rejection of the theater with a dependence on it.

This simultaneous rejection and dependence is the main feature of the modernist closet drama as I understand it, a feature exemplified in the works of Mallarmé, Joyce, Stein, and a number of other writers, ranging from Hofmannsthal to Lewis. It is more pronounced in Mallarmé's later work, but it appears as early as the revised versions of *Hérodiade.* Only three parts of *Hérodiade* were ever finished: an "overture," which consists of nothing but a dramatic monologue by Hérodiade's nurse that anticipates the ensuing tragedy of the murder of St. John the Baptist and possibly Hérodiade's own death; a dialogue between the nurse and Hérodiade, in which Hérodiade rejects the nurse's presumptuous intimacies and is concerned only with preserving the purity of her own body; and a concluding monologue by St. John the Baptist, which takes place after the dance and at the moment of, or rather after, his murder. Mallarmé fuses the figure of Salomé with that of her mother, Hérodias, and ignores many elements of the biblical story.[5]

More important than these changes in the story, however, is the manner in which Mallarmé transforms it into a closet drama. The *Ouverture ancienne,* composed shortly after Mallarmé's retreat from the stage, is a dramatic monologue that sets the ensuing scene and foreshadows its tragedy. More strikingly, however, the entire overture is an extended diegetic evocation of setting and characters, ninety-six lines of densely knit imagery describing a pond, a tower, the interior of a chamber, the nurse's own voice, and eventually the absent Hérodiade. This entire monologue is nothing but a particular kind of implied stage direction, implied because it is part of the nurse's direct speech, a speech that assumes the function of staging this play. Implied stage directions and extended diegetic passages are not unheard of in the tradition of the closet drama. On the contrary, the absence of a mimetic scene requires that the closet drama substitute mimetic theater with diegetic speech. However, in the case of Mallarmé, and the modernist closet drama more generally, this substitution is actively turned against what it putatively replaces, for this type of modernist diegesis seeks to foreclose the very possibility of theatrical, mimetic representation.

While the absolute dominance of diegesis is perhaps not as surprising in an opening soliloquy, Mallarmé extends diegesis, as well as its rivalry with mimetic, theatrical interaction, into the dramatic center of the text: the dialogue between Hérodiade and the nurse. From a theatrical point of view, this scene is structured around three gestures made by the nurse, each of which is interrupted and repulsed by Hérodiade.[6] The first gesture is the nurse's attempt to kiss Hérodiade, which provokes Hérodiade's angry response: "Retreat!" (*Oeuvres,* 142). The second is the nurse's offering Hérodiade some perfume, which Hérodiade refuses: "Leave those perfumes alone!" (143). Finally the nurse is kept from touching a lock of Hérodiade's hair: "Stop in your crime / this gesture, the known sacrilege, that chills / my blood back towards its origin" (143). These three moments of possible physical contact, which are not indicated through stage directions but encoded within the dialogue, mark the only moments of action in this closet drama, actions that are interrupted as soon as they are begun. *Hérodiade* indeed requires the physical theater of gestures and touching bodies, but only in order to reject it.

What stands behind this rejection and dependence on the theater is an aversion to embodiment and actors. When Mallarmé observed in an interview that "*Axel* should not be played," he added that the "theater created by poets" must avoid all the gross contingencies of the theater and instead should give us an "ideal representation" that cannot take place on a stage.[7] But how can Hérodiade's ideal representation be preserved from the vulgarity of the theater? At first glance Hérodiade seems to resemble the world-weary solitary figures who populate the aristocratic, aestheticist dramas of Villiers de L'Isle-Adam and Hugo von Hofmannsthal, whose *Die Frau im Fenster* (1898) is modeled on *Hérodiade.* Like *Hérodiade,* this play is based on the contrast between the common nurse and the lyrical heroine Dianora, who turns the external world, including her own hair, into a web of associations and symbols. Upon closer examination, however, it becomes clear that unlike Villiers or Hofmannsthal, Mallarmé is not content merely to rebuff the external world and physical human interaction in order to create a more refined and mysterious world in its stead. Rather, he attacks the very possibility of embodiment by pitting language against the theater's material mimesis: Hérodiade isolates herself and, once isolated, re-creates herself through speech that is directed against the very possibility of physical embodiment.[8]

The first interruption of physical interaction is motivated by Hérodiade's attempt to preserve the virginity of her hair: "Stand back. /The blond torrent of my immaculate hair /when it baths my solitary body" (*Oeuvres*, 142). A moment later we realize that this rejection is due to her investment in her own hair, which she proceeds to liken to the mane of lions, with whom she claims to have played in her childhood. But this is just the beginning of a process in which Hérodiade is increasingly obsessed with her appearance, an obsession epitomized by her looking in the mirror. The drama of her hair continues when she proceeds to liken it to a second series of attributes, this time consisting of metal and gold. As Hérodiade withdraws from the nurse, she moves on to new acts of self-fashioning that remove her from the human sphere and thus from the sphere of human actors, leading instead to the company first of animals and then of jewels and metals. With the main protagonist thus dehumanized, no actor would be able to impersonate this role.

Hérodiade's resistance to the theater emerges not just in this rejection of theatrical, mimetic interaction and her dehumanization but specifically in the manner in which she confronts her own figure with a diegetic discourse resembling that of the nurse in the overture. But this time diegesis is directed not at the world but at the speaker herself. What Hérodiade does can be done only in the poetic space of language, in which Hérodiade has full rhetorical control over her own image. No human impersonation would ever be able to replicate this process of diegetic dehumanization.[9] This poetic control over all visual attributes presumably was what Mallarmé meant when he observed that by giving up the theater, he would not lose but rather would "gain pose, costumes, decoration, furniture, let alone mystery" (*Correspondance*, 1:174). In fact the mystery that is the goal of this sentence and of Mallarmé's poetics more generally needs all these elements so that it can manipulate them at will. As Hérodiade sits in front of the mirror recreating herself through language, she can be taken as the figure of the closet drama itself, trying to control the imagined mimetic space of the stage through acts of spoken or textual diegesis. Hérodiade is thus involved in a struggle between mimesis—her potential physical interaction with the nurse—and diegesis—her self-creation and self-description. This strategy of diegetically foreclosing theatrical representation finds its most grotesque continuation in the last part, the "Cantique de Saint Jean," which functions as counterpart to the opening incantation of the nurse. Here, St. John the Baptist celebrates his own decapitation because it relieves him from the "old discord with the body" (*Oeuvres,* 148).

The struggle between diegesis and theatrical mimesis becomes particularly acute when it comes to the story's theatrical showpiece, Salomé's dance. Predictably, Mallarmé had deliberately left this part out of his play, as he reveals in a commentary (*Noces,* 51). The resistance to the dance, however, kept looming large over all subsequent revisions. At one point, for example, Mallarmé announces, "Today I will find again the dance," but once found, this dance does not take place on center stage, for Mallarmé immediately adds: "—displacement of/the dance—here—and/not anecdotal" (94). The dance will not be tied to dramatic "anecdote," which means here dramatic, or theatrical, mimesis; instead it will be "displaced." This displacement is necessary, for it preserves what Mallarmé calls the "ambiguity of Hérodiade and her dance" (111), an ambiguity between the old flesh *(la vieille chair)* and immaterial beauty. While the former makes Mallarmé think of the theater, the latter makes it impossible for him to envision Hérodiade dancing on a stage.

The precarious dance scene does not appear in the main text, but it does appear in a number of theatrical margin notes to which it is now displaced.[10] The form this displacement takes is that of a descriptive ekphrasis that recreates Hérodiade's dance of veils in the typographical layout of the text:

> se penche-t-elle d'un
> côté—de l'autre—
>   montrant un
> sein—l'autre—
>
>   et surprise
>   sans gaze
>
> selon ce sein, celui-là
>   identité
>   et cela fait—sur
> un pied l'autre,
>   eux-mêmes
>   sur les pieds
>   seins
> une sorte de dance

effrayante esquisse
—et sur place, sans
bouger
—lieu nul

[she leans from one
side—to the other—
showing one
breast—then the other—

and surprise
without veil

according to this breast, that one
identity
and this produces—from
one foot to the other,
they themselves
on the feet
breasts
a kind of dance
frightening sketch
—and when immobile, without
moving
—a nothing place.]

(113–14)

The text creates a series of references, "selon ce sein, celui-là/identité," that leaves out verbs and either postpones naming objects until after they are referred to by deixis, such as "ce," "celui-là," "cela," and "l'autre," or avoids naming them altogether. The sudden nudity of the breasts is evoked by four words that are separated from the rest of the text, "et surprise/sans gaze," and sequenced so that the reader is as surprised as the viewers of the dance would be. These ekphrastic notes do not fit into any of the categories offered by the classical textual apparatus of the theater, such as stage direction or stage script. Instead they form a diegesis of the dance, a type of writing whose typography is infiltrated by the theater, which it displaces but to which it nevertheless remains tied. What some critics, such as Mary Lewis Shaw, have called the "performance" of Mallarmé's texts can be understood then, I argue, in terms of Mallarmé's contentious relation to the theater, his particular form of anti-theatricalism.

Mallarmé continued his resistance to the stage with his most unusual and unsuccessful closet drama, *Igitur*. All we have of this prose text is heterogeneous fragments that are the products of a number of formal experiments. Nevertheless, we can surmise the outlines of a plot. Like the aristocratic protagonists of Huysmans, Hofmannsthal, and Maeterlinck, Igitur is the last, solitary descendant of an old family. He is dominated by an overbearing past that is epitomized by the mysterious castle, its decaying furniture, and its genealogical book, a past from which he hopes to escape by fleeing into a yet undetermined future. The promise of the future is symbolized by the clock and by a throw of dice, which will transform the different possible futures into one realized event. However, we never really know what is at stake in the throwing of the dice. This is all the more surprising since the play's few external objects and moments of action are supposed to be entirely in the service of abstract meditations undertaken in the language of transcendental philosophy: "the infinite," "the bottom of thing," "the absolute," "the necessary," "spirit," "thought," "chance," "idea" (*Oeuvres,* 473–500). The inability to connect single objects and gestures with these abstract ideas is therefore the most striking feature of this play, and it signals the play's overinvestment in single objects. It is this overinvestment that turns this play against mimetic, theatrical representation, which could only provide an insufficient rendering of these objects' and gestures' metaphysics. Although Mallarmé speaks about the attempt to bring together ideal and body in terms of the symbol, we can see here that symbolism is less concerned with the achievement of such a unity than with the desire for one. This desire leads Mallarmé to favor images—foam, fan, glass, gossamer—that are situated right at the limit of immateriality, which is also the limit of the theater.[11]

Mallarmé's primary strategy for counteracting the possibility of an adequate theatrical representation of *Igitur,* however, centers on the protagonist himself. Igitur is even less a "full" character than the dehumanized Hérodiade. We cannot imagine his being successfully impersonated on a stage; he too is infused with metaphysics.[12] In this metaphysical depersonalization Igitur emulates Hamlet, who, according to Mallarmé, also does not belong to the existing, physical theater but rather to a "theater of our mind" because, like Igitur, Hamlet is "half infused with abstraction."[13] And like Hamlet, Igitur is a protagonist who is characterized by a lack of action and is without, to use T. S. Eliot's formulation, objective correlatives. The lack of action defines the play as anti-dramatic (the Greek word for *drama* means "action"), and the lack of objective correlatives defines it as anti-theatrical (objective correlatives are what the theater demands). It is precisely *Hamlet*'s failure to provide objective correlatives that Mallarmé is drawn to. Mallarmé here shows an affinity to those nineteenth-century theorists, from Coleridge to Hazlitt, who deemed Shakespeare too precious for the vulgarity of the theater and preferred to read his plays as closet dramas.[14] *Igitur* takes this reception history to an extreme by reducing *Hamlet* to a set of metaphysical conflicts and by turning Hamlet into a grammatical marker, the Latin "therefore."

Even though *Igitur* is unsure about almost all of its features, it is sure of its resistance to the real, existing theater and therefore announces: "This story is addressed to the intelligence of the reader staging everything" (*Oeuvres*, 475). This note invokes not only the closet drama but also another genre, namely, that of a short story *(conte)*. *Igitur* is in fact as much a story as it is a closet drama because its main text is dominated by a narrative voice describing and commenting on imaginary events in the present tense, "And now [*Alors*]. . . . And now" (476–77). Only a few times does the main body of the text change abruptly to the first-person direct speech of the protagonist Igitur before suddenly changing back to the narrative voice. What this narrative voice does in this play is directly related to the play's failure to connect objects, gestures, and protagonist to their putative metaphysical meaning, for it is this narrative voice on which the play pins all its hopes for such a connection. We can conclude, therefore, that the insufficiency of mimetic, theatrical representation drove this play to create a narrator whose commentary might be able to explain everything the theater could not show.

The reason why we should care about *Igitur*'s desperate attempts to bridge the gap between body and meaning by means of such a narrative commentator is that it led Mallarmé to a formal innovation with far-reaching consequences: a new use of stage directions. For the place from which this narrator speaks is the stage direction. While Mallarmé had erased all stage directions as soon as he decided to turn *Hérodiade* into a closet drama, in *Igitur* he realized what was to become one of the main insights of the modernist closet drama: stage directions do not have to be abolished; they can be used to reinvent the dramatic form. Once a play is radically divorced from the stage and addressed to readers only, stage directions are no longer an awkward appendix to the primary text; they are free to realize themselves as a space for an independent narrative voice that not only describes hypothetical actors and action but also manipulates this action at will. Stage directions offer a mode of speech that is not tied to embodied actors and that can therefore be turned against them. And this is precisely what *Igitur*, like most modernist closet dramas after it, does: it uses stage directions as a weapon against the theater.

Igitur's first stage direction announces the break with the theatrical space when the direction "He leaves the room and enters the stairwell" (*Oeuvres,* 484) is followed by an appendix that can never be enacted: "instead of riding down the handrail." Mallarmé's stage directions not only position themselves against a possible staging through such counterfactual prescriptions, they also represent the voice of a narrator or commentator who tries to turn the imaginary stage into an abstract, metaphysical theater of ideas through observations such as, "Empty hours, purely negative" (498). The stage directions thus provide a place for a narrator attempting to bridge the gap between physical action and its metaphysical meaning, claiming, for example: "Actually, Igitur had been projected by his race outside of time" (498). Mallarmé discovered that once stage directions were no longer concerned with the technicalities of the theater, they could become a new element of the dramatic text to be used for a variety of purposes, such as commenting on the meaning of specific actions, creating alternative or even mutually exclusive worlds, dehumanizing actors, as well as isolating and manipulating specific features. The reason that the importance of *Igitur*'s stage directions has not been sufficiently recognized may lie in the fact that their achievement is so closely tied to the play's failure, for the commentary provided in the stage directions does not manage to bridge the gap between the play and its meaning. But the formal innovation at work in *Igitur*'s use of stage directions anticipates the new importance and changed functions of stage directions in modern drama at large, from Shaw to O'Neill and from Stein to Beckett.

Le Livre: Book and Theater

Even though the diegetic destruction of the theater in *Hérodiade* and the re-functioning of stage directions in *Igitur* constitute two paradigmatic ways in which the modernist closet drama resists the stage, these two plays appear cautious in their anti-theatricalism when compared with a project that has come to be known as the *Livre,* a project Mallarmé began envisioning shortly after *Hérodiade*'s failure on the stage.[15] In fact the rewritten *Hérodiade* was supposed to be one of the "pillars," as Mallarmé put it, of this new project, with which he meant to write back to the theater that had rejected him. Perhaps no work demands with more insistence than the *Livre* that we reexamine our notions about the relation between the field of literature (texts, books, readers) and that of the theater (spoken words, scenes, audiences). Neither dramatic text nor script for a theatrical performance, but a peculiar combination of book and theater, the *Livre* links the history of the theater and the history of the book in an unprecedented manner.[16] Mallarmé spent most of his life working towards this book-theater, extraordinary in its scope and ambition but disappointing in its unfinished and

fragmentary nature. All we have are two hundred pages of notes consisting of mathematical calculations, schematic charts, and small fragments of
writing. While it is almost impossible to deduce from them a plot or even
themes, they do provide somewhat clearer indications about their relation
to the theater. Mallarmé may not have had a clear idea about the content
of the *Livre,* but he did work out a plan for its theatrical presentation, and
so the desire to create a different sort of theater, a theater that would avoid
everything Mallarmé found objectionable about the existing theater, can
be seen as the driving force behind this project.

Arguably the nineteenth century's most ambitious project in theatrical
reform, the *Livre* remains stunning in its determination to reinvent the theater from scratch. First of all, like many modernists, Mallarmé seeks to
exclude at all costs the public, which he dismisses as the "Foule," preferring
instead a small and carefully selected group of invited and initiated audi-
tors.[17] The *Livre*'s militant distaste for the theatergoing public continues a
feature of symbolism and aestheticism at large: the jealous defense of an
autonomous aesthetic sphere against the public sphere. This isolation co-
incides with what has sometimes been called the religion of art, a form
of worship that endows the artwork with precisely the type of aura that
was subsequently attacked by the avant-garde.[18] Jean Paul Sartre saw in this
defense of the artwork against the mass audience a mechanism through
which the endangered petit bourgeoisie tried to create a pseudoaristocracy
of art.[19] Nevertheless, it would be wrong to understand Mallarmé's attitude
as implying the total rejection of any kind of audience; more nuanced critics of Mallarmé such as Barbara Johnson have argued against this reading
repeatedly. While excluding the "Crowd," Mallarmé in fact seeks to forge a
controlled audience with great care.[20] In the theater, which has always been
the most public and the most social of the arts, this is particularly important but also particularly difficult. For this reason, Mallarmé devotes a large
number of notes to determining the precise number of people to be invited
to each show, the style of the invitation, and the seating arrangement, thus
exerting total control over every external aspect of this intimate, theatrical
presentation.

For Mallarmé, the status of art is threatened not only by the mass audience flocking to the theater but also by the theater's particular modes of
representation. His mathematical calculations concerning the audience are
followed, therefore, by an equally meticulous control of what we can call,
in a preliminary way, the stage. This stage consists of a reading desk,
a lamp, curtains, and a diagonally placed piece of lacquered furniture
equipped with a specific number of pigeonholes (the number being arrived
at by another complicated calculation) to hold the loose sheets that consti-

tute the performance edition of the *Livre*.[21] It is important to remember, however, that the space in which this theater takes place is not a regular stage but Mallarmé's own library. Desk, lamp, curtains, and pigeonholes are not stage props in the traditional sense, for they can be thought of as Mallarmé's real desk and lamp, and they certainly belong to his library. This library does not become a mimetic or referential entity and never exceeds its own proper function: nothing in it is taken out of context, and nothing refers to anything beyond itself, the condition for establishing a mimetic relation to the world. The only circumstance that can be said to mark the theatrical nature of this space and its objects is the precise manner of this arrangement: these objects signify only because they are so meticulously placed in the space to which they already belong. If Mallarmé's library becomes a theater at all, it does so only by virtue of an almost obsessive-compulsive order that is imposed on a preexisting place of reading.

If mimesis is to be reduced and possibly exorcised altogether, the figure that must be controlled most rigorously and perhaps abolished entirely is the figure of the actor. Just as the stage and its props are not mimetic signs, the actor does not impersonate a character but rather Mallarmé himself. Every presentation, or performance, is organized by a double reading: announced by a sound, the reader enters the room in a particular manner, takes out a number of loose sheets from the pigeonholes, shows them to the audience, and then proceeds to read them aloud in a first session. After a short break the reader reappears and takes the same sheets, but in a different sequence, and reads them again. As Frantisek Deak has pointed out, the type of performance Mallarmé envisioned for the *Livre* is an extension of the poetry reading at his Tuesday gatherings. However, what distinguishes this "reader" from a mere reciter of poetry is that Mallarmé prescribes a set of ceremonial and repetitive gestures and movements that determine exactly how the reader should enter the room and distribute the loose sheets. His slow entry and hieratic gestures do not refer to the kind of primitivist ritual that the avant-garde would excavate from below the strata of civilization; on the contrary, they refer to a type of aristocratic ceremony that endows art with religious significance and *gravitas*.[22] More important, however, this elevation of art to quasi-religious ceremony, typical for most symbolism and aestheticism, implies also an anti-theatrical function: the ceremonial quality of the reading keeps the theater of mimetic impersonation at bay. Much more radically than in either *Hérodiade* or *Igitur,* the actor disappears and is replaced by a master of ceremonies, who must be seen, therefore, as Mallarmé's anti-actor.[23]

In order to differentiate this anti-actor from both regular actors and mere readers of poetry, Mallarmé uses the term "operator" [opérateur]. As

Jacques Scherer pointed out in what is still the most careful commentary on the *Livre,* the word *operator* carries with it the connotation of operating a machine. This connotation pleased Mallarmé because it removed the *Livre* and its presentation from the realm of subjective creation and turned it into a rigorously mechanical and therefore impersonal enterprise. His obsessive mathematical calculations concerning the number of invitees, the revenues derived from the readings, and the reading sessions themselves, which would have spanned a total of five years, are efforts in the same direction of making these readings impersonal and objective, governed by mathematical precision and necessity. What Mallarmé cherished above all were the different permutations achieved by the various arrangements of the loose sheets and the possibilities of meaning derived from such an *ars combinatoria.*[24] The operator of the *Livre* is the manipulator of a machinery of precisely numbered loose sheets, executing a specific number of operations to be applied to them.

Given Mallarmé's rebellion against the genre of drama and its relation to the theater, it is perhaps not surprising that he had difficulties giving a name to the theatrical and literary genre he was creating. Besides the notes detailing the formal makeup of the *Livre* and the choreography of its reading, we find a large number of schematic charts that try to capture the genre of the *Livre* in terms of its theatrical and textual form. These charts map out all imaginable types of performing arts, including opera, ballet, parades, and theater; music, including orchestral music, hymns, chant, and chansons; and literature, including verse, poetry, drama, and journals. But since these charts do not identify those aspects and attributes Mallarmé sought to include in what looks like a gigantic combination of most existing art forms, it remains almost impossible to determine anything from them besides the fact that Mallarmé aspired to an extraordinary fusion of the arts.

The few passages in which Mallarmé adds discursive sentences to these charts give but feeble hints of how these different genres or types of genre would come together. Sheet 103A, for example, indicates: "Reading/or/ middle-term/hiding and showing/THEATER to the extent [that it is] *mystery*/through an operation called *poetry*/and this for the benefit of the BOOK [*LIVRE*]." Mallarmé here seems to demand that above all else the theater retain a certain degree of *mystery,* a term with which he usually describes the effects of his symbolist aesthetics more generally. What assures this degree of mystery in the case of the *Livre* is the ceremonial nature of the reading, this "middle term," which seems to fulfill the function of mediating between theater and the book, preserving a sense of mystery by both showing and hiding itself. And it is in order to preserve this hidden mystery that

Mallarmé hopes to achieve an occulted theater, in which not everything would be dragged into the bright visibility of the stage. Such a half-hidden theater would be based on poetry and not on actors; it would be a form of ceremonial recitation that took its inspiration, as Jacques Scherer has observed, from the Catholic Mass and its ritual reading of the liturgical text.[25] The resistance of the *Livre* to the theater finally assures the modernity of the *Livre*: "The entire modernity is provided by the reader" (148A). What the mystery of the *Livre* and its modernity have in common is that both depend on the erasure of the actor, stage props, and theatrical mimesis. I take this anti-theatrical impulse to be the central characteristic of the *Livre* and therefore propose to call it a *closet* theater: taking place in Mallarmé's own study, the theatricality of the *Livre* consists of nothing but the ceremony of reading. Mallarmé's famous remark that the world was destined to end up in a book refers precisely to this book-theater of the *Livre:* for Mallarmé, the *theatrum mundi* is the theater of his closet.

Mallarmé's ambition to unite the largest number of art forms and genres, as well as his distrust of the theater and its actors, must be understood against the background of his relation to the inventor of theatricality as a value, Richard Wagner.[26] Nothing would seem to be more different from Wagner's *Gesamtkunstwerk,* with its commitment to actors and to total theatrical representation, than Mallarmé's closet theater. Nevertheless, by including ever more genres, by using ever more types of theatricality, and by referring to ever more modes of expression, Mallarmé tried to out-*gesamtkunstwerk* the *Gesamtkunstwerk.* In its wild ambition the *Livre* is not unique. The nineteenth century abounds in various megalomaniac works, from Goethe's *Faust,* which also hovers awkwardly between text and theater, to Beethoven's Ninth Symphony, which tries to fuse the choral and symphonic traditions. The hubris of an all-encompassing form that tries to swallow all smaller projects links the nineteenth century to early-twentieth-century modernism, especially Proust's *À la recherche du temps perdu* and Joyce's *Ulysses,* both of which also refer to Wagner as one of their predecessors. The avant-garde, equally fascinated by Wagner, tended in the opposite direction, promoting small and compressed pieces, such as the futurist *sintesi,* synthesized spectacles lasting only seconds.

Even as he competes with the *Gesamtkunstwerk,* Mallarmé shares with other modernist critics of Wagner, including Nietzsche, Adorno, and Brecht, a number of anti-theatrical and anti-mimetic values that make him suspicious of Wagner's absolute belief in the theater. Mallarmé denounces Wagner's use of nationalist myths, proposing instead, as Brecht did, the more abstract and impersonal fable, and he bemoans the passive trance into which Wagner supposedly lulls his audience. In addition to this concern about the effects of the *Gesamtkunstwerk* on the audience, Mallarmé critiques Wagner's strategy for fusing the arts into gigantic, theatrical spectacles. These objections are outlined in an intricate and allusive text—half essay, half prose poem—commissioned by his friend Edouard Dujardin for the *Revue Wagnérienne,* a text that in style and diction could not be further from Wagner's programmatic pamphlets, which were printed in the same journal. Mallarmé writes: "You have to submit to a sorcery, which to accomplish no means of enchantment derived from the magic of music is too much, to violate your reason, so taken by a simulacrum."[27] Like many of Wagner's subsequent critics, Mallarmé recognizes that Wagner's operas "violate" and "enchant" reason by means of a spectacle that offers an illusionist simulation, or a "simulacrum," of reality. The measures that Mallarmé proposes against this mode of simulation—replacing myths with abstract fables, infusing actors with the depersonalizing rhythm of music, and separating the different arts—are typical modernist strategies for breaking the illusionist spell these performances supposedly cast on their audience.[28] In particular Mallarmé opposes Wagner's "personal" theater, calling instead for "The Figure who is Nothing" ("Crayonné," 174). Only an actor who represents nothing could hope to remove, or "deliver," all gestures and attitudes from their mimetic and theatrical origin.[29]

The reader, or operator, of the *Livre* is not the only safeguard against the spell of Wagner's spectacles. The most important one is Mallarmé's particular use of the literary text. One effect of Mallarmé's almost fetishizing worship of the literary text is his insistence on attributing central significance to its visual appearance.[30] The text enters the presentation of the *Livre* as an object of worship when the operator is instructed to show the single sheets to the audience: the performance depends not only on the reading aloud of text but also on its visual display. The single sheets of paper are presented to the audience with the slow and precisely choreographed gestures derived from religious ritual. Writing to the Italian symbolist Vittorio Pica, Mallarmé creates what one could call the formula of the modernist closet drama: "I believe that literature, taken up from its source, which is art and science, will give us a theater, the representations of which will be the truly modern cult: a book" (*Correspondance,* 3:73). Modernism presents itself as a cult worshipping some new form of ultimate book, and this book cult is what will constitute the theater of the future.

Mallarmé here participates in the peculiar form of French Wagnerism begun by Baudelaire and continued by Dujardin and his circle, which was more a literary and poetic movement than a theatrical or operatic one. A whole generation of French modernist or protomodernist poets elevated Wagner as their champion, not because of but despite Wagner's relentless use of theatricality. What fascinated them in Wagner was not what would lead the avant-garde to an inflationary use of the term *total theater* but rather Wagner's use of synaesthesia, symbolism, and conjunction of poetry and music, all of which they sought to transform into poetry rather than a *mise en scène*. The symbolist theater, for all its evocation of Wagner, is not the predecessor of an avant-garde commitment to total theatricality, but remains skeptical of the effects of Wagner's theatricalizations.

Both the anti-theatrical form of the presentation and the worship of text had an impact on the content of the *Livre*. Given Mallarmé's critique of actors and his aversion to mimesis, it is not surprising that his characters could not be farther from traditional characters; all that Mallarmé cares to represent are single, isolated, and interrupted glimpses of attitudes and gestures:

> The attitude is that of leaving—
> Bent forward, one foot forward
> (but nevertheless still, forward—in the pose—
> diagonally)
>
> (14A)

This fragment of a scene is set by a type of descriptive stage direction, a narrative voice conjuring up a brief moment, almost a tableau. The single action is frozen into one pose, evoked by two details (bending, one foot forward) and specified by a geometrical term, "diagonally." The presence of the narrator is so strong that this short passage is infused with an explanatory vocabulary, for the narrator informs us of the general nature of this tableau—that it captures a moment of "leaving"—and reminds us, in the middle of focusing on the choreography of this scene, that indeed we are faced with the description of a "pose." Whoever is the agent of this pose, he or she is decomposed to the point where the fundamental entity of the *Livre* is no longer that of a person but consists of gestures and poses. It is in passages like this that we can find the most tangible application of Mallarmé's doctrine of an "impersonal art." In the theater, the value of the impersonal leads to a fundamental critique of actors and thus to an attack on the conception of character. For this reason, Mallarmé's theatrical texts do their utmost to avoid constructing characters that could be impersonated by actual actors.[31] Mallarmé's struggle to achieve an impersonal art, like most of his other aesthetic values, can thus be traced back to his resistance to the theater.

The technique of representing isolated and frozen gestures and postures makes the visual presentation of text as central as it is to any poem, but it does not yet fully demonstrate the role of visuality for Mallarmé's *Livre*. More elaborate is Mallarmé's arrangement of text in the following passage, which is akin to the ekphrasis of Hérodiade's dance:

la double troupe, est là cette . . .

fois tendant en effet les bras d'une
part et d'autre, ainsi que sur deux
grèves très lointanes,
mais entre lequelles, à travers l'esprit sans
doute (à travers lui)
                              et idéale
il s'opère un mystérieux rapprochement, chacune
tendant d'où elle est, y soit allée ou
les bras à son absence . . .
et rêverie bras croisés sur seins
                                        absents
de l'autre côté, à la fois future
et passée   (un bras bas, un
                                        autre levé, attitude de
                                        danseuse)

Tel est ce qui a lieu visible
lui omis

[The double troupe, is there this . . .

time pulling in effect the arms from
one side to the other, as if on two
very distant beaches
but between which, through the spirit
without doubt (through it)
                              and ideal
comes about a mysterious rapprochement, each one
pulling from where it is,
and should have gone or
the arms to its absence . . .
and daydream arms crossed over
                                        absent breasts
from the other side at the same time in
the future and the past   (one arm down
                                        the other raised, attitude of a
                                        dancer)
This is what takes place visibly
He is omitted]

                                        (17A–19A)

Spoken by an observer or narrator, rather than a character, this passage invokes Amazons, identified by their one "absent breast," reminiscent of the equally alluring Hérodiade, as well as a number of other figures. Here too the *Livre* "omits" these figures and instead extracts from them single details, usually momentary gestures, such as a pulling hand, stretched-out arms, or a specific attitude. In addition, parentheses separate from the main text a passage that is even closer to an actual stage direction, specifying nothing but particular gestures and postures (one arm lowered and one raised) and toying with the vocabulary of dance ("attitude of a dancer"). This is a page full of interrupted movements that are interpreted by a narrator in terms of a "mysterious rapprochement" supposedly taking place between these figures, a rapprochement that is somehow brought about by the workings of "time," "spirit," and "ideal." Again we find that the voice that conjures up this array of depersonalized gestures and poses is not the voice of a neutral, descriptive narrator but that of a commentator with specific investments, who demands that we consider this choreography in light of a particularly abstract frame of reference.[32]

This text is so caught up with these gestures (and their abstract significance) that it lets them affect its own typographical arrangement: single words or strings of words are detached from their grammatical functions; attributes are left hanging in the air; and gestures appear suddenly somewhere on the page, sometimes interrupted by parentheses. The logic by which these words are arranged on the page is not syntax or poetics but the logic of the gestures themselves. While the operator, or reader, is forbidden to imitate these gestures, they break through the surface of the text. The choreographic energy that was driven away from the stage is here channeled back into the visual arrangement of text on the page, leading to something Mallarmé in another context called "gesticulating prose" [prose gesticulante] (*Correspondance*, 1:343). Mallarmé here enacts the type of gestural language he had praised in the free verse of M. Vielé Griffin: "a gesture, . . . suddenly jumping up, out of passion, which scans."[33] It is at this point that it becomes possible to specify how Mallarmé came to think of writing as a theatrical activity: "Theater and book are fundamentally just two sides of the same idea" (*Oeuvres*, 786). Not only does the *Livre* resist the theater but in the process of resisting it is drawn back to the theater, hoping to sublate it, its actors, and their gestures into a textual and typographical form, a form of textual, poetic diegesis infused with remnants of mimesis.[34]

The abandoned theater returns in the form not only of this gestural typography but also of thematic and generic references. A kind of "entr'acte" refers to the space of the theater itself, another act seems to take place in a circus, and a further fragment has two characters costuming one another.[35] Most of the time, however, Mallarmé privileges the nonsignifying, nonreferential, or to be more precise, decorative, elements of the theater, such as chandeliers, curtains, and flies.[36] This interest in decoration can explain why Mallarmé would agree to be responsible, albeit under different female pseudonyms, for the magazine *La Dernière Mode,* which was dedicated to questions of fashion and jewelry, as well as the fashionable and ornamental aspects of the theater. These references to the theater should not, however, be confused with the presentation of the *Livre* itself. Clowns, dancers, actors, and mimes all belong to the demimonde of the theater and not to the ceremonial reading of the *Livre* in Mallarmé's library. Nothing in the reading-presentation of the *Livre,* not even the operator, is mimetic, referential, or representational. Indeed, this divergence between the represented (the world of the theater) and the mode of representation (the anti-theatrical closet theater) is Mallarmé's way of articulating his critical attitude toward the theater, his way of relating to the theater he had left at an early stage and to which he returned only by way of distanced and estranged allusions.

We can measure the distance between the *Livre* and the theater by analyzing the changes that were necessary for Jacques Scherer to turn the *Livre* into a script geared toward theatrical representation. Scherer explains his strategy for the *Livre*'s dramatic adaptation as one of extracting the usable and "poetic" parts of the manuscript without adding "a single significant word"; the only additions would be "personal pronouns" to avoid some of the text's "awkwardness" (383). The embarrassment caused by the absence of such personal pronouns and names is indeed great, but it is located right at the center of Mallarmé's anti-theatrical strategy. Granted that the personal names Scherer chooses are all taken from Mallarmé's oeuvre: "La Nymphe" from the dramatic fragment *L'Après-midi d'un Faune;* "Hérodiade" from the closet drama *Hérodiade;* and "La Sirène" from the poem *Salut.* And that the rest of the cast is even lifted from the *Livre* itself: "PERSONNAGES / Le Maître, *basse* / L'Opérateur, *baryton.* / Le Calculateur, *ténor* / La Nymphe, *contralto* / Hérodiade, *mezzo.* La Sirène, *soprano*" (387). Nevertheless, all of these added personages introduce a personal quality into the carefully constructed impersonal texture of the *Livre,* especially the listing of the operator, on whom Mallarmé had placed all his hopes for overcoming acting, as simply one more "personnage." The operator is not a "personnage" and should not be played by someone posing as an actor and in possession of an operatic voice, be it baritone or countertenor. What Scherer adds here is precisely what Mallarmé tried to avoid at all costs, namely, *dramatis personae,* which turn the *Livre* once more into a drama of persons.

The changes necessary for this little experiment indicate for us what separates the performance of the *Livre* from the theater, and they show that we should not mistake the "performative" elements of Mallarmé's scripted reading—the selection of sheets, the entry of the reader, the participation of the audience, and the decoration of the library—for a representational *mise en scène,* nor the operator or any other figure or proper name for *dramatis personae.* In fact, the semipublic reading and presentation of the *Livre* does not include a *mise en scène* at all. Rather, given its reliance on the reader and his narrative voice, the *Livre* takes place in a *mise en lecture*—what Julia Kristeva called the "theater of the voice" (*Révolution,* 562)—whose purpose is never to become visual theater.

Bringing the *Livre* into the theater has one further consequence: it reintroduces the theater's specific normativity associated with the drama of persons and impersonating actors. Mallarmé is less concerned here about censorship than about the aesthetic normativity of the theater, which is the normativity of the human actor. Many of the figures evoked in the *Livre* are ambiguous figures, such as sirens or amazons, definitely seductive but not clearly women. And his closet dramas feature illicit figures such as the Faune and Hérodiade. Apparently, the written text for Mallarmé constituted a space in which such figures could be evoked through isolated poses without having to be appear on a stage. In a similar vein, Mallarmé wrote under female pseudonyms, thus using the medium of text for a variety of female poses and roles.[37] For Mallarmé writing and in particular the closet drama were ways of working with and against these gender differences without having to expose them to the ocular proof of the theater.

Theater-Texts

Besides the closet dramas and the *Livre,* Mallarmé responded to the theater through a third group of texts, which, like the *Livre,* defy the usual literary genres and which I propose to call *theater-texts.* These theater-texts are not just writings *on* the theater.[38] As their title, "Crayonné au théâtre," claims, they are texts produced inside the theater under the direct stimulus of the theatrical performance. In terms of genre, they continue the French tradition of the literary theater and ballet review. The emergence of the feuilleton had provided the intellectual and economic basis for writers such as Théophile Gautier to devote considerable time and energy to short texts on theatrical performances.[39] Even though the theater was by and large an abject form of art, writing about it became an acceptable activity for a poet.[40] Publishing his theater-texts in the exclusive literary journal the *Revue Indépendante,* the successor of the *Revue Wagnérienne,* Mallarmé transformed the literary theater review and turned it into a venue for translating theater into text.

In a central passage from these texts, Mallarmé outlines a program that becomes the touchstone for his writings on the theater. At the heart of this program stands the complete depersonalization of the dancer, which also characterizes his closet dramas and the *Livre:*

> This means that the dancer *is not a woman who dances,* for these two juxtaposed reasons: *she is not a woman* but a metaphor summarizing some elementary aspect of our form, sword, cup, flower, etc., and *she does not dance,* suggesting, through miraculous *raccourcis* and *élans,* in a corporeal writing what would take paragraphs in prose dialogues and descriptions to express in the process of revising: a poem disengaged from the whole writing apparatus. ("Crayonné," 192–93)[41]

Mallarmé does not look at the ballet in terms of either dancer or dance but pursues a radically different interest that has nothing to do with the dancer herself nor even with the dance, but takes the dancing agent as a metaphor that operates by suggesting abstract forms and entities. Every time Mallarmé looks at the ballet, the dancer vanishes and is transformed into series of isolated signs, "when there emerges for the gaze an isolated sign of the scattered general beauty, a flower, a wave, a cloud, and a jewel, etc." (181).[42] Mallarmé wants to reduce the continually moving body to sets of distinct and detached movements. And it is striking that he dismisses the vocabulary of the ballet as a tool to describe these movements. Mallarmé knows the technical vocabulary of the ballet—such as *raccourcis,* a position in which the thigh is raised to the second position *en l'air,* with the knee bent so that the pointed toe rests against the knee of the supporting leg, and *élan,* which describes the manner in which a dancer attacks a step—but the act of viewing gestures requires imagination, an imaginative impulse, and not an expertise in the conventional terminology of the ballet.

As soon as the performer's gestures are isolated, in Mallarmé's vocabulary they become signs—"when there emerges for the gaze an isolated sign of the scattered general beauty"—and what one has to do with such gestural signs is "to ask oneself before each step, each attitude [pose] however strange, those tops [of the feet] and little steps [*taquetés*], stretchings [*allongés*], and bounces [*ballons*]: 'What might this signify'" (197).[43] In his attempt to answer this question, Mallarmé backs up his anti-mimetic stance with what could be called a symbolist theory of gestures centered around the notion of the sign.[44] However, he never outlines a matrix through which we could in fact begin to decode these gestural signs; rather, he chooses to provide only vague examples, such as "general beauty" or even simply "idea," to indicate the direction in which such successfully isolated gestures are supposedly pointing. The interest of this theory of symbolism lies, not in establishing different codes of performance, but rather in instituting a practice of reception that does not rely on the technical vocabulary of the ballet in the first place. Instead this symbolism of gestures proceeds in ways that Mallarmé alternately calls "allusion," "suggestion," and "indirect indication," all of which are modes of signification that revolve around the avoidance of direct naming: "To evoke, in a deliberate shadow, the silenced object, through allusive words, never direct, reduced to a similar silence, involves an attempt close to creation."[45] What one might call a protosemiotics of gestures here falls deliberately short of creating a true codex of gestures. Allusive, evocative, and suggestive — gestures always say less, and more, than mere linguistic signs.[46]

The difference between suggestive gestures and text has at times been downplayed by a critical tradition invested in continuing Mallarmé's own attempt to use the literary text as a bulwark against theatrical representation, a tradition epitomized by Jacques Derrida's reading of Mallarmé's text "Mimique," which belongs in this group of theater-texts.[47] Eager to escape a phonocentric fixation on speech, Derrida questions the priority of the theatrical performance that Mallarmé observed over the little text that was putatively written in response to it. Derrida proposes that we instead think of both the theater and the text as partaking in an "écriture générale" (La dissémination, 274). By subsuming theater under such a "general writing," Derrida indeed faithfully follows Mallarmé's manner of speaking about actors, dancers, and mimes, but it is because of his faithfulness to Mallarmé that Derrida does not fully see the dynamics behind Mallarmé's texts, namely, their resistance to the theater. Mallarmé, the inventor of the modernist closet drama and closet theater, and Derrida, the philosopher of the totalized text, can be seen as the bookends to a high modernism that must believe in the literary text in order to resist the theater.[48]

Mallarmé's relation to the theater has been at the center of a second critical tradition, ranging from Haskell Block to Frantisek Deak.[49] These critics made it their goal to show that Mallarmé was in love not just with text but also with the theater and that all of his texts are in one way or another theatrical.[50] Occupied with proving the text fetishists wrong, these theatricalist critics did not see that Mallarmé's own text fetishism was a consequence of his critique of the theater. In order to excavate Mallarmé's antitheatricalism it is thus necessary to relate these two traditions critically to one another. Only then can we see that the theater constitutes the horizon of Mallarmé's Livre, his closet dramas, and his writings in the theater, but it is a horizon that these texts work against; their particular poetic strategies and textual choices can only be understood in light of their struggle with and against the theater.

Thinking about Mallarmé within the frame of a resistance to the theater also means recognizing that however much he may try to turn the dance into a texture of signifying and suggestive gestures, he cannot and does not want to erase the performer onstage entirely. And indeed at least one performer was of particular importance for Mallarmé, namely, the American dancer Loie Fuller, who captivated Paris audiences with a revolution in ballet. Since her Paris debut in 1871, Loie Fuller had attracted attention with large veils that covered her body and accentuated its gestural expressivity.[51] Unlike the traditional ballet attire, which emphasizes the shape of the individual dancer, these veils represented for Mallarmé the model of a gestural ballet as disengaged as possible from the individual corporeality of the dancer and thus as close as possible to pure fiction. He notes of Loie Fuller that "the free scene, given to the order of fiction, let loose to the play of a veil by poses and gestures, becomes the most pure result" ("Crayonné," 200).[52] The impulse, then, to depersonalize the performer comes from a dancer who rebelled, in her own way, against the personalizing effects of the theater.[53]

The dance that made Loie Fuller famous was Salomé's "Dance of the Seven Veils." We may therefore suspect that Mallarmé never ceased to recognize in Fuller's veils the obscure gestures of his Hérodiade, whom he had displaced to the margin of his closet drama. In this sense, Hérodiade becomes a figure for the impossible and ambitious project of Mallarmé's symbolism itself, a symbolism of isolated gestures and poses, detached from the dancer on the stage and transformed into various genres of writing: the *Livre,* closet dramas, and theater-texts. What these three genres have in common is that they orient Mallarmé's texts toward the theater, even by way of resistance. The typography of gestures that characterizes the choreographic passages of the *Livre* and the margin notes of Hérodiade's dance, as well as the syntax of the theater-text, contain remains of the mimetic and gestural quality of the rejected theater. That these dispersed and textualized gestures can be traced to Hérodiade and then back to the actual dance of Loie Fuller shows that Mallarmé's work remained intimately tied to the theater it struggled so much to reject. Mallarmé's reliance on the literary text, his construction of the theater as a book, his distrust of public audiences, and his aversion to actors inaugurates a modernism that derives its values from a resistance to the theater, a resistance that keeps the theater at the center of literature.

James Joyce: 3
Novel and Drama in Ulysses

There can be little doubt that the history of the novel is a story of success. Drama, which Hegel considered to be the great synthesis of epic and lyric poetry, finds itself challenged and replaced by the novel as the culmination of literary history.[1] Perhaps the best account of the novel's victory over drama is given in Bakhtin's notion of heteroglossia, which describes the novel's ability to incorporate the most heterogeneous elements and voices and to sublate all other genres of literature.[2] And if someone should object that the novel, no matter how all-inclusive it may be, is nonetheless too limited a genre to figure as the summa of literary history, we can turn to Franco Moretti's notion of the "modern epic," a genre that outdoes the novel in containing even more heterogeneous elements and genres, including the novel itself.[3] One way of beginning my inquiry is to point to the persistence of the dramatic in Moretti's list of heteroglossic modern epics. Goethe's *Faust,* Wagner's *Ring,* Flaubert's *La Tentation de Saint-Antoine,* and Kraus's *Die letzten Tage der Menschheit* are literally plays, while Melville's *Moby Dick* and Joyce's *Ulysses* include dramatic sections such as *Moby Dick*'s "Midnight. — Forcastle" and the "Circe" chapter of *Ulysses* — eruptions of drama within the (epic) novel.[4] And perhaps it should come as no surprise that the quest for heteroglossia outlined by Bakhtin and Moretti would ultimately lead back to drama, for enacted drama is the only genre that speaks truly with different tongues.[5]

The attempt to include all other genres within the novel does have a counterhistory in the field of drama, one that goes by the name *epic theater.* According to this counterhistory, modern drama learns from the novel and begins to use novelistic strategies, not as a way of ceding ground to the novel but rather as a way of rejuvenating the dramatic form. Such borrowings, of course, are not new to modern drama. Confined by some version of the Aristotelian unities, the drama has always needed to constitute itself against the more loosely defined epic tradition. For this reason, most descriptive and prescriptive theories of drama since Aristotle have downplayed what has always existed in drama: narrative elements ranging from descriptive teichoscopy (a person onstage looking, *scopein,* over a wall, *tei-*

chos, and reporting what he or she sees) and messengers reporting events to the chorus and its modern incarnation, the *raisonneur.* In modern drama, however, these elements shift to the center. Even though Brecht, following Piscator, is one of the few who actually employs the term *epic drama,* the increasing importance of narrative elements — from Strindberg's episodic *A Dream Play* to the narrative prefaces and epilogues of Shaw, and from Yeats's chorus to Stein's narrative voices — has led many theorists, most prominently Peter Szondi, to apply an expanded notion of epic drama to modern drama at large.[6] We are now faced with two competing histories, one that tells of an increasing absorption of drama (and poetry) by the novel and one that describes the increasing use made of narrative elements, in particular narrative diegesis, by modern drama.

Between these two genres and histories Joyce, with great cunning, positions *Ulysses,* a novel so heteroglossic that it includes a play, but this internalized play itself relies on a number of narrative strategies and elements that place it within the history of epic drama. From the point of view of the novel, which is the view taken by most critics, the dramatic form of "Circe" constitutes just one narrative experiment among others. However, from the point of view of drama, "Circe" must be seen as a play, and more specifically as a narrative closet drama. Only an analysis that follows both of these trajectories and reflects on their conjunction can recognize the curious superimposition of novel and drama that characterizes this chapter of *Ulysses.*[7]

Drama had occupied Joyce from the very beginning of his literary career. Long before the publication of *Exiles,* Joyce had worked on a play entitled *A Brilliant Career* (which won him the attention of William Archer) and had written "epiphanies," short pieces of prose, many of which take the form of short dramatic dialogues.[8] In addition, we have Joyce's extensive dramatic criticism, devoted in part to the generic differences between drama and epic. As early as 1900 Joyce discussed the Dionysiac origin of Greek theater and formulated his first critique of Aristotle's *Poetics,* observing that "for good or for bad, it [Greek drama] has done its work. . . . Its revival is not of dramatic but of pedagogical significance," while praising the Irish Literary Theatre.[9] New drama can only arise by breaking with dramatic conventions, and Joyce's definition of drama revolves, therefore, around the notion of dynamic movement: "Drama is strife, evolution, movement in whatever way unfolded; it exists, before it takes form, independently; it is conditioned but not controlled by its scene" (*Critical,* 41). We can see the first signs of this "strife, evolution, movement" in Joyce's early dramatic exercises. However, their employment here remains tentative, for Joyce still understands these terms according to his dramatic idol, Ibsen — Joyce went to the trouble of studying Norwegian in order to read him—and thus within the confines of a somewhat altered well-made play. But just as Ibsen himself left this form behind, Joyce, in the third and last phase of writing *Ulysses,* began to rely on "strife, evolution, movement" to create a dramatic form closer to the "fierce, hysterical power of Strindberg" (*Critical,* 71) than to the discussions and psychological revelations of Ibsen. The result of this effort is the dramatic fifteenth chapter of *Ulysses.*

"Circe" has been considered by many to be the climax and center of *Ulysses,* and not just because of its extraordinary length. More than any other chapter, "Circe" encloses within its boundaries the entire novel, its characters, gestures, fragments of dialogue, and objects. By recycling leit-motifs, figures, and themes, "Circe," in the formulation of Hélène Cixous, puts all of *Ulysses* on an imaginary stage.[10] In this, "Circe" replicates the role of the Circe episode within the *Odyssey.* Circe's island is a place to which Odysseus returns, and it therefore functions as a false *nostos,* threatening to take the place of his real homecoming to Ithaca. And structurally this epi-sode anticipates his upcoming adventures because Circe tells Odysseus not only about his future dangers but also how he will survive them. Thus the Circe episode becomes something like a center around which Odysseus's wanderings revolve.

In order to understand the form and function of "Circe," it is not enough to register the struggle between drama and narrative; instead, it is necessary to mediate, or triangulate, this struggle through the category of the theater, for only then can we understand what Joyce means when he says that drama "is conditioned but not controlled by its scene." To some extent, the theory of drama has always included the category of the theater—the Aristotelian unities, for example, were usually justified by the confines of the stage—but in modernism theatricality becomes a term and value that occupies a central and often antagonistic role with respect to the dramatic text. We can attribute this development to the fundamental change in the practice and theory of the theater that begins with Wagner and continues with such figures as Adolphe Appia, E. G. Craig, Georg Fuchs, F. T. Marinetti, and Antonin Artaud, all of whom place unprecedented value on the theater or theatricality, often in opposition to the value and function of the dramatic text.[11] Their at times excessive valorization of the theater against drama puts new pressures on the dramatic form; from the later nineteenth century on-ward, drama is therefore forced to position itself explicitly against a theater by which it is regarded with great suspicion.

Reading "Circe" as not only drama but also theater, we must ask how it envisions its relation to the stage: how it could, in principle, be transformed into an actual production. Such a perspective demonstrates that "Circe" does not easily lend itself to being produced in a theater. With too many characters, too many concurrent events, parallel plots, and plays within plays, with sudden transformations of characters, scenes, and settings into hallucinatory sequences, "Circe" partakes in the tradition I call the phantasmagoric or *exuberant* closet drama. The genre includes Flaubert's *La Tentation de Saint-Antoine,* Karl Kraus's *Die letzten Tage der Menschheit,* and Goethe's *Faust,* whose *Walpurgisnacht* scene is one of "Circe"'s dramatic models. (That all four are on Moretti's "modern epic" list indicates the importance of the exuberant closet drama for this tradition.) Of these texts, "Circe" is perhaps the most extreme, exploiting the hallucinatory theatricality of impossible scenes with unprecedented determination, as if the exuberant closet drama had finally come to realize what it might mean to be "not controlled by its scene."

It is crucial to recognize that "Circe"'s exuberant theatricality does not mean that this text embraces the actual theater. Where restrained closet dramas, like *Igitur,* resist theatrical representation by minimizing action, exuberant closet dramas take theatrical action to an extreme so as to exceed the limits of the theater. One could call "Circe"'s resistance to the theater a structural form of anti-theatricalism, for "Circe" distances itself from the stage, not because Joyce despises theater managers and disapproves of the profession of acting, but because he uses the freedom from the constraints of theatrical representation to create forms of theatricality that can only unfold in the form of text. In order to resist being staged, however, "Circe" takes a path that is the safest of them all: it goes hiding within a novel that no one would ever dream of putting on a stage. The crafty strategy of pretending to be part of a novel, however, has a number of consequences for the dramatic form, the most important of which concerns the nature of stage directions. It is through a reconceptualization of stage directions from the point of view of the novel that Joyce invents the peculiar dramatic form that one might call the *narrative* closet drama.

"Circe"'s Narrative Stage Directions

The rise in the late nineteenth and early twentieth centuries of immensely detailed and at times excessively long stage directions was a response to a fundamental change in the institution of the dramatic text. Although drama had been printed since before the Elizabethan period, it was only in the course of the eighteenth and nineteenth centuries that contemporary dramas, and not just the classics, were generally considered to be literature and therefore were printed, taught, and read as literature. The international nature of modernism meant that some of the most influential plays circulated in translation, for example those of Strindberg and Ibsen, and censorship meant that some plays were more easily read than performed, as in the case of Wilde and Shaw. This gradual development toward reading drama had a profound impact on the form of modern drama. One consequence of this development was that stage directions now had to be conceived as being part of the literary text. Joyce's *Exiles,* printed before it was staged, fully participates in the literarization of stage directions. A page-long introductory stage direction sets the scene meticulously, each character is introduced with a detailed physiognomic portrait, and specific actions and carefully sequenced gestures are described and prescribed on every page of the play.

The most important effect of this literarization is that we can no longer take modernist stage directions to be prescriptive intrusions of a dramatic author on the turf of a stage manager, a direct and therefore paratextual communication of a technical nature.[12] Instead they are addressed to the general reader. The consequences of this fundamental shift have not been properly understood because theater studies still sees in stage directions the most direct attempt of the dramatic text to "dictate" theatrical performance. And since theater studies is still devoted primarily to "liberating" theatrical performance from the dramatic text, stage directions are usually condemned for representing the worst type of textual intrusion on the performance. In the debates about stage directions, both the detractors of stage directions, such as Patrice Pavis and Keir Elam, and their occasional defenders, such as John Searle, share the assumption that stage directions represent a direct authorial voice that must be either obeyed or ignored.[13] As soon as drama is directed at a general reader, this assumption becomes untenable. Now stage directions can no longer be seen as authorial hints occurring somehow outside the literary text proper but become integral parts of it. We are indebted to Joyce for recognizing the consequences of the process of assimilating stage directions to the primary dramatic text: if it is not the author who speaks through stage directions, then the only kind of figure to whom we can attribute them is a narrator. It is perhaps no surprise that it took a novelist such as Joyce (in addition to the poet Mallarmé) to recognize the narrative character of stage directions and that it was in the context of writing a novel that he did so, for there is no play in which this increasing reliance on narrative stage directions is more prominent than in "Circe."

Nevertheless, it took Joyce several rounds of revisions to arrive at a form that takes full advantage of the narrative character of stage directions. In fact, the first draft of "Circe" is not yet fully written in the dramatic form but consists of the words of a descriptive narrator, whose discourse is only occasionally interrupted by speakers and dialogue:

~~Faithful Place~~ Night town. Rows of grimy houses with gaping doors. . . . Whistles are heard in the distance {call{{ing}} and answer{{ing}}: Wait my love, and I'll be with you.} On a step a rag-picker crouches to shoulder a sack. . . . A girl's voice sings out, high ~~and hoarse~~, {still young,} from a lane:

> I gave it to ~~Kitty~~ {Molly}
> Because she was ~~pretty~~ {jolly}
> The leg of the duck
> The leg of the duck.

. . . The redcoats halt ~~with~~ {beside} the patrol and talk. {Their tunics are bloodbright near the lamp, their blond heads close cropped, their biscuits caps set on the side lobes are round ball-sockets.} . . .

Lynch
So That?
Stephen

So that the {art of} gesture renders visible not the lay sense but the first formal rhythm.[14]

The first draft of "Circe" is a peculiar combination of narrative and drama. The narrative voice both introduces direct speech ("A girl's voice sings out") and quotes it ("Wait my love"), thus fulfilling all obligations of a distanced and descriptive third-person narrator; the only formal difference from a novel is that Joyce's narrator speaks in the present tense, the tense of stage directions, rather than in the narrative past tense. The typography too veers toward the dramatic form, for most speakers' names are centered and set in italics above their spatially isolated direct speech. However, this feature is employed somewhat hesitantly, for the initial call and answer, the girl's voice, and a number of other noises are not introduced in this manner as *dramatis personae*. The only other dramatic element Joyce begins using a few pages into this first draft is a limited kind of stage direction, one that modulates the speech of characters:

{*Rudolf*
(severely) One night they bring you home ~~dead~~ drunk. as a dog. after spend your good money. (Herring, 214)

With the second draft, Joyce shifted this balance between narrative and drama in the direction of drama. New stage directions indicating tone and manner of speech are inserted where there had been none before.[15] In addition, all direct speech is now presented with the speaker's name centered above each paragraph; even "The Call," quoted by the narrator in the first draft, becomes an independent, if anonymous, agent:

The Call
Wait, my love, and I'll be with you. (*Ulysses,* 350)

And the "girl" acquires a proper name so that she too can be presented as a *dramatis persona:*

Cissy Caffrey
I gave it to Molly
Because she was jolly, . . . (351)

"Circe" is thus transformed into a standard dramatic form, consisting of *dramatis personae* and direct speech.[16] The simplest but also most consequential change, however, concerns the narrator of the first draft, for this narrator is now confined into the enclosed space of the stage direction. Besides the conventional short stage direction, inserted before a direct speech, "Circe" now has a much more substantial type of stage direction, one that is always set apart from the dialogue and contains the text's narrative voice.

What is striking about this narrative voice, however, is that even though it no longer has the novelistic power to introduce the characters and to quote their speeches and noises, it still acts as a dominating, self-confident narrator.[17] In the process of experimenting with a large number of narrative modes, Joyce came to the realization that a dramatic stage direction was nothing but a particular form of present-tense narration. More than simply one more narrative experiment like the other chapters of *Ulysses,* "Circe" therefore constitutes an important contribution to the history of the closet drama, one that demonstrates that the stage direction represents a particular form of diegesis.

That the stage directions are no longer commands from the author to the director does not mean that the diegesis of the stage directions is any less prescriptive or authoritative. On the contrary, it is because these stage directions are no longer directed at a stage director that their authority is in fact increased beyond all limits; as long as they are mere directives, they can be disobeyed, and in fact they are all the time. As soon as they are directed at a reader, however, their prescriptive force can range unchallenged. Joyce has no scruples in taking advantage of this absolute authority of stage directions in a modernist closet drama, as he willfully prescribes sudden changes of costume and appearance. When called "A cardinal's son," Stephen is transformed all of a sudden so that he "(appears in the doorway, dressed in red soutane, sandals and socks. . . . He wears a battered silk hat sideways on his head)" (427). In a similar situation, Leopold Bloom suddenly becomes Lord Mayor of Dublin and appears "(in alderman's gown and chain)" (390). There is no change of dress or scene too fast for this narrator to describe and no technical requirement that would stand in the way of making it happen.

But the power of "Circe"'s stage directions extends beyond the domain of dress and costume. As in the tradition of the dream play, from Strindberg's *Dream Play* through Apollinaire to expressionist drama, a word uttered onstage can lead to the appearance or transformation of its referent. When Bloom teasingly calls Zoe a "dear gazelle," that speech act transforms the word *gazelle* into immediate (theatrical) reality, and this transformation is conjured by the narrator in parentheses: "(Gazelles are leaping, feeding on the mountains . . .)" (389). In the same way, Bella's sex change happens simply by virtue of substituting the letter *o* for *a;* Bella becomes Bello (432), and nothing else is needed to bring this transformation about. That the gazelles and the sex change are triggered by a word does not mean, however, that they are only imaginary, although that has been argued many times.[18] Within the frame of the stage this transformation is a biological one.[19] At one moment, for example, Bello "(bares his arm and plunges it elbowdeep into Bloom's vulva)" (440), a prescription that indicates graphically enough, one should think, that Bloom has actually been transformed into a woman and that he has not simply changed his clothes.

We have no ground on which to challenge this matter-of-fact prescription. Because there is no human actor whose feigned sex change can be dismissed as some trick of theatrical illusion, we cannot help but accept that at this point, within the fictional frame of the text, Bloom actually does have a vulva.[20] "Circe" may evoke the physical presence and representational reality of actors and their organs, but this theatrical "reality effect" remains in the service of a phantasmagoric transformation of women into men and men into swine.[21] Many of these transformations turn upside down the understanding of language formulated by J. L. Austin, which Joyce seems to anticipate in chapter 9: "Speech, speech. But act. Act speech. . . . Act. Be acted on" (173). Austin had argued that within the frame of a theater, speech acts uttered actually do not have the same ability "to do things" that they have in real life. In the closet drama "Circe," by contrast, speech acts have absolute and immediate transformative power: to be spoken to—to be addressed and named—is to "be acted on." "Circe" thus shows how to do things with words—especially how to turn them into objects and then to personify them—as long as these words are overheard and then turned into reality by a narrator speaking from a stage direction.[22]

It is in order to preserve the absolute authority of stage directions and thus their phantasmatic reality effects that Joyce must constantly mark his difference from the actual theater. A substantial number of stage directions break openly with the frame of the theater, as when they use the cardinal directions south and east and thus refer to a real topography rather than the left-right schema of the represented space on stage, such as in the following with regard to Bloom: "(He points to the south, then to the east)" (360). Since the stage is not defined by terrestrial coordinates, it is impossible to comply with this stage direction in the theater; the direction can only be understood as a narrative representation, as opposed to a theatrical one, of Bloom's gesture of pointing. The distance of "Circe" from the stage is perhaps most apparent in those passages where Joyce endows stage directions with narrative functions that go beyond the faithful description of scenes. Some narrative stage directions, for example, summarize certain events rather than indicating their representation on stage: "(The instantaneous deaths of many powerful enemies, graziers, members of parliament, members of standing committees, are reported)" (396). In a similar way, a few pages later, a stage direction mentions that "(Bloom explains to those near him his schemes for social regeneration)" (400). Neither the report nor the explanation is a single event; rather they are condensed and compressed indications of processes that unfold over time and comprise, presumably, many different acts that the stage direction does not bother to depict in detail.

The narrative character of stage directions is taken to an extreme when Joyce uses them to represent a scene in which Bloom defends himself against charges of having assaulted one Mary Driscoll: "(Bloom, pleading not guilty and holding a fullblown waterlily, begins a long unintelligible speech. They would hear what counsel had to say in his stirring address to the grand jury. He was down and out but, though branded as a black sheep, if he might say so, he meant to reform . . .)" (376). The exterior description of a gesture — "holding a fullblown waterlily" — blends directly into a condensed report — "begins a long unintelligible speech." Then, all of a sudden, the narrative voice merges with Bloom's thoughts: "They would hear what counsel had to say in his stirring address to the grand jury." Finally, the narrator enters Bloom's speech altogether: "He was down and out but, though branded as a black sheep, if he might say so, he meant to reform." The stage direction then continues for another twenty or so lines to represent Bloom's speech by means of what by now we have surely identified as free indirect discourse; these words are not of the narrator's choosing but of Bloom's, and what we are hearing is a third-person — indirect — representation of his very speech. This is Joyce's most cunning stage direction because it turns the division between direct speech and stage direction upside down: while the stage direction is supposed to function as the space for scenic depiction and prescription, through the technique of free indirect discourse it here presents Bloom's direct speech veiled as narrative report.

An analysis not just of "Circe"'s form but of its content as well opens a different perspective for thinking about its particular mode of resistance to the theater. It is significant that Joyce chose the form of the closet drama to represent the most illicit scenes of the entire novel, that the closet drama, and not narrative, would be the form in which the novel's textual unconscious was acted out. The illicit has always been part of the history of the closet drama, which has tended to represent what otherwise could not or would not be put before the eyes of an audience, from Goethe's *Faust II* and Shelley's *The Cenci* to Flaubert's *La Tentation de Saint-Antoine* and de Sade's *Philosophy in the Bedroom*.[23] Indeed "Circe" is indebted to the latter because it derives its deviant and illicit scenarios from the classics of aberration, such as Leopold von Sacher-Masoch's *Die Venus im Pelz* and Richard von Krafft-Ebbing's *Psychopathia Sexualis*.

In "Circe," as in those other cases, the acting out of the illicit, the deviant, and the censored may be in some sense theatrical in that it takes place through role-playing, changes of costume, and changes in appearance. At the same time, however, this acting out cannot take place in a real theater because it everywhere exceeds the limits of theatrical representation, especially its reliance on real actors, with real appearances and genders, as well as the presence of actual censorship. Between these two factors, censorship and the reality of the actor's body, we find a range of limitations imposed on and by theatrical representation, including the number of people on stage, the speed of scenic transformations, and so forth. Not that these limitations cannot and have not been circumvented and even in some sense overcome. Indeed, they can be said to have inspired some of the more innovative reforms and revolutions in the history of the theater. But this does not mean that these limitations do not make themselves everywhere felt in the theater. It is the closet drama alone that is truly capable of resisting them; it alone can actually change a man into a woman, place thousands of people on an impossible stage, and even turn objects and fragmented body parts into agents. For Joyce, then, as for Mallarmé, the closet drama's resistance to the theater does not signify a purely negative retreat into an aestheticist sphere of *l'art pour l'art*.[24] Rather, this resistance is part of a larger resistance to the limitations of the theater and the normativity that stems from them. It is this possibility of resistance, built into the very structure of the closet drama, that necessitates what one might call an epistemology of the closet drama.[25] Such an epistemology would be devoted to tracing the forms of deviance, including but not limited to sexual deviance, that find their place in the closet drama, hidden from censorship, from the expectations of the audience, and perhaps most significantly, from the limits of theatrical representation.

The Choreography of Gestures

Thus unable and unwilling to rely on the stage, "Circe" must devise a way to represent theatricality in language.[26] Not only particular movements, gestures, and attitudes but also the characters' appearance and disappearance, change of dress, and gender must be described, since they will not be enacted, and for this a more precise language is required: the theatricality of the stage *(chora)* is transcribed into choreography.[27] One vocabulary through which gestures and postures can be easily integrated into writing is the choreography of dance and ballet.[28] For this reason, the languages of dance and ballet keep appearing in the tradition of textual theater with almost predictable frequency, from Mallarmé through Yeats to Beckett. Joyce's "Circe" too turns to the terminology of dance in the figure of a master of dance and ceremony, Maginni, to facilitate the textual presentation of gestures. Maginni's expert discourse on gestures begins to dominate the scene as soon as Zoe, the prostitute who is pursued by Stephen and Leopold alike, proposes a dance. It is through the voice of Maginni that the text offers to the reader a vocabulary of motion, whose language, naturally, is French:

> Carré! Avant deux! . . . Balancé! . . .
> Avant huit! Traversé! Salut! Cours de mains! Croisé! . . .
> Les tiroirs! Châine de dames! La corbeille! Dos à dos! . . .
>
> . . . .
>
> Dansez avec vos dames! Changez de dames! Donnez le petit
> bouquet à votre dame! Remerciez! (470–71)

While Maginni refers to these terms as "the poetry of motion, art of calisthenics" (469), what he actually says sounds more like a series of commands that are supposed to be immediately and accurately translated into gestures and poses, a dancing master's instructions to a class. In fact these instructions resemble the traditional stage direction in that they seek to dictate to the performers what to do.

Meanwhile, the "poetry of motion" Maginni claims for himself actually happens elsewhere, namely, in Joyce's own, much more elaborate stage directions. For example, "Carré! Avant deux! . . . Balancé!" becomes: "(The morning and noon hours waltz in their places, turning, advancing to each other, shaping their curves, bowing visavis. Cavaliers behind them arch and suspend their arms, with hands descending to, touching, rising from their shoulders)" (470). The description of descending and rising hands, suspended arms, and bowing bodies grasps only in part what it means to properly follow the commands "Carré" and "Balancé," and the specificity of the choreographic instructions of the classical ballet, whether they be accurately enacted or not, is certainly lost in the corresponding stage direction. All we get are glimpses of isolated gestures and movements, sketched moments of corporeal interaction, "descending" and "rising" hands, "suspended arms," and "turning" and "bowing" bodies. While this transcription may be partial, it is not without method, moving from the most general attitudes of bodies to those of arms and finally of hands, and it thus shows an interest, not in representing continuous action, but in the possibilities offered by carefully and economically isolating selected moments of attitude and gesture.[29]

In a second example, the transcription of Maginni's commands into Joycean stage directions leads to an even more elaborate textual effort: "(Arabesquing wearily they weave a pattern on the floor, weaving, unweaving, curtseying, twirling, simply swirling)" (471). "Twirling" and "swirling" do not have the defined meaning of "Les tiroirs!" and "Balancé!" but the stage direction compensates for this loss in specificity through the creation of a language that may indeed deserve to be called a "poetry of motion."[30] This stage direction includes internal rhyme ("twirling," "swirling"; "wearily," "weave," "weaving," "unweaving"), accentuated sound patterns ("twirling," "simply swirling"), and a neologism, namely, "arabesquing," which surely must claim poetic license.[31] While these stage directions compete with Maginni's specialized language, Maginni himself turns out to be anything but a guarantor of a proper and abstract terminology of dance; not all commands belong to the repertoire of dance, particularly "Chevaux de bois! Escargots!" [Hobbyhorses! Snails!] (471). The vocabulary Maginni uses cannot be trusted, and the stage direction is more poetic, more suggestive, and more "calisthenic" than anything he produces. One might say that this scene stages the triumph of a specifically Joycean stage direction over the older model of the stage direction as command. And this new "poetic" stage direction is made possible by the closet drama's freedom from the stage.

In its attempt to replace theatrical enactment with a new form of stage direction, "Circe" demonstrates that the closet drama not only rejects the theater but also needs to create a different, literary one in its stead. This need led Joyce to both draw on and reject the vocabulary of dance, which he used as something against which he could develop his own poetry of motion. A similar dynamic led him and his early critics to conceive of his own language as somehow inherently theatrical, and the name used for this theatrical quality of language was *gesture*.[32] A literary "art of calisthenics" must not only present a poetic description of gestures in the place of enacted ones; the very language of such descriptions must be infused with the gestural as well. The search for a gestural poetics was at the foreground of *Our Exagmination Round his Factification for Incamination.* A landmark collection of essays published in 1929 and dedicated to *Finnegans Wake*—then called simply *Work in Progress*—it includes, for example, an article by Robert McAlmon entitled "Mr. Joyce directs an Irish word ballet." McAlmon praises the gestural repertoire of *Ulysses* with the following words: "Also good comedy, clowning, pantomime, nonsense, slapstick, drollery, does not appeal to the sense of humour by explanation, but by gesture. . . . Prose too can possess the gesticulative quality."[33] A similar notion of a gestural, or "gesticulative," language is offered by Samuel Beckett in the same collection of essays. Using in part Vico's terminology, Beckett sees the trajectory of human development as a history of alienation, a process fueled by the increasing emergence of a conventional language. Caught in its last phase of total abstraction, this conventionalized language has lost touch with its earlier expressivity, based on figurative expressions and concrete forms. The real origin of language, however, resides in gesture—"In its first dumb form, language was gesture" (*Exagmination,* 11)—and it is through poetry and literature that we may mourn the loss of the gestural origin of language. In accordance with this gestural poetics, Beckett characterizes Joyce's language as an attempt to overcome conventionality by presenting a "quintessential extraction of language and painting and gestures" that initiates a "savage economy of hieroglyphics" (15). It becomes clearer and clearer that Joyce's words themselves have now acquired the character of gestures, so that they "elbow their way on to the page" (16) and even begin to "dance" (14). And through this gestural "dance" of words the realm of the theater is enfolded into the very language of the text.[34]

Beckett's scheme of the increasingly conventional and thus decreasingly expressive nature of language is reminiscent of what is sometimes called the early-twentieth-century crisis of language.[35] In response to a general dissatisfaction with language, writers and theorists as diverse as Hugo von Hofmannsthal, Nietzsche's follower Fritz Mauthner, and a number of expressionist writers began to devise ways of gaining access to a more authentic form of mimetic expressivity, for which gestures were the most promising candidate.[36] The search for an original language of gestures occurred not only in literature and philosophy but also in the performing arts, where it took the form of a search for a more authentic language of gestures that would not depend on conventional language. In fact McAlmon compares Joyce's gestures indiscriminately to the gestures of African tribes and to Isadora Duncan's dancing figures (107), a combination symptomatic of turn-of-the-century primitivism. The topos of a theatrical language of gestures keeps resurfacing in the history of modern theater and the performing arts, from Wagner's aesthetics of gestures to Stravinsky's ballet music, and from Brecht's notion of *gestus* to Artaud's call for a new grammar of gestures. As a closet drama, "Circe" is located between this search for a theatrical language of gestures and the search for a gestural language of literature, or more precisely, it superimposes the one onto the other. It is in the conjunction of a theatrical language and a literary one that "Circe"'s choreography takes shape.

Ritual Gestures

Hand in hand with the search for a gestural original of language and a language of gestures goes another particular modernist obsession: ritual and religious ceremony. Beginning with Wagner's theory of the theater and Nietzsche's *Birth of Tragedy from the Spirit of Music* and continuing all the way to Frazer's *Golden Bough,* various forms of ritual and ceremony promised to counteract the abstraction that threatened everywhere to annihilate artistic expressivity. The most common object of fascination for reformers such as Artaud and Grotovsky, but also Victor Turner and Richard Schechner, were the rituals they encountered on their anthropological excursions, a fascination that led to what is now called *theater anthropology.* The search for the exotic ritual that promises some form of authenticity is dominant in the performing arts but is not restricted to them. Joyce, for example, turns to a ritual closer to home, one that had also fascinated the high modernists Mallarmé and T. S. Eliot, for the type of ritual that furnishes the theatrical space of *Ulysses* is not some putatively primitive ritual but the ceremony of the Catholic liturgy.[37]

Like the vocabulary of dance and ballet, ritual gestures provide a vocabulary for conjuring movement through textual descriptions and thus serve as a paradigm against which Joyce can establish his own language of gestures. More significantly, however, the liturgy constitutes a matrix that endows such gestures with significance and meaning. The reasons for which "Circe" is drawn to and resists the theater of the liturgy appear more clearly when one turns to the theology of gestures that Joyce encountered in the late twenties through the Jesuit Marcel Jousse. Jousse's public lectures in Paris were devoted precisely to grounding the crisis of language — a critique of its conventional nature — in a theology of gestures based on the liturgy.[38] Mary Colum reports Joyce's fascination with Jousse's project: "At that time the Abbé Jousse was lecturing in Paris. He was a noted propounder of a theory that Joyce gave adherence to, that language had its origin in gesture — 'In the beginning was the rhythmic gesture,' Joyce often said."[39] It is hard to believe that Joyce gave full "adherence" to Jousse's theology of gestures. Indeed, Joyce reportedly "could not omit a piece of blasphemy when mentioning a heavenly gesture" (131). Nevertheless, it is important to recognize Joyce's fascination with a theory of the origin of language that so resembled the one proposed by Vico, which Joyce had recommended to Beckett for his essay on *Work in Progess.*[40]

Unapologetically taking the opening of *Genesis* as his point of departure, Jousse proclaims, "In the beginning was gesture,"[41] an axiom that Joyce slyly circulates back into his next text as "In the beginning was the gest he jousstly says,"[42] echoing Beckett's claim that "in its first dumb form, language was gestures" (*Examination,* 11). Jousse goes on to consider every form of human activity and expressivity in terms of gesture. Beginning with corporeal and manual gestures of the expressive body *(gestes corporels-manuels),* he extends the notion of gesture to language, differentiating between oral speech, which becomes a "gesture of the mouth" [geste laryngo-bucal], and writing, namely, "graphic gesture" [geste graphique]. Behind this reformulation of oral and written language in terms of gesture stands a critique of the conventional sign for losing touch with its gestural origin and falling prey to the danger of abstraction. This theory of gestures culminates in the gestures of the Catholic ritual. Endlessly troubled by the diverse translations and thus the danger of falsifying Jesus' words, Jousse turns to Jesus' gestures, which presumably do not have to be translated, to authenticate the ritual: "The words have been translated from Aramaic to Greek, from Greek to Latin. Everything has changed. . . . But the lasting gestures, profound, energetic, remain: This is my flesh. This is my blood" (128). Jousse thus reveals that what fuels a theological ontology of gestures is an anxiety about language, in particular about translation, changes of meaning, and so forth. Ultimately, however, gestures share the same fate, and we must say that Jousse's anxiety about language extends to gestures, including and particularly ritual gestures: they too lend themselves to being repeated externally, detached from the ceremony and its ritual meaning.

Joyce's use of ritual gestures in "Circe" is located precisely between a theology of original gestures and their external parody. Routinely, for example, Stephen presents mock imitations of the gestures of priests. Prompted by Lynch's speculation that Stephen must be "a cardinal's son" (427), Stephen—by the transformative power of words—immediately appears as a cardinal himself, and the stage directions conjure up his cardinal's dress and ritual movements: "(Releasing his thumbs, he invokes grace from on high with large wave gestures . . .)," and a moment later, "(his head aslant he blesses curly with fore and middle fingers, imparts the Easter kiss and doubleshuffes off comically, swaying his hat from side to side . . .)" (428). Not only the atheist Stephen, who still has the Jesuit blood running through his veins, "only injected the wrong way," as Buck Mulligan observes in the first chapter, but also the assimilated Jew Leopold Bloom performs mock liturgical gestures. When he engages in a masochistic play with his mistress Bella, Bloom kneels down to unlace her boots and recalls kneeling earlier that day during the mass held for Dignam's funeral: "I knelt once before today" (431). In this sense, "Circe" is the realization of Jousse's worst nightmare, namely, the theatrical corruption and mindless imitation of the most ontological and liturgical of gestures, a technique identified by Henri Bergson as one of the primary sources of comedy.[43]

This negative or parodic project, however, is only one side of "Circe"'s relation to liturgical gestures; the other side is a continued reliance on established systems of gesture that provide it with an aesthetic and ontological matrix. It is only by displacing and estranging such a matrix that "Circe" seems capable of establishing its own gestures. "Circe" certainly resists the liturgy, but what motivates this resistance is the more central if also more hidden necessity of employing a vocabulary of gestures and their meaning. In fact Stephen himself, echoing a similar remark made in *Stephen Hero,* evokes such a theological grounding of gestures: "Lynch: So that? Stephen: (looks behind) So that gesture, not music or odour, would be a universal language, the gift of tongues rendering visible not the lay sense but the first entelechy, the structural rhythm" (353).[44] While the text of the world (as well as the text of the Bible) remains disturbingly polysemic — the chapter mentions the vain hope for a universal language several times — the universal language of gestures promises direct expressivity: the original language of the world.[45] Here Stephen sounds surprisingly like Abbé Jousse.

Indeed, Stephen not only sounds like Jousse, he refers to precisely the gestures that stand at the center of Jousse's theology, the gestures of a priest during the transubstantiation, the gestures accompanying the speech acts: "This is my flesh. This is my blood." But Stephen refers to these gestures not without estranging them: "Anyway, who wants two gestures to illustrate a loaf and a jug? This movement illustrates the loaf and jug of bread or wine in Omar. Hold my stick" (353). No gestures have received more theoretical consideration than the gestures performed by a priest during the transubstantiation. They lie at the heart of the liturgy and have been variously theorized as signs, signifiers, symbols, and metaphors. Stephen takes a distinct position in this debate when he asserts that the gestures of the priest "illustrate" loaf and jug, for the gradual formation of the official Catholic doctrine had evolved through a discussion of the sign status of bread and wine and the ritual gestures associated with them.[46]

While participating in this theological debate, Stephen abruptly changes the context from the transubstantiation to the *Rubaiyat* of Omar Khayyam.

In doing so he not only exchanges the liturgical gestures with what are probably obscene ones but also displaces an entire doctrinal theology of gestures.[47] This displacement directly affects the choreography of the stage directions, for this choreography can no longer rely on the established vocabulary of the ritual: "(Stephen thrusts the ashplant on him and slowly holds out his hands, his head going back till both hands are a span from his breast, down turned, in planes intersecting, the fingers about to part, the left being higher)" (353). It is the obsessive precision of this stage direction—the position of fingers; geometrical relations; detailed measures—that registers the pressure of the Catholic theology of gesture on "Circe"'s descriptive project, but also the manner in which the effort of displacing this theology stands behind the creative effort of the chapter. "Circe" seeks out the most rigorous terminology of movement and gesture (dance and ballet) and its most theological foundation (liturgy), not to accept them, but to compete with them.

When thinking about "Circe"'s relation to the formal language of dance and the theological language of ritual one may begin to wonder how the rest of *Ulysses* relates to these discourses as well. Indeed, ritual gestures are central not just in "Circe" but also in other chapters, most notably perhaps the very opening scenes of the novel, in which the shaving Buck Mulligan gleefully impersonates a priest. But the significance of "Circe" for *Ulysses* goes beyond the representation of gestures, for even if we believe that the novel has successfully incorporated drama, this incorporation might at least have left more pervasive dramatic traces on the novel. Two of the most well-known techniques in *Ulysses*—the interior monologue and the use of leitmotifs—can indeed be seen as such traces. This was the opinion of Edouard Dujardin (whom Joyce credits with the "invention" of the interior monologue), who emphasized the theatrical quality of the interior monologue, attributing it to the desire to avoid a controlling and organizing narrator. By the same token Dujardin insisted that the leitmotif was a dramatic and theatrical technique as well, one he claimed to have derived from Wagner.[48] It is not the place here to speculate on the extent to which "Circe" might be only the most extreme manifestation of what one might call the "dramatization" of the novel, but an investigation devoted to this question might take as its point of departure an understanding of "Circe" as the twentieth century's most astonishing closet drama.

Ulysses Set in Nighttown

So seductive is the theatricality of "Circe" that the modernist theater could not resist staging this combination of a dramatized novel and a narrative closet drama. Under the supervision of Padraic Colum, Marjorie Barkentin "presented and arranged" what she called a "dramatized and transposed" version of "Circe," performed for the first time in 1958 at the Rooftop Theatre in New York City.[49] While this "dramatized and transposed" *Ulysses in Nighttown* focuses on the dramatic "Circe" chapter, the authors of the script extend the scope of their project by also including a dramatized version of the opening chapter and of chapter 6 to establish the two main characters, Stephen Dedalus and Leopold Bloom, before their entry into Nighttown. Transforming the scenic organization of the opening pages of *Ulysses* into a dramatic script does not really pose a problem, since the choreography of the novel represents isolated and identifiable gestures and movements in a way that comes close to stage directions. After Buck intones the formula "Introibo ad altare Dei," his gestures and actions that follow— "Halted, he peered down the dark winding stairs and called out coarsely" (3)—are simply transformed into a stage direction without further addition or change; the only other alteration needed is to turn the narrative past tense into the present tense. The same technique of transforming descriptive passages into stage directions is used for the short excerpts from "Hades," which are meant to introduce Leopold Bloom to the audience.

Given that descriptive passages are as central to the novel as is dialogue, it is perhaps not surprising that the adapters did not want these passages to disappear into stage directions. For this reason they took recourse to another mode of transposing *Ulysses* into a drama geared toward the stage: the figure of a narrator who tries to keep the exploding theatricality under control. Thus the first lines of *Ulysses,* which could easily be transformed verbatim into stage directions, are put into the mouth of a narrator, who speaks in the novel's past tense:

> NARRATOR Stately, plump Buck Mulligan came from the stairhead, bearing a bowl of lather on which a mirror and a razor lay crossed. A yellow dressing gown, ungirdled, was sustained gently behind him by the mild morning air. He held the bowl aloft and intoned:
>
> BUCK MULLGAN Introibo ad altare Dei. (Halted, he peers down the dark winding stairs and calls up coarsely) (3)

Speaking what would otherwise be a stage direction is the narrator's only function, and for this reason the narrator might be said to personify *Ulysses'* narrative form in the midst of its stage adaptation.

The difficulties of adaptation are entirely different for "Circe," which constitutes the largest part of the dramatic script. Even though this chapter formally follows the generic requirements of drama, with present-tense stage directions and dialogue, Barkentin and Colum must work harder to dramatize and transpose this chapter into a stageable script because they need to overcome the resistance "Circe" poses to the physical theater. This resistance lies not only in "Circe"'s vast scope but also in its hallucinatory structure, its legions of characters, and their sudden transformations, which project a type of theatricality that does not seem to fit the confined space of a stage. For this reason, Barkentin and Colum find themselves forced to reduce, simplify, and domesticate the exuberant theatricality of the text. The most difficult problem they encounter is that the closet phantasmagoria of "Circe" is capable of creating overlaps between realistic scenes and hallucinations, sustaining parallel strings of fantasy and reality, transforming one into the other, masking characters, changing their clothes and gender, and having them perform plays within plays and transformations within transformations. The stage version, on the other hand, must introduce a clear separation between these two levels, deciding what we, and the characters, see and do not see onstage. In fact the adaptation insists on two neatly separated levels, a "reality" level and a "hallucination" level, with square brackets indicating the exact moments of change.[50]

While "Circe" projects too much theatricality to be a usable dramatic script and must therefore be reduced to a more manageable scenic organization, at the same time it does not provide enough information for a continuous stage performance. Joyce's text freely introduces large numbers of characters without having to worry about their entries and exits and their continuous presence on stage. All this becomes a problem precisely at the moment when "Circe" most willfully subverts the dramatic form, namely, in Bloom's defense speech, which is represented in the original by means of free indirect discourse, but within a stage direction: "Bloom, pleading not guilty and holding a fullblown waterlily, begins a long unintelligible speech. They would hear . . . " (34). Perhaps sensing that there was something odd about this narrative speech in its shifts from present-tense narrative description to the past tense of free indirect discourse, the adapters try to anchor it in Bloom, the putative speaker, through the following set in symptomatic square brackets: "[Accompanied by pantomime of BLOOM]." Bloom here presumably goes through the pantomime of the speech that we hear from the narrator as if he, Bloom, were holding it himself, thus pantomimically regaining the voice taken from him. What we witness here is indeed an awkward attempt at bringing the technique of free indirect discourse onto the stage. Because the adapters are dedicated to the principle of not adding any text to the original, they do not find it possible to fill these additional stage directions with content. The bracketed stage direction "[Accompanied by pantomime]," which punctuates the text at the most crucial moments, thus marks a lack in "Circe"'s theatricality, a shortage of continuous scenic organization, and indicates for us the moments when "Circe"'s theatricality and the demands of an actual staging are most radically opposed to one another.[51]

The different interventions necessitated by the project of transforming "Circe" into a stageable script register negatively "Circe"'s various forms of resisting the theater. The stage version contains no huge crowds, no ambivalence between hallucination and reality, and no actual sex change. The absence of these features testifies to the closet drama's being located at the conjunction of a technical, an aesthetic, and a political problem: it is problematic to have a male actor turn into a woman because it goes against the laws of biology and the decorum of the theater and might provoke the activities of the censor. Some of these constraints are not unique to the theater, as the history of censorship, in particular of the censorship of *Ulysses,* demonstrates. Nevertheless, the closet drama has tended to allow more room for deviant practices, for political as well as for aesthetic and technical reasons. The stage version of "Circe," like the stage version of the *Livre* or the stage version of Gertrude Stein's *Four Saints in Three Acts,* suppresses part of what is allowed to dwell only inside a closet drama, and it can serve as a measure for these closet dramas' resistance to the theater. The provocation of *Ulysses* is not simply that it incorporates a drama within the novel but that it creates an entirely new genre: the narrative closet drama. We can recognize the creation of the narrative closet drama only when we suspend, at least temporarily, the success story of the novel and relate this dramatic chapter to the theater, which it resists and on which it therefore also continues to depends.

Gertrude Stein:
Four Saints in Three Acts —
A Closet Drama to Be Performed

Disregarding actors, arias, movement, gesture, and every other element of theatrical presentation, Gertrude Stein's *Four Saints in Three Acts* defies all formal conventions of the libretto. It lacks a list of *dramatis personae,* proper act numbers, designated speakers, and a discernible plot. In addition, it does not differentiate clearly between direct speech and stage directions and includes short passages written in the narrative past tense. Even after reading *Four Saints* it remains so utterly unclear how many saints appear, how many acts this play includes, and what is spoken on stage that one begins to wonder whether this text was written for the stage at all or should be regarded, along with most of Stein's so-called plays, as a particularly strange kind of closet drama.[1]

This claim that *Four Saints* belongs to the varied group of modernist closet dramas calls for a number of qualifications. I do not wish to suggest, of course, that it is impossible to stage *Four Saints,* a claim that would be belied by the surprising success of its original staging. Produced by The Friends and Enemies of Modern Music, it premiered in 1934 at the Hartford Atheneum before it was transferred to Broadway for a spectacular run. Since then it has been revived a number of times by such star directors as Bob Wilson. The so-called impossibility of staging, however, has always been a misleading and superficial description of closet dramas. Constitutive for this genre are the ways in which dramatic texts actively resist being staged and coopt the world of the theater. The plays and operas of Gertrude Stein participate in and even radicalize this tradition. Central features of *Four Saints* become visible only when we recognize that this text deliberately opposes actors, stage props, and the theatrical space itself. This resistance to the theater emerges with particular clarity in the process of staging, which requires that this resistance be first identified and then overcome. There is, after all, no better way of testing whether a dramatic text is in fact a closet drama than by observing what changes must be made in order to bring it onto the stage. This is a rule that applies to Scherer's stage adaptation of Mallarmé's *Livre,* to Barkentin's adaptation of Joyce's "Circe," and finally to Virgil Thomson's staging of *Four Saints.* Why Stein came to write a closet drama, however, is a question that can be answered only by taking into account Stein's own theory of modern drama, her understanding of the work of art, and most importantly, her conflicted relation to the theater.

Reading Drama, Viewing Theater

In a characteristic combination of autobiography and theory, Stein links her dramatic oeuvre directly to her disregard for the theater: "I practically when I wrote my first play had completely ceased going to the theatre. In fact although I have written a great many plays and I am quite sure they are plays I have since I commenced writing these plays I have practically never been inside of any kind of a theatre."[2] Stein's ambivalence about the theater lies primarily in what she perceives to be an almost unavoidable a-synchronicity, or "syncopation," between observer and action: "The time of one's emotion in relation to the scene was always interrupted" (xli). Subjected to the temporality of the theater, the audience cannot control the time, place, or speed of reception and must submit to the pace of the performance. There is no way of assuring that the performance conforms to the desires of any particular audience member, with the result that audience and performance are almost always out of sync.

One solution to this a-synchronicity is the act of reading, for readers, in contrast to viewers in the theater, can adjust the speed of reading, as well as its time and place, to their own sensibilities and needs. Stein's declaration "I rather liked reading plays, I very much liked reading plays" (xxxix) is thus grounded in her annoyance with "the bother of never being able [in the theater] to begin over again . . . and at no time had you been ready" (xli). Stein here participates in the value of engulfment that is characteristic of the modernist novel and its culture of solitary and silent reading, a mode of reception systematically shielded from the distractions of public spaces.[3] It is only in private and ideal circumstances, Stein and so many modernists argue, that a perfect synchronicity between story and the affective reader can be achieved. Much of Stein's reinvention of the dramatic form is motivated by the attempt to import this quality of synchronized reading into the dramatic form. For this project, Stein also may have drawn on a nineteenth-century American tradition that Alan Ackerman has aptly termed that of the "displaced" or "portable theater."[4] The "portable theater" includes most prominent postbellum writers, such as Melville, Whitman, Alcott, Howells, and James, who kept their distance from the theater while at the same time displacing it to such literary genres as theatrical and dramatic novels (*Moby Dick* is one of the few precedents for including a dramatic chapter within a novel), dramatic poetry, monodramas, and closet dramas.

In modernism, however, the portable theater acquires a new anti-theatrical foundation. Here the preference of reading text over viewing theater becomes part of a program devoted to preserving the autonomy of the aesthetic sphere, an autonomy that seems to be provided by the solitary artist and the isolated recipient, both utterly detached from the social reality surrounding them. And it is the insistence on the reclusive artist and the withdrawn recipient that determines what might be called the originary scene of modernist art: artist and reader, both confined in their studies, concentrate on the complex processes of production and reception, a concentration that demands their total absorption in what they are doing without the slightest distraction or interruption.

The modernist investment in the type of artwork requiring absolute concentration and absorption is related to what Pierre Bourdieu has called the "consecration" of the work of art, the process of endowing it with the value and significance that requires a reverent attention and attitude on the part of the viewer.[5] At the same time, we find an almost obsessive scorn for the "masses": just as the artist must despise and withdraw from these masses, so the recipient of the work of art must be isolated from these masses and their public gatherings as well. The theater, alas, is an art form that is produced collaboratively and seen collectively; and so theatrical production and reception become anathema to many modernists. A constant reminder of the public and political masses outside the autonomous aesthetic sphere, the theater is then seen as the Trojan horse of the extra-aesthetic intruding into the field of art, and for this reason there is a tradition within modernism that defines itself through an opposition to the theater. From this perspective, it becomes clear that critics have tended to overstate Stein's allegiance to both dadaism and surrealism.[6] The "radical" nature of her poetry, prose, and drama and the "experimental" appearance of her texts suggest all too easily an affinity to the equally "experimental" writers of the avant-garde. But for all its insight into particular literary strategies, such an approach ignores the fact that Stein's writing is based on the high modernist values of engulfment and solitary reading, an aesthetics that is directly opposed to the distracting and interruptive nature of the theater as it was systematically celebrated by the avant-garde. Stein's understanding of the work of art and, in particular, her suspicion of the theater put her in the company of Mallarmé, and not of Tristan Tzara.

The theorist who has articulated this modernist version of anti-theatricalism most succinctly is Michael Fried. In fact, Fried has become something of the anti-theatrical straw man of theater and performance studies even though his brand of anti-theatricalism is not primarily directed against the theater, but against theatricality.[7] Fried's aesthetics departs from the position that "the theater and theatricality are at war today not simply with modernist painting (or modernist painting and sculpture), but with art as such."[8] And the value that is to be preserved through such a war against the theater is that of "absorption," Fried's version of the modernist value of concentrated engulfment. The modernist artwork is here portrayed as being in constant danger of being "corrupted or perverted by theater" (20). The theatrical arts are deemed "aggressive" (16) and attention-mongering because they are eagerly "waiting for a beholder" instead of subsisting in a state of self-sufficient complacency and introspection. Fried's measure for theatricality is the degree to which an artwork is tailored toward or conscious of the beholder. But the beholders themselves are negatively affected by the theater as well, for the eager artwork creates a kind of theatrical atmosphere that makes them feel as if they were in a theater, in the awkward company of other people, "distanced, or crowded, by the silent presence of another *person*," (Fried's emphasis), an experience that is deeply "disquieting" (16). Being absorbed by the artwork requires a reception that is not interrupted by the presence of others in the audience.

Fried's anti-theatricalism is not only based on a particular form of absorptive reception; it also is concerned with the other component of modernist anti-theatricalism, namely, a critique of human actors. In a remark on cinema, for example, Fried adds, in the fine print of a footnote, that he is bothered not only by the other people in the audience but by the people onstage, for the cinema escapes the pitfalls of the theatrical only because "the actors are not physically present" (23 n. 16). But what does it mean to critique certain forms of painting and sculpture for being theatrical, when they, surely, do not require actors for the work of representation? Fried argues that since the theater so centrally relies on actors, every "theatrical" artwork, be it painting or sculpture, acquires a personal or "anthropomorphic" quality (19); the artwork, in other words, starts behaving as if it were a physically present actor standing on a stage.

Fried's anti-theatricalism captures central components of Stein's resistance to the theater. What Fried and Stein share in particular is an aversion to distracting audiences as well as to human actors on the stage.[9] Stein's critique of the actor is based on what she experiences as the effects of impersonation on the stage, the "nervousness of the theatre excitement" ("Plays," xxxix). Stein's explanation of this "nervousness" is one of the most idiosyncratic versions of modernism's critique of actors. Again, Stein turns to the act of reading, this time with reference to the ways in which both reader and viewer are "getting acquainted" (xxxix) with the actor. In the act of reading a novel the characters or agents—Stein sometimes calls them "actors" as well—take shape gradually, with the reader becoming increasingly acquainted with them as the story progresses. First we have only a name. Then this name is increasingly fleshed out by description, speech, and interaction with other characters until we finally arrive at an imagined, three-dimensional figure. In the theater, by contrast, characters cannot gradually take shape in the same way, since they are present on the stage from the beginning, making their sudden, corporeal appearance onstage and thereby forcing themselves onto the audience, which has no way of escaping this sudden assault. In Stein's diction, this means that "when the actors are there they are there and they are there right away" (xxxviii). This sudden "thereness" and presence of the actor is at work, for Stein, even in the act of reading a play. Here the list of *dramatis personae* establishes the cast of characters, and often their functions or relations as well, instead of letting the story itself introduce them to the readers. The immediate presence of the characters on the first page in the form of names is even required in order to keep track of them, making it necessary "to keep one's finger in the list of characters for at least the whole first act" (xxxviii).[10] Stein's critique of actors applies equally to actors onstage and to the characters in the dramatic text whom these actors will impersonate.

Stein's reform of the dramatic text seeks to avoid the "thereness" of actors and characters from the beginning, to make the act of viewing theater more like the act of reading. For this purpose, Stein disassembles the entire apparatus of theatrical representation, but most importantly the figure of the actor. Meyerhold and Craig would do this through a reform of acting, but Stein attempts instead to reform the dramatic text. Insofar as the dramatic text encourages theatrical representation and impersonation, it must be radically changed. And so Stein devises a dramatic form that would make regular impersonation impossible, an anti-theatrical drama.[11]

Anti-Theatrical Drama

Stein's numerous and diverse plays have one thing in common: they do not take the dramatic form for granted. Her early conversation plays, for example, *Not Slightly* (1914), have no *dramatis personae* at all, not even proper names that could be construed as identifying speaking agents. The speaker of each line must be surmised from the almost nonextant context, and while the play is divided into five acts, the category of the fifth act is used three times, first simply as "Act Five," then as "Continuation of an Act Five of the Act Five," and finally, with false innocence, as "Act Five."[12] Counting the number of parts, acts, and scenes is an activity any reader of Stein's plays is asked to perform time and again, notably in the play *Counting Her Dresses* (1917), which includes "XLI" "Parts," which in turn are subdivided into seven "Acts," most of which consist of one line only. Because such texts are always on the verge of ceasing to be plays, Stein calls her next play *I Like It To Be A Play*. This title acknowledges that the status "play" constitutes a program that has yet to be implemented and might very well never come to be—unless the mere intention of writing a play were already enough to determine its genre. Needless to say, all of these plays were published in collections of texts, and most of them were never intended to be performed. The title *Four Saints in Three Acts* continues these number games and includes a similar generic designation in its title by referring to the "Three Acts" of a text that thus cannot be anything but a play.

Stein reiterates this need for generic names in her essay "Plays," where she writes, "I think and always have thought that if you write a play you ought to announce that it is a play and that is what I did" (xliii). The determination with which Stein designates so many of her texts "plays" certainly looks like a generic overcompensation. At the same time, however, it is part of a poetics grounded in her laconic statement that "anything that was not a story could be a play" (xliv). Like Plato and the poetic tradition indebted to him, Stein here appears to define drama in opposition to narrative intervention: while the novel is organized by a narrator who tells stories, drama represents action directly, without the mediating figure of such a narrator. Since "something is always happening" and "anybody knows a quantity of stories of people's lives," she finds "telling stories" (xliv) a superfluous activity. In order to avoid replicating these ubiquitous stories, it becomes imperative to create a form of non-narrative drama: "And the idea in *What Happened, A Play* was to express this [the relation between characters] without telling what happened, in short to make a play the essence of what happened" (xliv). Again, the opposition within which Stein seems to operate here is that between (narrative) diegesis and (theatrical) mimesis: the narration, or description, of action through language (be it stage direction, commentary, or descriptive narration) and the direct theatrical presentation of action on the stage (the characters' dialogue, gestures, and use of theatrical space). This distinction between mimesis and diegesis, between things happening and stories that tell of them, is calibrated to Stein's first play, *What Happened, A Play*. *What Happened, A Play* does not "tell" what happened (diegesis) but instead aspires to represent "the essence of what happened" in a mimetic manner: "A play was to express . . . without telling what happened." This theory, along with the confusion experienced by many readers, has led to the conclusion that Stein sought to invent a non-narrative theater.

However, a cursory look at *Four Saints* demonstrates that Stein does not simply oppose mimesis to diegesis, direct expression to distanced narration, the way classical dramaturgy from Aristotle on has done. In fact, her relation to Aristotle is exemplary of her relation to genre in general: rather than coming up with new terms of her own, Stein uses traditional terms but carefully reworks and displaces their meaning. The opposition between drama and narrative is no exception. The opening part of *Four Saints,* for example, which could be considered a kind of prologue or preface, slyly yokes together this ominous "happening" of things and narration: "What happened to-day, a narrative" (440). Stein here suddenly seems to think narrative suitable for the genre of drama. And indeed, *Four Saints* includes actual bits of narrative, written in the traditional narrative past tense: "We had intended if it were a pleasant day to go to the country it was a very beautiful day and we carried out our intention"; or a little further, "He came and said he was hurrying" (441). What we begin to see here is that *Four Saints* is a text that does not shy away from narrative and diegesis but makes extensive and strategic use of a variety of narrative elements.

This qualified understanding of narrative is specified in Stein's essay *How to Write* (1931), which is the counterpart to her thoughts on drama. Here Stein insists that narrative must no longer be used to describe past events: "Never describe as a narrative something that has happened."[13] A little later in the same text Stein reveals that what stands behind her opposition to the traditional role of narrative is its explanatory function: "To know a narrative to know now now to know a narrative is like explanation it says so. A description is not like narrative it does not say so" (285). Narrative tends to connect events in an explanatory manner, endowing a sequence of events with causality. Description, on the other hand, conjures only glimpses of events and static tableaux and tends to avoid explanatory causality. Once this critique of explanation is specified, however, Stein proceeds to salvage narrative and thus to rethink its function. Nonexplanatory description, for example, does not lie entirely outside narrative, but within, and Stein consequently speaks of a "description narrative" (238). While narrative as explanation, as something that tells us what happened in a mode that might be construed as an explanation, must be avoided, descriptive narrative is still allowed.

Descriptive narrative is a term that can be applied to *Four Saints,* which gives up the narrative past tense after the prologue but continues to use descriptive narrative or descriptive diegesis derived from portraiture, landscape, and ekphrasis. Portraiture is the art to which Stein likens her plays most closely: "in my portraits I had tried to tell what each one is without telling stories and now in my early plays I tried to tell what happened without telling stories so that the essence of what happened would be like the essence of the portraits, what made what happened be what it was" ("Plays," xlv–xlvi).[14] The portrait promised a way out of the a-synchronicity between dramatic action and the audience because it allowed Stein to get rid of dramatic action altogether and to approximate and replicate, through a new dramatic form, the stasis of portraiture. Even in *How to Write* she mentions portraiture as a privileged form of descriptive narrative (234).[15] Stein here represents a modernist version of the recurring oscillation within theater history between the pictorial and the narrative, basing her static and pictorial dramaturgy, to use the distinction made by Martin Meisel, on eighteenth-century tableaux rather than on nineteenth-century narrative theater.[16] In fact, a good number of twentieth-century dramatists, from Cocteau to Beckett, can be said to have shared this fascination with static tableaux.

The insertion of painting into drama also motivates Stein's well-known notion of the landscape play, of which *Four Saints* is the primary example.[17] The term *landscape play*, akin to her fascination with static portraiture, might even be taken literally. Like the impressionists, as well as her declared master, Cézanne, Stein began to write actually "in nature," moving her chair about in order to get different perspectives, while Alice B. Toklas would bring her whatever she needed.[18] Here too Stein was working, according to Alice B. Toklas, with the desire "to describe something without mentioning it," but she was doing so, one might add, with the "it"—the landscape—present all around her (*Virgil Thomson*, 72). The term *landscape play*, however, also has a more conceptual meaning. It is the stasis of the landscape, in opposition to dramatic movement or action, that Stein foregrounds: "The landscape [is] not moving but being in relation" ("Plays," xlvii).[19] While the notion of the landscape play, like that of the portrait, thus addresses the potential a-synchronicity of dramatic action (if there is no movement, you don't feel that you are either ahead of or behind the action), it responds even more directly to Stein's other anti-theatrical concern, namely, the sudden, unmediated appearance of physical actors at the beginning of a play, actors to whom one had not been properly and gradually introduced: "The landscape does not have to make acquaintance" (xlvi). When Stein observes that "In Four Saints I made the Saints the landscape" (l), she does not suggest a picturesque arrangement of actors, but a depersonalized drama that forecloses the "thereness" of impersonating actors.[20]

In "Plays" Stein mentions a third anti-theatrical strategy, the most classical method for interrupting movement and action, namely, ekphrasis. St. Ignatius, Stein writes, is the textual transcription of a porcelain statue, a circumstance that is even alluded to in the text: "Saint Ignatius could be in porcelain actually in porcelain standing" (*Four Saints,* 450). Similarly, Stein used the photograph of a young girl in conceiving St. Therese, and even the process of writing was determined by the presence of this static image:

"I was writing Saint Therese in looking at these photographs" (li). While most of Stein's descriptive techniques refer to imaginary entities or natural ones (landscape), here Stein had actual representations, in another artistic medium—the porcelain statue, the photograph—in front of her, representations that she proceeded to translate into the medium of drama. As Wendy Steiner has pointed out, Stein was confronted with the difficulty—which sometimes threatens to take the form of a paradox—of how to transpose the static, spatial art form of portraiture into the temporal one of literature and drama. This dichotomy between the temporality of dramatic action and the almost static quality of absorption or engulfment turned painting into a productive model for dramatic literature. One might say that Stein transposed the old doctrine *ut pictura poesis* (that poetry should aspire to the condition of painting) to drama.[21]

The place where Stein was able to put her understanding of nonexplanatory, descriptive, or ekphrastic diegesis to work is in her unusual stage directions. Stage directions are the most abject part of the traditional drama, and for this reason they proved most useful for its reform, as they also did in the writings of Mallarmé and Joyce. Direct theatrical presentation depends on the distinction between direct speech (monologue or dialogue) and the so-called secondary text, or paratext, which includes various kinds of stage directions, a list of *dramatis personae,* and act numbers. The secondary text is never spoken on the stage; rather, it determines how a dramatic text is supposed to be represented through actors, stage props, and lighting. This means that the secondary text is a descriptive or prescriptive rendering of the stage, a form of descriptive diegesis. The mingling of secondary text with the speech and dialogue of the characters that happens in *Four Saints* thus causes an intrusion of diegesis into the dialogue of the scene.

When extracted from the text and separately compiled, these descriptive fragments compose an array of movements, gestures, attitudes, objects, and situations, a cut-up stage without a unifying perspective or continuity of space and time: "Saint Therese half in doors and half out of doors . . . Saint Therese in a storm at Avila . . . Saint Ignatius not there . . . Saint Therese silent . . . Saint Therese seated . . . Saint Therese seated and not standing" (445). If Stein's stage directions were isolated—and the stage adaptation of *Four Saints* in fact does isolate them—they might be seen as the building blocks of an imaginary but utterly fractured stage in which alternative poses and constellations are evoked without consideration for the unities of space, time, or action. The stage directions in *Four Saints* are both the proof that this text is not geared toward the theater and also the technique through which this text constructs its own, utterly broken and fragmentary stage.

We can see in this decomposition of theater something akin to Plato's anti-theatricalism. Attacking direct theatrical representation and actors impersonating different roles, Plato proposed to transform all direct speech (mimesis) into third-person narration (diegesis). Stein integrates into the dramatic form those elements of the dramatic text that can be said to belong to the category of the descriptive and the narrative, namely, stage directions. Instead of simply mediating theatrical representation through a narrator, Stein undermines the spatial and temporal continuity of the theater, inventing a dramatic form that pits theatrical mimesis and diegesis against one another, interrupting the flow of narrative time and theatrical action. There is no distinct narrator or narrative voice to whom these diegetic fragments could be attributed, as in Joyce, but scattered pieces of diegesis that are mixed up with fragments of dialogue. This technique can be compared to the kind of cubism Virgil Thomson recognized in Stein's texts, a cubism that created "static pictures in spite of a non-fixed eye-point" (*Virgil Thomson,* 173).[22] Betsy Alayne Ryan compiled a useful chart classifying generic traits of Stein's seventy-seven plays; except for a few short late pieces, the only trait her plays have in common is what she calls a narrator-description perspective.[23] When one examines Stein's use of narrative, however, it becomes clear that it never amounts to one privileged diegetic perspective, but rather a multiplicity of diegetic fragments that interrupt the representation of mimesis and action, what one might call a cubist diegesis.[24]

Staging a Closet Drama

Most of Stein's plays are texts that were never intended to be performed and in fact still have not been performed even in our time, which does not easily shy away from bringing every text onto the stage. *Four Saints,* however, together with a handful of other plays, was staged. And even though its resistance to the theater is as extreme as that of technically "purer" closet dramas, it comes with the imperative subtitle *An Opera to be Sung.* Stein also referred to the text as "a drama" and "a play," but she kept *opera* in the subtitle and insisted in various letters and exchanges, to the surprise of her friends, that this text's sole purpose was to be performed.[25] Writing to Mabel Dodge, for example, Stein explained that she did not want to have the play printed at all: "No, decidedly not. I do not want the plays published. They are to be kept to be played."[26] Not even a workshop-like reading was enough. A similar commitment to performance is also apparent in the formulations Stein used in her brief exchanges with Thomson: "I think I have got St. Thérèse onto the stage," she told him and promised "that we will talk some scenes over."[27]

Both the subtitle demanding performance and Stein's refusal to publish the play before its staging are surprising for a number of reasons. First, all of her previous plays had appeared in print, with no indication that this form of publication was a second choice, a substitute for a theatrical performance. Her first collection, entitled *Geography and Plays*, for example, had been published, at Stein's own expense, by a small publishing house in Boston (where the student Virgil Thomson discovered it and fell in love with it).[28] Second, by the late nineteenth century it had become common practice to publish plays. And third, everything in Stein's text indicates a deeply rooted suspicion of the theater and the desire to keep theatrical mimesis at a distance. Even though she had stopped frequenting the theater and had developed a distrust of its modes of presentation, her anti-theatricalism is thus not a simple rejection but a more conflicted form of resistance, a resistance that entails a simultaneous attachment to the theater. *Four Saints* appears to be a kind of closet drama, but one that seeks to be put on a stage: a closet drama that is to be performed.

Performed it was indeed, but only after the intervention of Virgil Thomson, who needed to overcome Stein's resistance and thus transform her text into a script that could be sung in the first place. The transformations that were necessary for staging *Four Saints* can serve as a measure for the distance Stein's text maintains from the theater. The first thing Thomson had to do in order to comply with Stein's subtitle was to create a list of characters who could then be impersonated and performed by singers. Since Stein's text did not present such a list and did not specify which lines were to be sung by which character, Thomson simply used several of the recurring proper names as the main characters and grouped them according to the traditional musical forms of chorus, quartet, duet, and solo aria. In reverence to the opera's title, perhaps, four Saints—St. Stephen, St. Settlement, St. Plan, and St. Sarah—form the opera's central quartet, assisted by a chorus of saints who remain unnamed. In addition, St. Teresa (whose name Thomson changed from Stein's French "Thérèse" or "Therese") is split into a Teresa I and Teresa II for the purely musical reason, as Thomson explained, that she would be able to sing duets with herself.[29] In the course of the opera additional saints, certainly more than four, make their appearance, such as St. Celestine, St. Lawrence, St. Jan, and St. Chavez. This translation from proper name to character radically alters a central anti-theatrical feature of Stein's text: it reintroduces the practice of impersonation, from which Stein had willfully deviated.

While all of these characters appear in Stein's text at least as free-floating proper names, Thomson went so far as to add a pair of characters that do not appear in the original text at all: Commère and Compère. What is striking about these two characters is not, however, that they are Thomson's invention but that they fulfill the specific role, as Thomson himself put it, of "nonsaintly commentators" (*Virgil Thomson,* 107) and are therefore kept apart from the "saintly" primary cast. And the reason why they are thus segregated is that they are assigned precisely the diegetic parts—narrative, stage directions, commentary—of Stein's confusing text.[30] Thomson thus gathers the dispersed diegetic fragments and attributes them to these two characters (as well as to a chorus); in Thomson's rendering diegesis thus acquires a voice, a face, and a figure. The first lines sung by Compère at the very beginning of act 1, for example, are stage directions, describing a first scene: "Saint Teresa in a storm at Avila . . ." (22), while Commère observes, "Saint Teresa silent" (23).[31] The other scenes are likewise introduced by a descriptive text that is spoken by these commentators. Scene 3, for example, begins: "Compère: Saint Teresa as a young girl being widowed" (25). It was Thomson's strategy to maintain Stein's characteristic use of dispersed stage directions and other forms of diegetic text, but at the same time he sought a particular theatrical solution—or equivalent—to this diegetic technique of Stein's text: commentators who remained largely outside the set of regular characters and were therefore able to project stage directions, description, and narration onto the mimetic space of the theater.[32] And since Commère and Compère are not part of the primary cast and only speak secondary, diegetic text, they can be considered diegetic and secondary characters.

Maurice Grosser, who wrote the scenario for *Four Saints,* continued the play's adaptation in the same vein and transformed the separation between primary and secondary action into a theatrical, spatial manifestation: a curtain divides the stage into two designated areas, for the primary and secondary action, respectively. While the inner stage is reserved for the primary cast, the diegetic characters are placed on the outer stage, from which they comment on the action taking place within. The action itself unfolds in a series of tableaux, translating Stein's fascination with pictorial stasis into a principle of *mise en scène.* In fact, some of the tableaux refer explicitly to Stein's ekphrastic process of writing. The second tableau, for example, exhibits the photograph of a young girl that was supposedly Stein's inspiration for the figure of St. Teresa; it shows St. Teresa II holding a dove in her hand while being photographed by St. Settlement (Grosser, 9). Pictoriality returns in the next act when St. Plan brings a telescope through which the two St. Teresas can behold a vision of the Heavenly Mansion. In act 3 St. Ignatius has a vision of the Holy Ghost, which he describes, diegetically, to the audience on and off the stage. Both the static pictorial quality of the inner stage and the narrative, ekphrastic, and diegetic commentators on the outer stage turn central features of Stein's anti-theatrical text into theatrical form, thus creating an anti-theatrical theater.

As they speak Stein's secondary text, Commère and Compère bring into the foreground and onto the stage another central feature of *Four Saints:* its particular form of self-referentiality. While it is difficult to discern what Stein's text says about its alleged subject matter (St. Teresa and her life near Barcelona), it becomes increasingly clear that a large portion of Stein's text depicts, not St. Teresa, but the process of writing an opera about her. The story of St. Teresa, with its numerous saints, pigeons, gardens, photographs, and the invocation of Barcelona, never quite gets under way; or rather, it is constantly being interrupted by the predominant secondary "meta"-story of writing an opera. Indeed, Virgil Thomson first recognized Stein's affinity to such a topic and suggested to her "the working artist's working life" as the subject matter of the collaboration that became *Four Saints.*[33] Stein's text keeps returning not so much to the artist's life but to the process of creation, posing such questions as, "How many acts are there in it," as if such structural decisions had not yet been made. Endless variations on stage directions, such as "Saint Teresa half inside half outside of the door" or "Saint Teresa not half inside and half outside of the door," similarly show that we are confronted with a present-tense narrative about the process of creation. Almost twenty years later, in Thomson and Stein's second collaboration, *Mother of Us All,* Thomson replaced Commère and Compère with Stein and himself, thus making explicit the extent to which these two secondary characters were bound up with the opera's process of production.[34]

Once we see *Four Saints* onstage, the context of these self-referential elements changes: the text is no longer about the process of writing a dramatic text but about the process of staging a play.[35] In Thomson's theatrical rendering, then, this (secondary) action of staging a play becomes the privileged subject matter of the dialogue between the diegetic figures Commère and Compère. In the prologue, for example, they debate the number of benches with which the stage should be furnished:

> CP: Imagine four benches separately.
> CM: One in the sun. Two in the sun. Three in the sun.
> CP: One not in the sun. Not one.
>
> (Thomson, *Four Saints,* 19)

At the same time, they both function as stage directors, giving signals and commands to the other players, for example, at the moment when Commère addresses the chorus: "Begin suddenly not with sisters." The secondary action of staging a play emerges perhaps most clearly in the "inter-mezzo" (so labeled by Thomson, not by Stein) between acts 3 and 4, in which Commère and Compère discuss whether there should be a fourth act at all, apparently revising a previous plan. For this purpose they step out in front of the curtain to discuss the formal shape of the play that is in the process of being created, asking structural questions such as Commère's "How many acts are there in it" or Compère's "How many saints are there in it" (45). Finally they both seem to come to one conclusion: "One two three four all out but four one two three four four four or four or more" (46). This sense of accord is finally expressed in a unison finale: "Act four." It does not matter exactly what happens in act 4; what matters, and what happens, is that we can follow the process through which this act is created.[36] With Thomson and Grosser's *mise en scène,* the secondary plot of creating a play becomes more visible (because there are now designated diegetic characters speaking it), as does its commentary on the mimetic space of the inner stage, which is simultaneously present. And Grosser's tableaux keep to a minimum the temporality of dramatic time and thus the possibility of a-synchronicity between audience and play. Both Grosser and Thomson managed to adapt the stage to Stein's anti-theatricalism; they imported anti-theatricalism into the theater.

There is one more consequence of bringing Stein's closet drama onto the stage: together with turning Stein's textual experiment into a play that can be represented by human actors and singers, all the expectations and norms associated with public theater return to the play as well. Commentators who praised Stein's writing as a pure *écriture feminine* have tended to see in Thomson's version a violation of this purity, at times even a reinscription of a heterosexual melodrama between St. Teresa and St. Ignatius into Stein's female writing.[37] While the essentialism of an *écriture feminine,* on which some of these readings are premised, might seem untenable today, what they register is the return of the forms of social normativity, which the theater can never entirely escape and against which the closet drama rebels.[38] In the stage version, the difference between female and male is no longer simply a function of proper names fractured by the cubist diegesis and fragmented mimesis of Stein's text; it becomes once more human and therefore social. Nothing can keep the audience from projecting onto these humans a romance, whether Thomson intended it that way or not. That staging a closet drama is a process that must necessarily deal with the reemergence of these human and social categories shows the extent to which closet dramas are marked by a negative gesture: the refusal of or withdrawal from social normativity. Mallarmé imagines the illicit figure of Salomé only in a few sketched words; Joyce, the transgressive fantasies of

Bloom in some stage directions; and Stein, the life of a saint in a collage of diegetic and mimetic fragments loosely held together by a proper name.

These forms of rejection, however, do not mean that the closet drama wants to foreclose the political altogether. While Stein's text withdraws from the (theatrical) scene, it practices, to borrow a phrase from Barbara Johnson, a "politics of the penultimate," a writerly resistance to the constraints and normativities of the social and the political to which the theater gives rise.[39] Thomson's act of staging *Four Saints,* like other stagings of closet dramas, forces into the theater of human bodies a dramatic text that had taken great pains to decompose them entirely. Its normativity is not, in the first place, the return of one sexual preference over another but a return of the type of normativity grounded in the requirements of theatrical representation, in particular in the necessary reliance on human actors. This is not to say that Stein's text or any other closet drama is a "pure" space that is completely free from any kind of normativity. The social world, human bodies, and everything associated with them intrude into the closet drama from all sides, through moments of diegesis, mimesis, proper names, associations, and insinuations. Many of Stein's texts willfully tease the reader with such references, but they owe the freedom that allows them to tease in this way to the resistance to the theater that keeps these norms at bay.

The importance and productive nature of such resistance does not mean, however, that a theatrical rendering always signals a simple choice of normativity over resistance. The theater, with its actors and singers, is capable of making different kinds of interventions from those of the closet drama. The première of *Four Saints* in 1934 bears witness to the possibility of interrupting theatrical norms within the theater, an interruption that in fact derives from Stein's textual resistance. The group that brought this opera onto the stage included the British choreographer Frederick Ashton, the reclusive upper-class painter Florine Stettheimer, and Chick Austin, the director of the Hartford Atheneum, where *Four Saints* premiered. Many of them, especially Austin and Thomson, knew one another from Harvard, forming what Steven Watson calls the Harvard Moderns.[40] These upper-class modernists formed an astonishing alliance with a second group of artists, singers from Harlem. That an all-black Harlem cast would perform a modernist opera that was not "about" an African American subject matter was a break with the customs of the music and theater industries at the time.[41]

One might speculate that *Four Saints* was able to dissociate the race of the performer from the subject matter depicted because Stein had avoided writing a drama calibrated to human impersonation in the first place. Nothing in the play signals how it is to be brought to the theater, so that the norms and practices of racial casting could not be anchored in a reading of Stein's text. Even though many of the white collaborators, including Stein, both praised and critiqued the Harlem cast in ways that were often patronizing and primitivizing, one can see the collaboration of Harvard, Hartford, and Harlem as a theatrical resistance that arose from Stein's resistance to the theater. *Four Saints* thus bears witness to both the return of social normativity in the staging of a closet drama and the manner in which the closet drama's anti-theatricalism enabled the avoidance of other theatrical norms and practices.

It is important to remember in this context that Stein, who agreed with Thomson's plan of turning her text into a stageable libretto, certainly did not vilify the theater; what she insisted on was a particular form of resistance to the theater. Marking this difference in the genre of drama not only led Stein to invent a new drama but forced Thomson and Grosser to invent a diegetic theater based on narrative figures and tableaux to accommodate Stein's text.

The introduction of narrative characters mediating between mimetic actors and the audience and a stage divided between an area for diegesis and an area for theatrical mimesis are not just ad hoc solutions to the problems of staging Stein's text but standard features of a theater devoted to bringing an anti-theatrical and an anti-mimetic impulse onto the stage. The last part of this book is devoted to examining three writers and directors — Yeats, Brecht, and Beckett — whose works, for all their differences, represent ways of reacting to a modernist anti-theatricalism by incorporating this anti-theatricalism into the theater. They accomplished this task by employing precisely the types of diegetic techniques that surfaced in Thomson's staging of *Four Saints*. If modernist theater can be described as a theater marked by anti-theatricalism, it is an anti-theatricalism that returns in the form of diegesis. Modernist theater, therefore, can be seen as diegetic theater.

Part III

The Diegetic Theater

William Butler Yeats: 5
Poetic Voices in Theatrical Space

Voices on Castors

> I am certain that there was something in myself compelling me
> to attempt creation of an art as separate from everything hetero-
> geneous and casual, from all character and circumstance, as some
> Herodiade of our theatre, dancing seemingly alone in her narrow
> moving luminous circle.[1]

Yeats may find it compelling to imagine his poetry taking the form of
Hérodiade's alluring dance, but at the same time he betrays an ambivalence
about the theater, or to be more precise, he ignores one of its central features: the relation between live performer and audience. Hérodiade is completely self-absorbed, "seemingly alone," as if no audience threatened to
disturb this rare spectacle, and this solitude ensures that Hérodiade's dance
is in fact "separate from everything heterogeneous and casual" for which
the audience stands. Yeats, it seems, is compelled by the theater, but he is
also worried about some of its central features, and those two conflicting
attitudes signal an ambivalent attitude toward theatrical representation.

As we try to picture this *fin-de-siècle* dance of dances, we may think, as
Yeats did, of Mallarmé's efforts to capture Hérodiade's dance in the margin
of his play.[2] For this purpose, Mallarmé had used his most daring poetics, disassembling the dancer's body into isolated movements and gestures
and scattering them freely over the page. But even transposed into poetry,
Hérodiade's dance still struck Mallarmé as too vulgarly theatrical, and so
he removed it from the margin of his page. Yeats, for all his dedication to
poetry and his distrust of performers, had no such scruples. Not only did
Hérodiade's alluring dance enter his mind whenever he thought of art but
he brought his symbolism, his poetry, and his Hérodiade into the theater.
And so there is no better place than Yeats's dramatic oeuvre to ask what
happens when a poetic closet drama is confronted with stage props, actors,
spotlights—and an audience.

We can find symptomatic clues of what happens when a closet drama
is staged in the attempts to perform Mallarmé's *Livre,* Joyce's "Circe," and

Stein's *Four Saints in Three Acts.* The main feature of these stagings is that they transpose the closet drama's textual diegesis to various forms of diegetic speech, spoken by narrators, raconteurs, poets, and choruses. This transposition also lies at the heart of what I call the *diegetic theater,* which systematically uses diegetic figures to control, confront, and interrupt theatrical representation. For this reason, diegetic theater is a theater marked by the closet drama's distrust of the stage and continues the closet drama's techniques of dissociating gestures from their actors, of isolating stage props and spaces—in short, of utterly fragmenting the theater by means of diegetic language. Diegetic theater thus comes into being when the anti-theatrical techniques of the closet drama are brought into the theater. The most fundamental reforms of the theater, from Yeats through Brecht to Beckett, are derived, in different ways, from the return of anti-theatricality to the stage.

In his acceptance speech for the Nobel Prize in 1925, Yeats articulated the relation between his poetry and his work in the theater in the strongest terms, singling out his work in the theater as the foundation of his lyrical poetry: "Perhaps the English committees would never have sent you my name if I had written no plays, no dramatic criticism, if my lyric poetry had not a quality of speech practised upon the stage" (*Autobiography,* 378). Even though Yeats suggests that his poetry grew out of the theater, he was in fact already an accomplished poet when he turned, with difficulty, to the dramatic form. In order to transplant his poetics from the lyrical to the dramatic, Yeats was forced to overcome his dependence on the organizing force of the lyrical voice and to develop, within a single work, a multitude of voices, characters, and diction. In the many revisions of *Shadowy Waters,* for example, Yeats gradually endows the common sailors with a more everyday idiom through which to confront the aristocratic protagonist, Forgael, and his private symbolist system, a system that seems dangerously close to Yeats's own.

In addition to the dramatic form, Yeats also had to come to terms with the theater, where he faced the problem of how to integrate poetic speech with the reality of the stage and its actors. Yeats's initial reaction—the reaction of a lyric poet—was to keep this reality to a minimum. Particularly at the beginning of his career, Yeats considered the *mise en scène* to be nothing more than an instantiation of the poetic text.[3] This attitude was fueled by an ingrained distrust of actors, who were prone to be unfaithful to the spirit of his text and whom he accused of adding excessive mimicry and gesticulation to his delicate lines.[4] In an essay published in *Samhain,* the newsletter of the newly established Irish National Theatre, Yeats outlines, manifesto-like, a theater reform grounded in the elevation of lyrical speech at the expense of the actor: "But if we are to restore words to their sovereignty we must make speech even more important than gesture upon the stage" (*Explorations,* 108). In this privileging of the spoken word, Yeats begins to imagine the ideal actor as one who is not an actor at all but a storyteller in the fashion of a medieval minstrel singer. Such a minstrel, or "reciter," does not work, Yeats insists, by (theatrical) "illusion," but by (poetic) "allusion" (215). He does not impersonate and "speak for another person" (214) but tells of something "that is always distant," as a messenger would do: "The reciter cannot be a player . . . but he must be a messenger" (215). In these fantasies of an actor who is not one, Yeats returns to the origin of the Greek actor as a messenger addressing the lyric chorus; he attempts to resurrect an actor who is still, basically, an extension of the lyrical voice, an actor who has not yet learned to fool the audience by means of illusion.[5] The transposition of poetry into the theater, it seems, leads to a critique of the impersonating actor.

It is indicative of Yeats's attempt to limit theatrical performance to a recitation of poetry that the figure of the bard, musician, singer, or singing poet occupies a central place in almost all of his earlier plays. Forgael in *Shadowy Waters* (1911), for example, is prefigured in *Countess Cathleen* (1892) by Aleel, the poet who alone has access to a world beyond the cruel and calculating reality of the here and now. In *The Land of Heart's Desire* (1894), the first of Yeats's plays to be performed, a similar function is filled by Mary, the dreamer, reader, and ballad-maker who tries to escape everyday, domestic life; Seanchan, the master poet and musician in *The King's Threshold* (1904), stands up for the ancient rights of the bard, which are threatened by calculating and philistine politicians who consider poetry to be mere entertainment; Martin and Andrew are the dreamers who desire to go beyond "common things" in *The Unicorn from the Stars* (1908); and the poet Septimus, in *The Player Queen* (1922), tries to convince an angry and violent crowd of the symbolic beauty of the unicorn. Usually alone in their opposition to the everyday world, most of these figures speak in verse, and they fight the good fight in their heroic defense of poesy. These singing poets embody and personify lyrical speech, and their language is set apart from the speech of everyday life, used by the other characters, who thus stand in for the plays' reality principle. This reality principle, which never ceases to threaten the poet, is also the principle of the theater, with its multiple actors and voices; in Yeats's work, the privileged but threatened figure of the poet is a sign of an ambivalence toward both the dramatic form and theatrical representation.

Yeats's dream of finding authentic poet figures in the Irish countryside was never fulfilled. Furthermore, "making speech more important than gesture" is not an easy thing when the stage is full of actors who must do something not only during their own speeches but also during the speeches of other actors. Should they just stand still in order to comply with their subservient role, like messengers who had dutifully delivered their message? Grappling with this question, Yeats preferred amateurs, who in his opinion had less professional vanity and were thus more likely to respect his ambitious verse. Their inexperience, he thought, sometimes led them to suspend acting altogether, inducing them "to keep still enough to give poetical writing its full effect upon the stage" (*Explorations*, 86).[6] Yeats's most radical proposal, however, later so slyly transformed into theatrical reality by Beckett, was to have actors rehearse in barrels so that they would be perfect mouthpieces for his texts and unable to spoil his poetry with their gestures. These barrels would force them to "forget gesture and have their minds free to think of speech for a while." Realizing that this strategy would create completely static scenes, Yeats came up with the following handy solution: "The barrels, I thought, might be on castors, so that I could shove them about with a pole when the action required it" (*Explorations,* 86–87). Yeats's ambivalence about theatricality and, in particular, about actors is nowhere as clear as in this proposal for creating a truly literary and purely poetic theater whose action would reside solely in the movement of voices: a theater of voices on castors.

This continued aversion to actors left an anti-theatrical imprint on Yeats's dramatic oeuvre, most visibly so in *The Player Queen.*[7] Begun in 1907, at the time of Yeats's commitment to a literary theater, this play is centered on the familiar anti-theatrical conceit that an actor can impersonate a role, in this case the role of a queen, more convincingly than the original.[8] In Yeats's treatment, Decima, an actress of dubious descent—"born/in a ditch between two towns and wrapped in a sheet/that was stolen from a hedge" (735)—claims that she is born to play a queen, even as the Queen, exclusively devoted to ascetic prayer, does not know how to play the role society demands of her: "The Queen cannot play at all, but I could play/so well. I could bow with my whole body down to/my ankles and could be stern when hard looks were/in season" (735). Because of the Queen's failure to adapt her actions to the ceremonial requirements of the court, a band of peasants suspects that she is a witch and arrives at the castle to kill her. Decima takes the Queen's clothes and so convincingly presents herself to the peasants, who have never seen her, that the Queen's entourage is unable to contradict her in front of the enraptured mob. Decima exclaims triumphantly, "I am Queen. I know what it is to/be Queen" (757), and she can therefore become the real thing.

This exchange of roles is by no means the only anti-theatrical topos of the play. Early on, we witness Decima's professional vanity when she refuses to play any role in which she would be older than thirty. A little later, various actors speculate, in a ridiculously self-aggrandizing manner, that the peasants' revolt was incited by local actors jealous of the traveling players' success; little do they know that the reason for the peasants' rage is not the players' acting but rather the Queen's refusal to fulfill her role adequately. The most astonishingly anti-theatrical turn happens at the very end of the play, when the Player Queen, having successfully replaced the real Queen, banishes all the players from her kingdom, as if to erase the memory of her past playacting in order to merge with her new role for ever.

While there can be no doubt about the anti-theatrical provenance of these topoi, it is surprising that the play itself resists, at least in part, the anti-theatrical implications of its plot. Even though Yeats began the play as an experiment, to study role playing's effect on character, he does not denounce Decima as an imposter. Commentators have tried to make sense of the endorsed substitution within the frame of Yeats's symbolist *Weltanschauung,* codified in *Per Amica Silentia Lunae,* which calls for a new beginning with each new cycle of history; the old, ascetic Queen, in this reading, has to be replaced by a new and vital one.[9] Whatever Yeats's world system may say about Decima, it is clear that the play relies on an anti-theatrical narrative. However, Yeats's attitude toward this narrative is not to be confused with the anti-theatrical lens through which critics such as Yvor Winters and Helen Vendler view Yeats's plays, including *The Player Queen,* as pieces of lyrical poetry concealed in dramatic form.[10] Yeats's anti-theatricalism does not seek to erase the category of the theater. Rather Yeats turns his resistance to the theater into a productive force that leads to a wide-ranging reform of theatrical representation.

Poetry in the Theater

The Player Queen adds a curious ending to this halfhearted denunciation of deceitful acting. Before the play ends and the players are ordered to leave town—reminiscent, perhaps, of Plato's verdict against actors in *The Republic*—the new queen not only prevents the players from performing the play they have been rehearsing but also orders them to dance: "They had some play they were to perform, but I will make them dance instead." The last line of the play is her final command, "Come, dance" (760): impersonation is replaced by abstract dance.[11] This ending envisions a different solution to the problem of acting: turning mimetic players into dancers. The poet figures in Yeats's early plays repeatedly speak of some mysterious world of dance. At roughly the same time dancers start to appear more frequently in his poetry, from the dialogue "Michael Robartes and the Dancer," which addresses the dangers of the body, and the appearance of Loie Fuller in "Nineteen Hundred and Nineteen" through "The Dancer at Cruachan and Co-Patrick," to the famous concluding question in "Among School Children" about the difference between dancer and dance. With the cycle "Plays for Dancers" (1917), however, Yeats began to take his own figure of symbolist art, the dancing Hérodiade, literally, for dance now occupies a central place on Yeats's stage.[12]

Dance is an alternative to the crisis of acting as it is registered in *The Player Queen* because it does not primarily rely on make-believe. The actor pretends to be another person, but we know that the actor's playing is only a deceit—it is always possible to know the actors from the characters they are impersonating. And this is not the case with dance. Yeats's rhetorical question "How can we know the dancer from the dance?" addresses precisely this difference between acting and dance, for we cannot know the dancer from the dance; there is no mimetic project that would allow us to do so. Rather than hiring amateurs, who would only "play themselves," Yeats therefore started to engage dancers, who would never do anything but "dance themselves." This turn from acting to dance indicates Yeats's changing attitude toward the theater, his gradual realization that the acting body need not be hidden away in a barrel and that when properly trained, it could become a vehicle for a truly lyrical theater.[13]

The most important component of Yeats's reform of acting is a fundamental critique of mimesis: "We have to prepare a stage for the whole wealth of modern lyricism, for an art that is close to pure music, for those energies that would free the arts from imitation, that would ally acting to decoration and to dance" (*Explorations*, 258). How can we begin to imagine such lyrical gestures? Keeping the stage clear of imitation demands a type of acting that does not use gestures as the exteriorization of human affects and passions but rather allies them with formalized dance or impersonal decoration. In order to become part of such an anti-mimetic lyricism, gestures must be at least partially removed from their connection to the human agent. Yeats's fascination with non-mimetic gestures and dance does not imply, as is sometimes argued, that he had overcome his old aversion to actors.[14] On the contrary, once he no longer relied exclusively on the actors' speech, hiding their gestures away in barrels, the obsession with controlling actors became even more imperative, if also more complex. Acting was no longer forbidden in the Abbey Theatre, but it had to be radically transformed.[15]

In search of a theatrical model for a non-mimetic mode of dance-acting, Yeats reacted enthusiastically when Ezra Pound, who had edited the manuscripts of Ernest Fenollosa, an eminent American scholar of the Nôh tradition, acquainted him with Japanese theater. The Nôh theater supplied Yeats with not only a vision of theatrical reform but also a scene that captured, for him, the origin of the actor's mimesis. In the following Nôh anecdote Yeats triumphantly relates how actors are denounced for their practice of copying gestures:

> A young man was following a stately old woman through the streets of a Japanese town, and presently she turned to him and spoke: "Why do you follow me?" "Because you are so interesting." "That is not so, I am too old to be interesting." But he wished, he told her, to become a player of the old women of the Nôh stage. If he would become famous as a Nôh player, she said, he must not observe life, nor put on an old voice and stint the music of his voice. He must know how to suggest an old women and yet find it all in the heart.[16]

The anti-mimetic tradition, which abounds in such polemical depictions of the origin of acting, always arrives at the same, predictable conclusion: acting and the theater can only be transformed into an art of suggestion and suggestive gestures when it overcomes the mimesis from which it originates and from which it can be freed only with the greatest effort.

The manner in which not only Yeats but also writers and theater reformers as different as Craig, Brecht, Meyerhold, Claudel, and Artaud all turned to Asia to find tangible models for their various polemics about theater reform is indicative of a specifically theatrical orientalism dominant in the late nineteenth and early twentieth centuries. This orientalism appears particularly clearly in Yeats's obsession with Michio Ito, the Japanese dancer who Yeats hoped would authenticate his use of Nôh theater: "My play is made possible by a Japanese dancer whom I have seen dance in a studio. . . . All imaginative art remains at a distance and this distance once chosen must be firmly held against a pushing world. Verse, ritual, music, and dance in association with action require that gesture, costume, facial expression, stage arrangement must help in keeping the door" (*Classic Nôh*, 153). Ito, for Yeats, became something like a figure for a new dance theater, the orientalist counterpart, one might say, to Hérodiade. Ito, however, was an orientalist creation also in the sense that Yeats's vision of him bears almost no relation to Ito's actual background. He had had little of the laborious training of the Nôh theater, having instead been trained in eurhythmics in Hellerau; there is even reasonable doubt whether he ever had any formal training in Nôh at all.[17] And as if to bring orientalism full circle, Ito, after leaving the Abbey Theatre, went to New York and then to Hollywood; forced by the war to return to Japan, he ended up staging such works as Gilbert and Sullivan's *Mikado* for the American occupying army.[18]

Since Yeats used the Nôh theater as a projection screen for his own poetic *mise en scène,* he routinely ignored the established meanings of Nôh gestures and instead indulged in the aesthetic experience of their appearance.[19] In his essay on Nôh, this necessary and, one might add, aestheticized ignorance reveals his desire to read into Nôh his own symbolism: "The interest [in Japan and China] is not in the human form but in the rhythm to which it moves. . . . There are few swaying movements of arms or body such as make the beauty of our dancing. They move from the top, keeping constantly the upper part of their body still, and seem to associate with every gesture or pose some definite thought" (*Classic Nôh,* 158). Intrigued by the stylized gestures of Asian actors, Yeats would surely have been disappointed to learn their conventional meaning. Instead, he took great pleasure in merely imagining that this tradition seems "to associate with every gesture . . . some definite thought" as long as he did not know what those definite thoughts might be.

What is interesting about Yeats's orientalist projection is that it addresses the relation between body and meaning that stands at the center of what he calls the symbol.[20] Like Mallarmé, Yeats speaks of a poetic theater in terms of suggestive symbols: "I desire a mysterious art, always reminding and half-reminding those who understand it of dearly loving things, doing its work by suggestion, not by direct statement, a complexity of rhythm, color, gesture" (*Explorations,* 255).[21] Unlike Mallarmé, however, Yeats wants to create such suggestive, gestural symbols on the stage. Literary and dramatic critics tend to feel a certain degree of embarrassment when asked to comment on the symbols of symbolism because symbolist writers distinguish the symbol with such determination from the "mere" sign.[22] These critics celebrate the symbol for its refusal to participate in an economy of signification; they consider any material form as an instrument for indicating indirectly and mysteriously a meaning that is at the same time incarnate and hidden: the idea shines through the symbol's materiality, but it ultimately remains inaccessible.[23] For Yeats this precarious notion of the symbol acquired particular importance in the theater, where the symbolist subordination of materiality to idea stood on particularly shaky ground because it could not escape from the continuing presence of actors and objects. The actors could not be considered symbols because their own agency, as well as the contingencies of their acting, kept interrupting the idealized unity of material and ideal. Actors thus proved resistant to serving as vessels for symbolist meaning as long as they did not inspire a beholder to project onto them a hypothetical meaning as Yeats had done with Nôh actors.

Ultimately, it was not enough to train human actors to stop imitating and start dancing; they had to be depersonalized in a more fundamental way. This necessity is registered particularly visibly in a figure that promises to rid the acting body of all agency and personal whims: the marionette. In his introduction to Fenollosa and Pound's *Classic Nôh Theatre of Japan* (1916) Yeats reveals the underlying connection between his fascination with Nôh actors and his interest in marionettes: "It is natural that I go to Asia for a stage-convention, for more formal faces, for a chorus that has no part in the action and perhaps for those movements of the body copied from the marionette shows of the fourteenth century" (*Classic Nôh*, 155). Marionettes, for Yeats as for most theater reformers at the turn of the century, were the only Western model for a fully depersonalized mode of acting, one that successfully rid the stage of the awkward presence of live human beings. Indeed, most symbolist playwrights from Maeterlinck to Hofmannsthal envisioned their plays to be exclusively enacted by marionettes, for marionettes did away with the independent agency of the actor, which was so adversarial to the project of symbolism on the stage. While the living organism of the actor always claimed its own right and therefore continued to oppose being instrumentalized for signifying ideas, the marionette presented a type of materiality that was capable of suggesting movement without such an interference. The problem with marionette theater was, however, that it constituted the most debased form of spectacle and was therefore considered by many unfit to herald a new, lyrical theater. And here the Nôh theater offered an "aristocratic" alternative, a combination of lyrical drama and a theater of gesture in which all naturalist mimesis was exorcised from the stage.

The violence of symbolism's polemic against the presence of the actor onstage is perhaps nowhere as stark as in the writings of Edward Gordon Craig, who also shared Yeats's fascination with Asian theater.[24] In fact it was through Craig that Yeats came first into contact with a general *japonisme* well before he read Pound's edition of Nôh plays.[25] As early as 1902 Yeats began using Craig's famous screens in many of his plays and invited him to design the costumes and screens for a revival of *On Baile's Strand*;[26] Craig in turn published Yeats's play *The Hour Glass* in his journal, *The Mask*. The particular sensibility they shared, however, was their common aversion to actors. After a brief career in acting at a young age, Craig began to envision a theater entirely without actors as we know them, calling instead, at least rhetorically, for his notorious "Über-Marionette." The "Über-Marionette" was part of a plan, reminiscent of Heinrich von Kleist's *Über das Marionettentheater,* for replacing actors with mechanical figures, which would be placed under the total control of the director to ensure that the stage was clear of any accidental imitation. What Mallarmé had tried to achieve with his closet dramas, Craig took much more literally: he removed the gestures of actors from their mimicking bodies by creating disjointed limbs ready for assembly by a director-puppeteer, who would use them to build a gestural work of art. Craig, therefore, justified the figure of the marionette by means of a polemic directed against the embarrassment of impersonating mimesis:

> They [the actors] must create for themselves a new form of acting, consisting for the main part of symbolical gestures. . . . To-day the actor impersonates a certain being. He cries to the audience: "Watch me; I am now pretending to be so and so, and I am now pretending to do so and so;" and then he proceeds to imitate as exactly as possible, that which he has announced he will indicate. For instance, he is Romeo. He tells the audience that he is in love, and he proceeds to show it, by kissing Juliet. This, it is claimed, is a work of art: it is claimed for this that it is an intelligent way of suggesting thought.[27]

The actor's body stands in the way of achieving "symbolical gestures" because of its mimesis, which must consequently be overcome in order for the body to "suggest thought." As in *Axel* and the plays by Mallarmé, Rachilde, and Maeterlinck, symbolism is enamored with abstraction and must mold bodies and their materiality in the spirit of abstract thought.

Like Yeats, Craig has his own version of the degraded origin of the actor's mimesis. His "street scene" not only foregrounds the vanity of the actor but also points to the vanity of poets, more particularly their attempts to use actors as mouthpieces for their poetry: the writer flatters the man with the better "countenance" into reciting not his but the writer's lines (*Art of the Theatre*, 58–59). We can see here that for Craig the deception in the theater of illusion stems not exclusively from vain actors but also from seductive writers, who know how to manipulate the actors into proclaiming speeches that are not theirs. In his Platonic dialogues on the theater, Craig even sides with the actor against the writer who wants not only to supply the dialogue but also to prescribe by means of stage directions the gestures the actor should perform. When The Playgoer asks naively, "Then is all the stage direction in the world's plays worthless?" the Stage-Director, who always gets it right, answers, "Not to the reader, but to the stage-director, and to the actor—yes" (*Art of the Theatre*, 151–52). Like Adolphe Appia, Craig envisions an art of the theater that strategically ignores stage directions and thus prevents the writer from interfering in the business of the stage. When comparing Yeats's and Mallarmé's attempts to turn the actor into symbols with Craig's project, it is important to remember that Craig belongs to an anti-textual tradition and was therefore championed by such avant-garde theater reformers as Marinetti, Schlemmer, and Alexander Schawinsky. Despite this difference, it is striking that the textual tradition would arrive at some of the same conclusions as the theatrical one, namely, the abolishment of the actor.

The Divided Stage

Although the figure of the marionette keeps coming up in Yeats's oeuvre, Yeats never literally enacted Craig's plan of introducing marionettes onto the stage. Instead, he adopted another anti-theatrical technique, one borrowed from the closet drama and the Nôh theater alike, namely, a form of anti-theatrical diegesis. The use of spoken diegesis against theatrical mimesis appears most strikingly in his play *At the Hawk's Well* (1914–16), the first play Yeats wrote after his encounter with the Nôh theater.[28] The action of the play is as sparse as in any of Yeats's works. The young Cuchulain approaches the mysterious site of a well that purportedly promises eternal life. He meets there a man who has grown old waiting for the well to be filled with water. The Old Man warns Cuchulain that the Guardian of the Well will distract him or put him to sleep whenever it is full, but Cuchulain is not deterred. He waits for the water, only to discover by the end of the play that he has missed the life-preserving water himself.

The formal difficulty Yeats needed to resolve in this play was how to mediate between the theater and poetry, between Craig's marionettes and Mallarmé's textual dancers. The solution he derived from the Nôh theater was diegesis, specifically the use of diegesis as a weapon against the mimetic theater. As early as 1904, in one of his *Samhain* essays, Yeats foregrounds the competition and struggle between poetic diegesis and the theater, a struggle that has also been elucidated by William Worthen: "The actors must move, for the most part, slowly and quietly, and not very much, and there should be something in their movement decorative and rhythmical as if they were painting on a frieze. They must not draw attention to themselves at wrong moments, *for poetry and indeed all picturesque writing is perpetually making little pictures which draw the attention away for a second or two from the player*" (*Explorations*, 176–77, my emphasis). The image-making power of poetry competes directly with the visuality of the stage, seeking to "draw the attention away . . . from the player." Writing in his early anti-theatrical phase, Yeats concludes the passage by saying, "I have been the advocate of poetry against the actor" (177).[29] However, even after Yeats's turn to the theater the competition between poetry and the theater continued: Yeats transferred this anti-theatrical power of poetry to the diegetic narrators and commentators he found in the Nôh theater.[30]

In *At the Hawk's Well* the stage is framed by three musicians, who introduce the play and the players to the audience, add explanatory notes, and provide commentary on the action in the manner of a Nôh chorus. However, in addition to reflecting on the action of the play, these musicians also take over the function of setting the stage: "I call to the eye of the mind/ A well long choked up and dry/And boughs long stripped by the wind" (399). This imaginary scene replaces the stage with a diegetic description spoken by a diegetic narrator. This phrase is repeated almost verbatim in Yeats's second Nôh play, *The Only Jealousy of Emer,* which a musician opens by saying: "I call before the eye a roof/. . ./I call up a poor fisher's house" (531–33). What distinguishes *At The Hawk's Well* and *The Only Jealously of Emer* from the closet drama is that in these plays a mimetic space is presented alongside the diegetic one. This diegetic space does not exist, however, somewhere offstage but is instead projected right on top of the mimetic scene. The "little pictures" of ekphrastic diegesis compete with the theater and try to "draw the attention away for a second or two from the player."

There are two ways to describe what happens in this scene. On the one hand we could say that the mimetic space of the theater is simply doubled by diegesis. On the other hand we can recognize in this doubling a more contentious relation, a confrontation, cooptation, and interruption of theatrical mimesis by diegesis. This latter version points to the anti-theatricalism of Yeats's theater. One response to the collision between diegesis and mimesis is to reduce the mimesis of the stage, its props and gesticulating actors. Indeed, Yeats participates in this tradition not only in his crusade against mimetic acting but also by representing the well in *At the Hawk's Well* with nothing more than a square blue cloth on a stage that is free of naturalist clutter. However, even as a blue cloth, the well is mimetically present on the stage, as are the players, no matter how much Yeats terrorized them to rid themselves of mimetic acting.

In order to deal with the continued presence of stage props and actors, Yeats introduces an element into the theatrical setup of the stage that becomes the trademark of his Nôh plays: just as the musicians describe for "the eye of the mind" what the audience is to imagine, they unfold a curtain adorned with an emblematic hawk that veils the main stage from the view of the audience. This cloth serves as the projection screen for their poetic and diegetic ekphrasis of the stage and its props, hiding the mimetic space entirely. Only when the musicians begin to introduce the action of the play do they fold up the curtain again, giving the stage over to the play's three agents, the Old Man, the young Cuchulain, and the Guardian of the Well.

The curtain epitomizes the struggle between diegesis and mimesis by giving their confrontation a tangible and theatrical form. The curtain neatly separates the two modes of representing space (diegesis and mimesis) and the two sets of characters (diegetic narrators and mimetic actors) by situating them at the back of the stage and on the main stage, respectively. In this way Yeats systematically enacts what had been more of an ad hoc solution in Thomson's stage version of Stein's *Four Saints,* which was also divided into two areas and two types of characters, one diegetic, the other mimetic. But what will happen once the cloth is folded up and the theatrical space and its action is revealed? As if trying to evade a direct confrontation between diegesis and mimesis, the musicians direct their attention away from the stage, describing the entry of the Old Man:

> That old man climbs up hither,
> Who has been watching by this well
> These fifty years. He is all doubled up with age;
> The old thorn-trees are doubled so
> Among the rocks where he is climbing.
>
> (401)

For a moment, diegesis is put to a more conventional use, announcing the approaching Old Man, who is not yet visible onstage. The musicians call to the audience's mind his features and bearing, but through the established technique of teichoscopy, the description of events that happen offstage.

But this evasion is necessarily brief. So heavily does Yeats depend on narrators and their power to project objects and figures onto the physical space of the stage that the doubling—or clash—between diegesis and theatricality erupts in the scene that immediately follows, a scene during which the Old Man is, without a doubt, physically present on the stage. And the First Musician provides a detailed account of all of the Old Man's actions:

> He has made a little heap of leaves;
> He lays the dry sticks on the leaves
> And, shivering with cold, he has taken up
> The fire-stick and socket from its hole.
> He whirls it round to get a flame;
> And now the dry sticks take the fire
> And now the fire leaps up and shines
> Upon the hazels and the empty well.
>
> (402)

While the first line describes a finished action in the present perfect, "He has made," the second line already switches to the present tense, "He lays," providing a commentary that runs simultaneously with the silent action, "And now . . . And now. . . ." The doubling that is the unavoidable result of this simultaneity is revealed most starkly in the stage direction that describes in detail the actor's gestures during the running commentary of the First Musician: "He [the Old Man] crouches and moves his hands as if making a fire." For all of Yeats's attempt to rid his theater of imitation by "keeping the door shut," as he puts it, "against a pushing world," here imitation enters through the back door: through the double representation of narrative commentary and silent action, which, however stylized it may be, cannot help but resemble a pantomime in which the Old Man silently goes through the movements of "making a fire."

This imitative doubling does have an anti-mimetic effect, one that is in line with many modernist attacks on the actor. Yeats instructs the Old Man to act in as stylized a manner as possible at precisely the moment when he is reduced to this imitative pantomime of making fire: "His [the Old Man's] movements, like those of the other persons of the plays, suggest a marionette" (401). This marionette-style acting, which is required for the entire play and for all characters, is demanded just when the doubling of text and actor leads to an imitative pantomime. However, the diegetic description of making a fire is not the same as its pantomimic enactment. The passage only singles out discontinuous, individual actions. One might say here that like the ekphrasis of movement in Mallarmé, this diegesis dismembers the actor and his pantomime into isolated acts and gestures, so that the instruction to act like a marionette only confirms what was already effected by the text. This scene then also indicates that Yeats's diegesis is in fact akin to the type of depersonalization achieved by introducing marionettes onto the stage, that both constitute techniques for keeping under control the mimetic drive of actors and the continuing, mimetic presence of the actors' bodies themselves.[31]

It is in the competition between diegesis and theatricality that we can perceive Yeats's real debt to Nôh theater, as well as his difference from it. The Nôh stage is framed by the chorus on one side and musicians and attendants on the other side. The attendants remain silent and perform subservient functions, such as rearranging the players' dress or bringing in and taking away the few stage props. The musicians—three percussion players and one flutist—remain at all times at the back of the stage, opposite the audience. Besides playing their instruments, the three percussionists also produce guttural sounds that accompany the players' song and movement. The chorus, finally, is exclusively devoted to commenting on and describing the action that is simultaneously represented on the main stage, if in an extremely stylized manner, by the main players. From this schematic description of Nôh theater we can see that Yeats fuses the musicians, the attendants, and the chorus into one diegetic function under the name of either Musicians or Attendants. What he retains from them, however, is what he needs most, namely, a way of coopting theatrical mimesis through diegesis.

The project of a diegesis that frames, controls, and doubles mimesis marks Yeats's entire dramatic oeuvre. Yeats used attendants or musicians positioned at the back of the stage to introduce the play that will be represented on the main stage for the first time in *Deirdre* (1907) and then subsequently in most of his plays, including such late plays as *The King of the Great Clock Tower* (1935). This technique is used in the Cuchulain cycle, the Nôh-inspired "Plays for Dancers," as well as in his so-called Christian plays. Yeats included it even in his play *The Resurrection,* which was originally conceived without it.[32] These narrators also helped Yeats to overcome his fixation on the figure of the bard, which dominated his early plays. One could say that Yeats tried to come to terms with the problem of the privileged lyric subject by relegating this figure to the back of the stage and turning it into a diegetic commentator. Indeed, the overinvested poet figures of his early plays disappear miraculously as soon as he employed them as musicians for the specific and defined purpose of framing the main stage. Banishing the bard to the back of the stage did not fully guard Yeats's plays against dominating poetic voices. But once these voices were placed on the margin of the stage, the power of their speech was channeled to diegetic projection.

Poetic drama always has to struggle with the problem that the lyrical voice derives its power and authority from remaining unchallenged by other voices. In dramatic situations this entitlement is taken away and the lyrical voice is confined to particular actors and characters who find themselves confronted with opponents and thus with a multiplicity of voices. Yeats's banishing poets to the back of the stage was, therefore, also a way of maintaining parts of this lyrical authority: it was the only way of keeping it outside and thus above the drama of interaction and conflict. The peculiar power of language when it is removed from mimetic interaction might be another reason for Yeats's fascination with puppet theater, including Japanese puppet theater (which he wrongly believed to have influenced Nôh theater, whereas it was really the other way around).[33] In Japanese puppet theater all voices are spoken by a narrator, so that theatrical mimesis and speech are kept apart, a separation that preserves the power of a lyrical voice that contains all other voices and stands above the messy mimesis of theatrical action.

Despite this ideal of the pure diegetic voice, as removed from the mimetic stage as that of a puppeteer, Yeats remained too much a part of the tradition of mimetic theater to rigorously maintain the separation between mimetic actors and diegetic rhapsodes. While mimetic actors, such as the

Old Man in *At the Hawk's Well,* take on diegetic functions, such as describing the actions of the Guardian, the musicians, conversely, are drawn into the sphere of mimesis from which they were so carefully removed. In his notes on this play Yeats insists: "There will be no scenery, for three musicians, whose seeming sunburned faces will, I hope, suggest that they have wandered from village to village in some country of our dreams, can describe place and weather, and at moments action, and accompany it all by drum and gong or flute and dulcimer" (*Classic Nôh,* 151). What kind of mimetic illusion do these musicians have to create? Are they supposed to be authentic Irish peasants, with their sunburnt faces, rather than alienated city dwellers and office workers? Are they members of a traveling group of actors? It is this interest in the appearance of the musicians — they should "seem" as if they have been working in the sun — that reveals Yeats's investment in their illusionist mimesis, for they have to try to look different from what they are. The "mistake" (from the point of view of the Nôh theater) Yeats makes in having these musicians wear masks that ensure their participation in the mimetic sphere of the theater is therefore symptomatic of his more general difficulty of keeping mimesis and diegesis apart.

The Diegesis of Dance

The question that remains to be asked is whether the diegetic control of the stage also applies to dance, for one might think that after Yeats enthusiastically embraces dance, dance does not need to be mediated by diegesis. His last play, *The Death of Cuchulain,* even opens with a producer who seems to suggest that no language should intrude on the dance: "I promise a dance. I wanted a dance because where there are no words there is less to spoil. . . . But I was at my wit's end to find a good dancer; . . . I spit upon the dancers painted by Degas. I spit upon their short bodices, their stiff stays, their toes whereon they spin like peg-tops" (1052). While dismissing classical ballet dancers (Degas), the passage signals a retreat of diegesis from the dance, but at the same time this producer seems unable to find an adequate dancer — Ito had long since left for Hollywood. Even when Ito was still with the Abbey Theatre, however, Yeats retained too much ambivalence about the theater to ever let the dance alone. In the opening scene of *At the Hawk's Well,* for example, the First Musician paints an ekphrastic image and explains the figure of the dancer playing The Guardian of the Well, who remains entirely silent and motionless until the climax of the play:

> The guardian of the well is sitting
> Upon the old gray stone at its side,
> · · · · · · · · · · · · ·

> Her heavy eyes
> Know nothing, or but look upon stone.
>
> (400–401)

Even the climactic dance is not left to the awe-inspiring dance of the Guardian. In fact all three layers of the play—musicians at the back of the stage, the Old Man and the Young Man, and the silent Guardian—are superimposed onto one another. The First Musician comments on the Young Man—"For he grows pale and staggers to his feet" (410)—as the Young Man proclaims his determination to confront the Guardian. The dancer becomes integrated into a network of commentaries, diegetic projections, and direct speech.

The degree to which Yeats wants to have it both ways, poetic diegesis and dance, is perhaps most visible in two of his last plays, written under the influence of Nôh drama, *A Full Moon in March* and its structural sequel, *The King of the Great Clock Tower*. *A Full Moon in March* is Yeats's own version of the Salomé material, which had shaped nineteenth-century writing from Heine's *Atta Toll* and Flaubert's *Salambô* to Huysmans, Wilde, and, of course, Mallarmé.[34] *A Full Moon in March* is only indirectly related to the biblical story of Herod's daughter and the prophet St. John the Baptist, because Yeats transposes it to an Irish setting and fuses it with Anderson's fairy tale of the queen and the swineherd. Salomé is replaced by an Irish queen, and St. John by a swineherd who has come to sing his love and whose wooing song will be either accepted or punished by beheading.[35] However, there can be no doubt that *A Full Moon in March* is Yeats's answer to Mallarmé: like Hérodiade, the Queen describes herself as being "crueller than solitude" (392) and boasts of her "virgin cruelty" (395); when she feels insulted by the Swineherd, she demands his execution at once. Indeed, in several letters, Yeats confirms that this play is in fact an estranged and transposed version of the Salomé story.[36]

At the end of his career as a dramatist, then, Yeats finally introduces the dancing Salomé herself into his theater: the Queen dances with the Swineherd's severed head. As in *At the Hawk's Well,* Yeats creates different spatial areas by placing two attendants at the back of the stage, who operate the curtain that separates them from the main stage and who provide a continual diegetic projection of the action.[37] After an exchange between the Swineherd and Queen, the main stage is closed off by the curtain only to be revealed again, this time displaying the Queen with the severed head of the Swineherd. In contrast to the dancing Guardian of the Well, who remains silent because no speech is attributed to her, the Queen remains silent even though she is supposed to sing a song. For the duration of this song, the

First Attendant takes over her voice, "[singing as Queen]" (987) the song of the Queen's virgin cruelty. The real Queen is reduced to a visual spectacle, the First Attendant has become her voice, while the Second Attendant joins in and lends his voice to the Swineherd's head, which, although severed, has the last word of the main play (comparable to the severed speaking head of St. John in "Le Cantique de Saint Jean" in Mallarmé's *Hérodiade*). A similar switch happens in *The King of the Great Clock Tower,* where the attendants take over the voices of the Captain of the Guard and the Queen before her dance with the severed head of The Stroller. The split between silent gestures—pantomime or dance—and dialogue is here externalized by removing voice and language from the dancer altogether. In this split too Yeats follows the Nôh tradition, which does not restrict the chorus to third-person commentary on the action taking place on the main stage; at times the chorus switches to the first person, speaking for one of the main players. This switch only serves to foreground the power of those diegetic voices located at the margin of the stage.

Since the attendants have themselves become involved in the drama between the Queen and the Swineherd by lending their voices to these dancers, Yeats has no diegetic narrator left to control the mimetic theatricality of the dance. For this reason, perhaps, he intervenes in the choreography of the scene, projecting the dance through his own authorial voice in an extended stage direction: "[Queen takes the head and lays it upon the ground. She dances before it—a dance of adoration. She takes the head up and dances with it to drum-taps, which grow quicker and quicker. As the drum-taps approach their climax, she presses her lips to the lips of the head. Her body shivers to very rapid drum-taps. The drum-taps cease. She sinks slowly down, holding the head to her breast]" (989). This stage direction does not dictate every detail of the Queen's dance, but it outlines its basic structure. In both *At the Hawk's Well* and *A Full Moon in March* Yeats thus holds onto diegetic control, whether through narrative commentary at the back of the stage or by means of stage directions.

The technique of a stage divided between diegesis and dance is tied to the difficulty of negotiating the relation between the present world and the mythical worlds—from Cuchulain to Jesus—that these plays depict. In his earlier plays, the figures of the bard—Aleel, Mary, Seanchan, Martin/Andrew, Forgael—find themselves confronted with the dull, "common" reality of the everyday. In the later plays the mythical and ritual quality of the main plot and language is distanced and estranged through the attendants, who are the links to the contemporary world and who are set apart from the action on the main stage.[38] Before the Queen's dance in *A Full*

Moon in March a small exchange between the two attendants moves the argument of the play back in time:

> SECOND ATTENDANT: What do we sing?
> FIRST ATTENDANT: An ancient Irish Queen
> That stuck a head upon a stake.
> SECOND ATTENDANT: Her lover's head;
> But that's a different queen, a different story.
>
> (985–86)

This removal of the mythical worlds works as a kind of estrangement. The opening speech of the First Musician in *Deirdre,* the first play to use framing narrators and curtains, announces such an estrangement univocally: "I have a story right, my wanderers, / That has so mixed with fable in our songs / That all seemed fabulous" (345). The musicians and the curtain continue to keep us at a distance, and they keep us from conflating our world with that of mythology. In Yeats's last play, *The Death of Cuchulain,* this distance is additionally ensured by a dismissive comment made by the Old Man, who refers to the mythological subject matter of the play as "antiquated romantic stuff" (1051). Even though Yeats may not have placed estrangement at the center of his dramaturgy, the narrators and commentators, even as they create the doubling of speech and action that constitutes the central challenge of his plays, frame the mythical world of the play in order to demarcate our distance from it.

The mediation between mythical past and present is tied to a second mediation, that between the world inside the theater and the world outside. The perspective proposed by the term *diegetic theater* offers a way of specifying what has puzzled many commentators, readers, and audiences of Yeats's plays, namely, their relation to the cause of Irish nationalism, for which they were also conceived. For if it is true, as I have argued, that the modernist distrust of the theater was caused also by the perceived affinity between the public gathered in the audience and the political public, then Yeats's halfhearted attempt to bring the closet drama back to the theater must imply an equally conflicted, but not entirely negative, relation to the public sphere. Whereas Mallarmé had withdrawn into his closet, Yeats sought out a stage that was after all the stage of the Irish National Theatre. Indeed, Wagner's Bayreuth has often been cited as one model for the Abbey Theatre, not the least by Yeats himself, and the *Ring,* for Yeats's Cuchulain cycle.

At the same time, the persistence of anti-theatricalism in Yeats's work bespeaks a hesitation to celebrate the audience in the National Theatre,

Wagner-style, as the apotheosis of some Irish *Volk* and thus to propagate emphatically a total theatricality through which this *Volk* may finally come to itself. In fact Yeats became increasingly wary of any direct link between theater and politics and sought to distance himself from Griffith and Sinn Fein, insisting on the personal as opposed to the political nature of his theater (*Explorations,* 115), and later demanded that his thoughts "should be skipped by Politicians and Journalists" (429). It is true that Yeats's political ambitions did not disappear, but they were mediated by his remarkable relation to Synge, whose political plays he defended, risking his own reputation and the future of the Abbey Theatre in the process. Always prone to lyrical theater, Yeats in 1919 confirmed his plan to withdraw into something of a closet himself, demanding an "aristocratic" theater and not a popular one, a small chamber and not an arena for the assembled *populus.* In his notorious "A People's Theatre: A Letter to Lady Gregory" (1919–23), he retrospectively attacked the Abbey Theatre for having become a place where such things as "mechanism and politics" (*Explorations,* 313) found expression. Such developments, for Yeats, were nothing but "discouragement and a defeat" (313), and he drew from this observation the following conclusion: "I want to create for myself an unpopular theatre and an audience like a secret society where admission is by favour and never to many" (335).

After his early nationalist plays, Yeats started to become suspicious of the audience and wanted to turn it into a secret society. Instead of hoping for Wagner's Bayreuth, Yeats sought out something resembling Mallarmé's closet. There Yeats tried to implement what might be called a politics of anti-theatricality, a politics that sought to interrupt the theatrical, which it regarded with suspicion. In this, for all his difference to this near contemporary, Yeats set the stage for a writer whose distrust of Wagner's politics of theatricality led to a more openly disruptive politics of anti-theatricality: Bertolt Brecht.

Bertolt Brecht:

The Theater on a Leash

The Spell of the Theater

So unquestioned is Brecht's impact on the canon of the modern theater that his term *epic theater* has frequently been used to describe modernist theater at large.[1] The half-curtain, Lotte Lenya's rough voice, Mother Courage's cart, the fake elephant in *Man Equals Man,* Helene Weigel's acting, Kurt Weill's and Hanns Eisler's tunes, and the theory of the estrangement effect are classics of the modernist *mise en scène.*[2] Brecht's contemporaries admired the epic theater for somehow managing to "modernize" the theater, to rid it of its nineteenth-century dust and bring it up to par with what Brecht called the "scientific age." Brecht's shadow looms large over postwar theater from Germany (Peter Weiss and Heiner Müller) to Brazil (Augusto Boal); even studies of more contemporary drama use him as a point of reference, as, for example, Elin Diamond and Janelle Reinelt do to analyze British feminist theater.[3] And finally, Fredric Jameson recognized in Brecht's dialectic method a usable model for a contemporary political theater.[4] In the history of the theater and in contemporary criticism, then, Brecht continues to be seen as one of modernism's most successful innovators of the theater.

What is neglected in these accounts of Brecht's lasting success in the theater is that his work is not so much a modernist reform *of* the theater as one directed *against* it. Indeed, the most central features of Brecht's theater arise from a vehement and at times fundamental polemic against actors and the audience. And so we must recognize that Brecht counts as one of modernism's most successful theater reformers because he was most successful in making his resistance to the theater productive for a reform of the theater. This resistance to the theater is visible in Brecht's attacks on expressionist plays, on the theater industry, and on Max Reinhardt's seductive spectacles. His most categorical and fundamental condemnation of the theater emerges, however, when he, like many turn-of-the-century and early-twentieth-century reformers, speaks against the figure whose exploitation of theatricality never ceased to haunt modern theater, namely, Richard Wagner. Indeed, Wagner's relentless dedication to the theater and to theatricalism led Brecht to define one of his own operas, *The Rise and Fall of the City of Mahagonny,* explicitly against Wagner's *Gesamtkunstwerk.*[5] I will take the resistance to the theater as my point of departure for analyzing Brecht's work in the late twenties and reinterpret the main elements of his theater reform, such as epic acting, intertitles, and *gestus,* in light of this resistance.

Like Nietzsche, Mallarmé, and Adorno, Brecht fears that Wagner's *Gesamtkunstwerk* may unleash an all-consuming theatricality that would draw everything into its vortex. What Brecht finds so problematic about Wagner is precisely what had been a source of irritation for Nietzsche, namely, the theater's power and influence over the other arts, its unlimited capacity of "theatricalizing everything" [es theatert alles ein].[6] Brecht attributes this dangerous capacity to the "melting-pot process" [Schmelzprozess] (17:1010) of the *Gesamtkunstwerk:* the theater "melts in" everything, a process that affects every dimension of the theater, from actors to scenery, from music to the dramatic text. However, the theater not only "theatricalizes" the other arts by "melting" them together, it also melts the audience with the theater. Hence Brecht's concern about the intoxicating effects of Wagner on innocent audiences, who might be politically manipulated at will. The theater thus becomes not only aesthetically suspect but politically suspect as well. Brecht calls the Wagnerian opera a "culinary" [kulinarisch] art (17:1006), made only to be consumed like food and causing "drunkenness" [Räusche] (17:1011), an accusation that echoes verbatim Nietzsche's polemical description of the effects of Wagner's deceptive theatricality as a "repeated use of alcohol" [fortgesetzter Gebrauch von Alkohol].[7] Brecht drew the only possible conclusion: a lasting "mistrust of the theater" [Mißtrauen gegen das Theater] (17:991). It is this mistrust, a mistrust of Wagner but also of the theater more generally, that becomes the driving force behind Brecht's work in the theater.

Brecht shares his mistrust of the theater with the modernist anti-theatrical tradition, and the central concepts of his reform—the estrangement effect, the epic theater, the *gestus*—come directly from this anti-theatrical heritage.[8] That Brecht would articulate his mistrust of the theater in his critique of Wagner must be seen as yet another indication that Wagner had turned the theater and theatricality into an absolute value, a development that fundamentally changed the terms of the debate about theater reform. In declaring the theater to be a new and absolute value, Wagner had reversed the widespread scorn for the theater that characterized the nineteenth-century hierarchy of the arts, causing a polarization of the cultural field with respect to the value attributed to the theater.[9] Neither Wagner's admirers nor his critics could simply be for or against a particular form of theater, be it naturalism, realism, symbolism, or expressionism; they had to position themselves against the theater as such.

Given Brecht's resistance to the theater, it does not come as a surprise that Brecht's most programmatic early opera, *The Rise and Fall of the City of Mahagonny*, would take as its subject matter and also as its object of critique the institution of the theater itself. Brecht's primary strategy for dispelling the magic of operatic theatricality is to turn this spell into the subject matter of the opera, to thematize it. *Mahagonny* presents culinary, alcoholic, and sexual pleasures as they become commodities in an imaginary American town devoted exclusively to what one could call the pleasure industry. Increasingly, the satisfaction of pleasures develops its own dynamic; the laws and regulations concerning these pleasures are gradually abandoned until everything is allowed. What follows is a veritable apocalypse: one character, Jakob, eats himself to death; another is killed in a bloody prizefight; and the protagonist of this morality tale, the innocent logger Paul, is arrested and finally convicted for having no money, the most severe sin in this capitalist Sodom and Gomorrah. Finally, the commodification of pleasure self-destructs when the war of everyone against everyone is declared.

The central maxim of *Mahagonny*—that pleasures are allowed only if you can pay for them—prevents us from easily enjoying the opera, for which, surely, we have paid as well. Brecht's master project of representing, rather than obscuring, the mechanisms of capitalism and of making them available to our critical assessment must be applied to the opera, for the institution of the opera is itself a perfect example of the despised and dangerous pleasure industry against which his critique is directed: "Mahagonny may be as culinary as always—as culinary as it is proper for an opera—it nevertheless has a social function; it subjects the culinary to discussion, it attacks the society that needs such operas" (17:1016). *Mahagonny* thus announces its break with the history of opera first and foremost by exposing the economic logic governing the commodification of pleasure in which it participates.

Years after the opening of the first version of *Mahagonny*, Brecht and Kurt Weill began to see that their strategy of simply "subjecting" the opera "to discussion" left the institution of the opera basically intact, that it did not ensure the absolute break with the genre's history and power that they had hoped for. One cannot help but detect an almost naive Enlightenment belief in the hope that if audiences became conscious of the druglike effects of the theater, they would no longer fall prey to them. The popular and catchy songs in particular threatened to become counterproductive to the analytical mission *Mahagonny* was supposed to fulfill.[10] Brecht's 1930 essay on opera ends, therefore, on a skeptical note: "The opera Mahagonny was written three years ago, in 1927. In subsequent works attempts were made to emphasize the didactic more and more at the expense of the culinary element. And so to develop the means of pleasure into an object of instruction" (17:1016). The balancing act of using the culinary opera against itself remained too much bound up, it seemed, with what it had intended to resist.

This retrospective conclusion is perhaps too sweeping because it downplays the extent to which *Mahagonny* not only thematizes pleasure but also takes formal measures to protect the theater from the dangerous effects of theatricality in general and of the Wagnerian *Gesamtkunstwerk* in particular, namely, the "separation of the elements [arts]" [Trennung der Elemente] (17:1010). The separation of speech, music, acting, and set design from one another was supposed to check the numbing effects of the theater.[11] Brecht and Weill are no longer concerned with the integration of the separate arts, but only with their total independence from one another. Brecht formulates this project by using Wagner's language of the sister arts, observing that he would "invite all the sister arts of the drama, not in order to create an 'integrated work of art' in which they sacrifice themselves, but so . . . that they estrange one another" (16:698–99).[12] For Brecht and Weill, the only way to control the opera's total theatricality is to turn the arts against one another so that they interrupt and dissolve the totality of the total work of art. This, then, is the sense in which Brecht creates an anti-theatrical work: while theatricality for Wagner was the concept that assured the unification of the sister arts, Brecht's attempt to break this unity apart is necessarily directed against this understanding of theatricality.

Actors on Trial

Brecht's anti-theatricalism, like that of other modernists, also emerges when one considers that the figure with which he is most dissatisfied, and whose theatricality must therefore be reformed most thoroughly, is the figure of the actor. Actors bring out modernism's ambivalence about mimesis because not only do they make the act of mimesis tangible and material, they also give rise to a kind of mimesis that seems the least capable of abstraction and estrangement. In a move or slippage that is characteristic for modernism, a critique of the actor is thus extended to a critique of theater as such. This slippage may strike us as a mistake, taking only a part for the whole. Could there not be a theater without actors or at least one that is not centrally dependent on them? Although this might be a possibility and in fact is a common utopia, there have been few practical and convincing models for such a theater, and for now the theater continues to depend on the actor. Peter Brook's necessary and sufficient definition of theater is therefore representative, for it is based on the existence of an actor and an audience member: "A man walks across this empty space whilst someone else is watching him, and this is all that is needed for an act of theatre to be engaged."[13] This dependence of the theater on the actor turns an anti-mimetic critique into an anti-theatrical one. While the mimetic arts, such as painting or photography, can become anti-mimetic without questioning their own material condition—paint, canvas, celluloid—the theater, if it feels the need to abandon mimesis, must turn against its own material, namely, the human performer. Brecht's anti-theatricalism follows the same scheme. The audience Brecht liked to imagine, resembling the expert audience of sport events, would be fed up once and for all with the mimetic mimicking of actors: "Impossible that actors would dare to present to such people those few pounds of mimic art [*Mimik*]" (17:993). In his numerous treatises on acting and in his work with actors he does everything to make such illusionist mimicking and deceptive theatrical mimesis impossible. Again Brecht uses a terminology inherited from anti-theatrical polemicists and their denunciation of "aping" actors to prevent the actor from becoming what he himself called a "parrot or monkey" (16:687).

Brecht's solution to the actors' "pounds of mimic art" is indicative of the slippage between mimesis, actor, and theatricality: rather than advocating a new style of acting, he commands actors to suspend acting altogether. There is no better characterization of what this suspension requires than Brecht's own model of the "Street scene" (16:546–57), which replaces the actors' art with the act of bearing witness. Actors must not attempt to fuse with the roles they are impersonating, thus creating an illusionist and mimetic theatricality; instead they must perform their roles as if they were witnesses re-creating an accident for a court or the police. This change from acting to witnessing puts a halt to illusionist acting by demanding that the actors keep their distance from the roles they are impersonating; they remain themselves even as they are engaged in the re-creation of the accident they have hypothetically witnessed. Performer-witnesses need not represent all aspects of the reported event through mimesis since they can rely on explanatory speech to comment on, interrupt, and complement their acting. Instead of merging with their roles, they can use their own voices to represent events by means of explanatory commentary, a practice that enforces the dissociation between reporting actor and reported character. This act of distanced reporting is put into practice most directly in Brecht's "Directions for Actors," where he advises actors to practice their roles in the third-person singular, thus turning their direct speech into third-person narration about the characters they represent (15:410). In the final analysis, the separation of actor and role leads to a switch from impersonating theatrical mimesis to a reliance on narration and commentary.

The technique of rehearsing in the third person left its traces on Brecht's plays. Indeed, many of Brecht's characters speak as if they were reporting about someone else in the third person. Paul, in *Mahagonny,* for example, lets us know right away where he comes from and who he is:

> Deep in the woods of ice-bound Alaska
> Seven winters I toiled with three buddies together
> Cutting down trees and hauling logs through the snow
> And I lived on raw meat and saved my earnings
> Seven years it's taken to get me
> Here where I now am.[14]

In fact, all actors in Brecht's plays are such commentator-narrators, speaking about themselves and explaining what motivates their actions. They do not usually do so in the third person, but their speech is nonetheless as distanced as if they were speaking about somebody else. What is even more striking is that Paul is speaking directly to the audience. Such direct, explanatory speech violates the rules of dramaturgy demanding that the audience be introduced to the characters and the action of the play indirectly, as if it were peeping through a hole in the fourth wall.

While Paul's distanced self-introduction seems like a brutal violation of basic laws of dramaturgy, it is more in tune with the dramaturgy of the opera and, to an even greater extent, with the oratorio. The operatic libretto, with its limited dialogue and emphasis on monologic arias, has to revert to such self-introductions much more frequently than does drama. The stylization of the genre, the emphasis on aria, and most importantly, the limited space allowed for dialogue and interaction make it difficult for the opera to avoid such explanatory directness. However, these moments of explanatory speech violate the fourth-wall standard of the bourgeois opera, connecting these operas to a more popular tradition, precisely the tradition Brecht sought to continue. The oratorio relies even less on theatrical mimesis and must therefore revert more frequently to explanatory and diegetic speeches and arias, which then take over the task of setting an imaginary stage. Although Brecht usually denounces the opera as the most culinary of the performing arts, its artificiality helped him conceive of a stage free of theatrical naturalism, which had become the new doctrine in the theater of the late nineteenth century.[15] It is for this reason that almost all of Brecht's theater productions in the second half of the twenties were conceived of as operatic productions, from *Man Equals Man,* for which the original score has been lost, and the *Three Penny Opera* to *Mahagonny.*

The reliance on distanced commentary is a feature Brecht shares with Yeats's equally operatic stage, and it is in relation to Yeats's diegetic narrators and musicians that Brecht's dramaturgy can be more precisely defined. Brecht and Yeats in fact derive some of their shared anti-mimetic use of diegesis from a common source, their fascination with Nôh theater.[16] *Der Jasager,* Brecht and Weill's adaptation of the Nôh play *Taniko,* and its counterpart, *Der Neinsager,* are in many ways more faithful to the Nôh tradition than are any of Yeats's "Plays for Dancers."[17] *Taniko,* a relatively late Nôh play, which itself incorporates more dramatic and mimetic action than the plays of classical Nôh authors such as Zeami, depicts a dangerous pilgrimage in the course of which a young boy, who had convinced his teacher to take him along, falls ill.[18] An old custom demands that he be hurled down the mountain, and the teacher and the pilgrims must eventually comply with this custom. In his adaptation Brecht uses Elisabeth Hauptmann's German translation of the play, which in turn is based on Arthur Waley's partial English translation of the original.[19] While it is tempting to see in this text, twice removed from the original, a symptom of the distance between Brecht and the Nôh tradition, it is equally significant that Brecht would use the text of this doubly translated play almost word for word, thus maintaining as much of its original character as possible. His only change was to remove the religious nature of the pilgrimage so as to turn this play into an allegory of the progress of communism and the sacrifices it demands.

Brecht does not adopt certain aspects of Nôh theater, such as the dance or the suggestive gestures that fascinated Yeats, but contents himself instead with using the translated and altered dramatic text. On the face of it, then, Brecht and Yeats are involved with Nôh on quite different levels. While Yeats uses selected elements of Nôh theatricality—its characteristic emphasis on poetic speech, a climactic dance, minimal mimesis, and diegetic musicians and attendants at the back of the stage—in order to create a new lyrical drama, Brecht uses the text and plot of a Nôh play for the purpose of writing a didactic *Lehrstück,* a play that resembles in all ways his notorious *The Measure Taken.*

The question that remains to be asked, however, is how it was possible for Brecht to adopt the text of *Taniko* without also adopting the theatricality with which it is so inextricably linked.[20] Brecht did not have to adapt his practice of staging to that of the Nôh theater because certain features of his own reform of the theater already resembled Nôh dramaturgy. The most prominent of these features is Brecht's vision of the distanced, reporting actors, who introduce themselves directly to the audience. Waley's translation of *Taniko* and Brecht's adaptation, for example, both open with a scene of such distanced self-introduction, a scene that could have been taken straight from *Mahagonny:* "Teacher: I am a teacher. I keep a school at one of the temples in the City. I have a pupil whose father is dead; he has only his mother to look after him. Now I will go and say good-bye to them, for I am soon starting on a journey to the mountains."[21] Brecht's formal affinity to Nôh is reflected not only in his retaining this self-introduction, so similar to his own technique, but also in his use of the chorus. It is one of the functions of the Nôh chorus (and of Yeats's attendants) to speak about the main characters in the third person, sometimes even switching to the first person and taking over the characters' voices.[22] At the climax of the story, when the three students confront the boy with the choice between forcing them to return or allowing them to hurl him down into the valley so that they can continue their mission, Brecht overlays the direct speech of the students with the reporting third-person narrative of the chorus: "We will ask him (they asked him), whether he demands (demands)/that we return (return) because of him" (*Der Jasager,* 25; in the German, all verbs are given in their singular as well as in their plural forms). Brecht uses the diegetic chorus of the Nôh play in order to fuse it with the direct speech of the students; even if the actors failed to practice their roles in the third person, the chorus would make sure that their direct speech was marked by third-person reporting. Brecht here turns to the Nôh theater not because he is amazed by their stunning costumes or the spectacular nature of their performance, as so many early-twentieth-century reformers, from Meyerhold to Artaud, had been; instead Brecht, like Yeats, borrows from the Nôh a technique of diegesis that controls the mimesis of the actor.

From the perspective of the struggle between diegesis and mimesis we can now reconsider Brecht's acting. Rather than relying on specialized diegetic actors, Brecht envisions a style of acting and a manner of speech that infuses the performance of every actor with the function of a commenting chorus: actors would speak in the first person, but with the distanced attitude and in an explanatory mode as if they were reporting their speech in the third person to a court of law. Unlike Yeats's theater or the Nôh theater, Brecht's stage is not divided into an area of diegesis and an area of mimesis; the division between the two happens everywhere and, more precisely, in every actor, leading to what Bert States has called "Brechtian schizophrenia."[23] Because actors are distanced from their role, because they are agents of both mimesis and explanatory diegesis at the same time, the space of the stage is endlessly interrupted and broken into mimetic gestures and commenting diegesis. What in Yeats was a neat division between mimesis and diegesis, and then a superimposition of the latter on the former, becomes, in Brecht, a fractured ensemble of interpretation, commentary, and distanced enactment.[24]

Brecht's revision of Wagner's theatricality operates not only on formal grounds. It is also directed against the political function with which Wagner entrusted the theater, in particular Wagner's hope that a total work of art would forge the passive audience into a unified whole. Brecht's own attitude toward this Wagnerian fusion is a negative one: only if Wagner's total theatricality can be broken, if the theater can be turned against itself, will it be possible to use the theater as a critical instrument. And since *Der Jasager* and *Der Neinsager* employ Brecht's anti-mimetic diegesis most deliberately, Brecht's anti-theatrical politics should appear most clearly in these plays. A discussion of the politics of Brecht's Nôh-inspired plays leads necessarily to his notion of the *Lehrstück,* or didactic play, of which *Der Jasager* and *Der Neinsager* are early examples. Brecht's *Lehrstücke* in fact combine the two levels on which Brecht's resistance to Wagner's theatricality operates. While Brecht relies in his *Lehrstücke,* as he did in his other plays and operas, on diegesis as a formal means of separating the arts and of ensuring a distance from, and hence a critical attitude on the part of the audience toward, the theater, his *Lehrstücke* take this anti-theatrical strategy further, for in them he abandons the audience altogether. Brecht conceives of his most political plays entirely as workshop productions from which the audience is to be systematically excluded.[25] This exclusion is backed up by another anti-theatrical position, a suspicion of visual pleasure, what Brecht calls the dangerous "desire to see" [Lust am Betrachten] (17:1023). Brecht here attacks the theater at its very essence, namely, in the original Greek meaning of *theatron* as the place of *thea,* "seeing." This position almost reminds one of St. Augustine's attack on the sense of sight as being prone to a type of *curiositas* that finds its most dangerous instantiation inside the place that is meant to satisfy all visual pleasures: the theater. Rather than indoctrinating the audience with propaganda, the *Lehrstücke* demand that its participants rotate through different roles in order to partake in an active discussion of the political problem the play proposes, usually the necessity of an individual to consent to his or her own murder. We can see here the bifurcation between a traditional anti-theatricalism and Brecht's modernist one: while one recurring form of the anti-theatrical prejudice objects to the role-playing that happens inside the theater because such role-playing is seen as subverting social hierarchies and classes, Brecht endorses it, for his objection is founded on an anti-theatricalism that is concerned with the act of mimetically impersonating another human being for the curious eyes of an audience that may be easily manipulated through breathtaking spectacles.

Brecht's critique of Wagner and of the avant-garde is also a critique of the hope that the assembled audience would be something like an ideal version of a national assembly. Despite his commitment to engaged art, Brecht did not share the avant-garde's hope that theatrical spectacles would spill over to the social sphere, erasing the difference between art and life.[26] For Brecht, in contrast, viewing theater was an analytic exercise, one requiring concentration, critical distance, and an active audience. Brecht, like other modernists, recognized that his contemporary theater did not lend itself to these values, and he suspected that the theater in general might be at odds with them. Brecht's reform of the theater, including its actors, its audience, and the act of viewing a performance, was so fundamental because it was born from a fundamental mistrust of the theater, a mistrust that, despite his success on the stage, he never abandoned.

Text on the Stage

Brecht's suspicion of impersonation and of seeing is part of a common modernist anti-theatricalism: the privileging of reading text over seeing theater. Explaining his insistence on reading, Brecht observes: "The spoken word was no more important than the written word (of the titles). Reading seems to encourage the audience to adopt the most relaxed attitude toward the work" (17:1012). This "relaxed attitude" does not imply indifference but is the prerequisite for the critical attitude Brecht wants his audience to adopt. In his essay "The Literarization of the Theatre" Brecht reveals that he indeed thinks of the act of reading as an activity directed against the theater: "it seems desirable that the spectator should read plays whose aim is not merely to be performed in the theater but to change it: out of mistrust of the theater" (17:991). What stands behind Brecht's belief in text and reading is the presumption that the theater, despite the presence of other spectators, hard chairs, and, often, bad acting, tends naturally to overwhelm the critical capacities of the audience, which are, on the other hand, kept alive in the act of reading a compelling book in the tranquility of one's living room.

This assumption is not uncommon, but it is also not self-evident. We may object, for example, that literature, especially when read in undisturbed solitude, manages to draw us into its fictitious world and compels us to identify with its characters much more successfully than distracting public spectacles. Recurring anxieties about private reading and sensationalist fiction indicate that we should not take Brecht's assumption about the nature of reading for granted. What matters for Brecht, however, is not so much the question of absorption as the question of control, the type of control readers have over the act of reading but not over manipulative spectacles premised on a passive audience. One of Brecht's reasons for insisting on the critical potential of reading is that reading offers a great degree of external control, allowing the reader to determine the pace, place, and time of reading and to turn back and forward at will. For this reason, Brecht singles out "footnotes, and the possibility of flipping through a text in order to compare passages" (16:992), as the features of reading he wants to transpose into the theater. In Brecht's view, it is precisely the audience's lack of external control in the theater that is responsible for its being passively "drawn in" and subjected to the dictates of the performance. The critical, distanced, and "relaxed" attitude Brecht desires in his audience can only be assured when the audience retains control over the theatrical performance in the same way that a reader controls the act of reading.

Like Stein, Brecht seeks to introduce something of the act of reading into the theater. However, rather than changing the dramatic form as she does, Brecht does something more literal: he covers the stage with writing. Text becomes a device for channeling, controlling, and interrupting theatrical mimesis. This technique is employed most clearly in *Mahagonny*. Brecht introduces the plot of each scene in a text written across a half-curtain covering the lower part of the stage, a device he first employed in the *Three Penny Opera*. These narrative titles provide a frame for the action performed on the stage, and this action is even called, in narrative terms, a "story" rather than a "plot": "One day there came to Mahagonny among others a man called Paul Ackermann. We are going to tell you his story" (2:508). The play continues to be punctuated by narrative frames that condition the reception of its theatrical mimesis. In addition to titles and intertitles, Brecht uses other occasions as well to place text on stage. A changing price list hanging on the sign that reads "To Mahagonny" indicates the economic ups and downs of business, as do the statistics of currency fluctuation projected onto the backdrop in scene 7. When in scene 9 Paul Ackermann becomes increasingly annoyed by the petty laws governing Mahagonny, the stage is covered with printed notices bearing such inscriptions as "Do not wear down the chairs" (2:520). During the climactic scene 12, in which a hurricane is moving straight toward Mahagonny, this crisis is shown exclusively on the backdrop, where a map of Mahagonny and an arrow represent the drama of the hurricane's approach and then its circumvention of the city. Brecht's reliance on writing goes so far that the typhoon itself is represented by nothing but the word "TYPHOON" projected in "enormous letters" onto the backdrop (2:524). This text-only mode of representation is repeated in the last scene, which portrays the self-destruction of capitalism as groups of people parade signs with political slogans such as "For the battle of all against all" (2:561) across the stage, inscriptions that presumably demonstrate the contradictory nature of capitalism in its final phase.

The ability of these texts to frame theatrical mimesis is operative most strongly in the four middle scenes, which represent the moral allegories of eating, loving, fighting, and drinking: Jake eats himself to death; Begbick oversees the business of prostitution; Joe is killed in a bloody prizefight; and Paul indulges excessively in whiskey. The allegorical meaning of these scenes is controlled by four subscriptions that are projected, again in "enormous letters," at the back of the scene—"EATING," "LOVING," "FIGHTING," and "DRINKING"—projections that evoke the convention of the *subscriptio* in Christian moral allegories. In this tradition, the *subscriptio* produces and ensures the meaning of an image: while the *imago* must necessarily present an excess of visual (or theatrical) detail, the textual *subscriptio* ensures that the figure is ultimately subordinated to the abstract meaning indicated in the subscription. No matter how long the hair of the blind woman with scales or the gestures with which she holds them, the *subscriptio* invalidates all those unnecessary details and subsumes the picture under the abstract meaning of justice.

In *Mahagonny,* however, one promptly discovers ruptures and contradictions in the smooth surface of allegorical meaning suggested by the four subscriptions projected at the back of the scene.[27] The grim prostitution is countered by an overdone romantic love scene between Paul and Jenny; Paul's desire to bet all his money on Joe in a prizefight is motivated by their common nostalgic memory of Alaska and not by his capitalist greed; and drunkenness is not as much a problem as Paul's inability to pay for his drink. While the *subscriptio* still ensures that we look at these scenes in terms of eating, loving, fighting, and drinking, we do not have available to us a moral frame presenting them as vices. Instead, we are asked to transport them to the context of capitalism and its self-destruction, but for this application we are given but few instructions. And as long as this function must be performed by the audience, the textual subscriptions do not fully control, but only frame, the scene. The titles on the backdrop indicate the possibility of controlling the meaning of the scene in the manner of an allegory, but the conventions that govern the relation between image and abstract meaning have been suspended and must be established anew. Brecht thus does not reduce this theatrical scene to a mere allegorical sign that points away from its material particularities. Instead, he leaves a gap between text and scene, which the audience must try to bridge by exerting its own interpretive power.

We may take this gap between word and scene as an indication of the relation between text and theatrical mimesis in Brecht's oeuvre at large: the text written across the scene never erases completely the mimetic and theatrical complexities of the play. However, it forces audiences to acquire a double vision: to relate the abstract text, which is nevertheless typographically integrated in the design of the stage, to the mimetic scene, which remains infused with all the contradictions that need to be resolved. While these texts never fully control the theater, they force audiences to recognize this failure and to respond to it by themselves attempting to come to terms with the theater's mimesis. We can thus recognize on the stage a struggle between theatrical mimesis on the one hand and spoken and textual diegesis on the other, a struggle over the control of theatrical representation.

Brecht's mistrust of the theater acquires a new dimension when it is viewed from the perspective offered by his friend Walter Benjamin. In 1931 Benjamin wrote an essay on Brecht—"Was ist das epische Theater?"—that became central not only for all subsequent interpretations of the epic theater but also for Brecht himself, who lifted from this essay some of the terms with which he proceeded to theorize his own work. In this essay Benjamin wants to ground theater history in a history of technology. For this purpose he identifies the main features of epic theater—its stop-and-go episodic structure; the interruption of scenic action through intertitles and projections; the witness-actor—as means through which the theater is brought "up to par" with technology.[28] This call for an advanced theater, however, did not mean that Brecht integrated into his theatrical productions the then new media of radio and film, as, for example, Piscator did. Rather it means that the epic theater took from those media the cues for overhauling the most elementary aspects of theatrical representation.[29]

Behind Benjamin's admiration for the epic theater stands the assumption that radio and film expose the theater's archaic nature and that it would take a radical critique of the theater to turn it into a contemporary art form. Benjamin elaborated these assumptions a few years later in his essay "The Work of Art in the Age of Mechanical Reproducibility" (1934–35). Here he articulates the theater's premodern character by arguing that it, more than any other art form, participates in what he calls the "aura": the investment in the uniqueness of the artwork that stems from its ritualistic origin. The theater is particularly ensconced in this aura because not only are its works unique and nonreproducible but they require the presence of a live audience. Both radio and film dismantle this uniqueness through their irreverent reproducibility. In particular, however, they challenge the live actors in a more direct manner by displacing their voices (radio) and even their entire bodies (film) through close-ups and montage. It is precisely this dismantling of the live presence of the human actor that Benjamin recognizes in Brecht's epic theater. Like radio and film, the episodic and epic theater can "be switched on and off" (*Versuche*, 22), proceeding through series of tableaux and framed stills rather than through a continuous flow that characterizes the presence of the living human actor on stage.[30] As a result, actors in the epic theater cease being mimes and become what Benjamin calls "functionaries" (18) and "philosophers" (28). Benjamin here recognizes that the epic theater implies not just a change in the style of *mise en scène* but an assault on theatrical representation that is as fundamental as that caused by the emergence of radio and film. In fact, Benjamin comes close to formulating Brecht's reforms in terms of anti-theatricalism when he speaks of Brecht's desire to keep the theater "under control" (26) and aligns him with a kind of counterhistory of theater ranging from Plato's dialogues to the German *Trauerspiel,* a history that Benjamin himself calls "un-dramatic" (34) but that in fact describes the tradition of the anti-theatrical closet drama.

Gestus: How to Control the Theater

Benjamin's essay not only provides a new, technological frame for Brecht's anti-theatricalism, it also employs a term that Brecht would later use to theorize his own work in the theater: *gesture.* "Epic theater is gestural," is the first sentence of the essay, and all the features of epic theater—interruption, montage, episodic nature, quotation—are defined as gestural: "The more we interrupt an action, the more gestures we gain. The interruption of action is therefore the central concern of the epic theater" (19). What is significant about Benjamin's term *gesture,* and Brecht's version of it, *gestus,* is that it ties Brecht's anti-theatricalism to the dismantling of actors into isolated gestures. Even though there is no direct indication that Brecht chose this term explicitly in response to Wagner's aesthetics of gesture, *gestus* appears for the first time in Brecht's anti-theatrical polemic against the *Gesamtkunstwerk.* Indeed, it can be understood as a modernist defense against Wagnerian theatricality.

Brecht will ultimately distinguish *gestus* from the gestures of actors, but there can be no doubt that the term originates in his interest in acting. In 1929 Brecht uses the term *gestus,* then still untheorized, simply to describe different styles of acting (15:187), for example, the "ceremonial gestus" (15:204) of the actor Wachtangow. A few years later, however, in 1935, we find that *gestus,* or the gestural principle, has become a category decidedly dissociated from its mimetic origin, so that Brecht can proclaim: "The mimic principle is replaced by the gestural principle" (15:475). In between these two statements, with the help of essays by Kurt Weill and Walter Benjamin, Brecht turned *gestus* into a general theory of controlled theatricality. Actors now do not automatically produce a *gestus* by simply gesticulating on stage. On the contrary, they depict or present a *gestus* only when they begin to select, consciously and critically, isolated gestures, such as the agressive gestures of a master. It is through this demand for social legibility that *gestus* acquires the ethical dimension it has in its Latin meaning.[31]

Brecht is careful to distinguish this selection process from the kind of stylized depersonalization that Craig and Yeats propagated at the same time,
emphasizing that "the naturalness of gestures and intonations must not be
lost in the process of selection. I am not talking about stylization" (15:370).
Actors must select a number of distinct gestures that they deem typical and
relevant for the situation they are depicting, in contrast to the expressive
and involuntary gestures they may otherwise happen to perform.[32]

While Wagner cherished gestures *(Gebärden)* as the language of the unsayable, for Brecht a given *gestus* is selected based on its intelligibility. The
intelligibility of the *gestus* is assured not only by selection but by a particular
mode of theatrical presentation, a mode through which the theater's mimesis is brought under the control of meaning. What is required for *gestus* to
begin functioning like an iconic sign is that it stand out visibly and dis-
tinctly in the continuum of theatrical mimesis. Herein lies the difference between gesticulation and *gestus*. Brecht's own way of saying this is itself gestural, namely, by way of *deixis,* the gesture of gesture. The actors point toward
themselves (and the role from which they maintain their distance), and this
demonstrative gesture ensures the distinct isolation of *gestus*. In this sense,
the gesture of pointing structures Brecht's theater reform more generally,
leading to what one might call *deictic theatricality*.[33] Instead of simply replacing theater with language, Brecht's deictic theatricality is at once ostenta-
tious and controlled, channeling the gestures of the theater into signifying
structures by way of disrupting the continuum of material mimesis. If we
feel that the deixis of *gestus* resembles the raised finger of a didactic gesture, we may remember that the complexity of Brecht's work depends on
what he calls the "art of watching a play" [Zuschauerkunst] (15:428) and on
the insistence that "complex seeing must be practiced" (17:992). As Austin
Quigley has pointed out, it was Brecht's conviction that scenes, even if they
were somewhat simpler than life, would still provide enough material to
function as a critical inquiry and thus to provoke our critical faculties.[34]

Like Wagner's theory of gestures, Brecht's notion of *gestus* does not refer
to acting alone but encompasses the entire range of expression onstage,
including music and poetry. And it is in its critique of a Wagnerian fusion
that the anti-theatrical orientation of *gestus* comes more clearly into view:
instead of fusing the arts, *gestus* seeks to play them off against one another.[35]
Brecht took the term *gestus* and, along with it, the distancing and critical
function of music from his musical collaborator Kurt Weill.[36] For Weill,
music was an instrument that was not meant to heighten, but to undermine,
the theatrical effects of scenic action and actors. In fact Weill harbored the
fantasy of having music prescribe the *gestus* of a given scene and thus control the actors involved in it: "Ideally," Weill muses in *Musik and Theater,*

music "may fixate the *gestus* to such a degree that a false representation of the action is no longer possible" (64). Actors are prone to make mistakes, and only music has the power to prescribe the *gestus* that is supposed to guide their mimetic rendering of the scene. Weill reiterates this ideal in his notes for *Mahagonny,* where he states that his music could be used as a veritable script for the opera's *mise en scène:* "The attitude of the person is already fixated in music" (78). Weill here continues Wagner's and Appia's hope for an integrated notation of the *Gesamtkunstwerk,* albeit one with a critical spin: the musical *gestus* becomes a device for disciplining and channeling the theatrical mimesis of the actor.[37] Gestural music, music geared to a theatrical *gestus,* can be seen as yet one more form of diegesis directed at controlling mimesis; therefore, gestural music is diegetic music.[38]

While Brecht relied on Weill to define gestural music, he himself transposed *gestus* from acting to the domain of language and poetry, thus moving into — and against — the territory of Wagner's gestural poetics of alliteration.[39] Comparing two Shakespeare translations, Brecht notes, "How much more powerful were the actors' speeches when they spoke the rough verses of the old translation by Schlegel and Tieck, which was difficult to read" (19:396). Brecht favors those lines that have a "(changing, syncopated, gestural) rhythm" (19:395) instead of a smooth and regular one. However, Brecht does not stop at grounding a gestural rhythm in the body of the speaker but envisions, more generally, a language that bears the imprint of the body even when it is not actually spoken on stage: "A *gestus* can be put down in words alone . . . in that case certain gestures and mimic elements have marked that word and are easily legible in it (a devout bowing, a patting of the shoulder)" (15:409). Brecht's famous example of such gestural language is a sentence from Luther's Bible. In Brecht's opinion, the translation "If your eye is offending you: tear it out!" [Wenn dich dein Auge ärgert: reiß es aus!] is gesturally richer and purer than the hypothetical translation "tear out the eye that is offending you" [Reiße das Auge aus, das dich ärgert] (19:398). The gestural elements that Brecht singles out are the following: In the first sentence, the "illocutionary" act of the assumption, "If . . . ," is neatly separated from the act of giving advice. What matters is not only the strict separation of these two attitudes, which in the second sentence are separated by a comma, but also their effective sequencing. The first sentence begins with an assumption, is then followed by a small pause, indicated not by a comma but by a colon, to burst into the advice that comes, all of a sudden, as a surprise, emphasized by an exclamation mark. The sequence and the use of punctuation indicate that what is really at stake in the difference between these two sentences is their dramatic impact. The assumption hangs in the air; the expectation is heightened by a pause, which may be drawn out at will by the actor until the perplexing advice hits the listener over the head. The first sentence thus has built into its syntax and punctuation the drama of its performance onstage. Language is gestural to the extent that it is capable of translating this performance into its very syntax.

It is the gestural quality of language that enables it to control the stage. By virtue of including indications about the *gestus* of the actor, Brecht's text delimits the actor's freedom of interpretation. Like Weill's musical notation of gestures, Brecht's gestural speech thus becomes an extended stage direction through which Brecht retains control of actors and their modes of declamation. It is therefore important to recognize that the theatrical quality that comes along with the *gestus* of music and speech, the orchestra on the stage and the declamatory quality of syntax, is not meant to heighten the theatricality of the stage, amplifying its effects on the audience. On the contrary, it pits one dimension of the theater against the other, so that the stage ends up being composed of checks and balances that undercut, interrupt, and coopt the effectiveness of its different components.

Even though Brecht and Weill think of *gestus* as an ideal notation, for all practical purposes they have to settle for the second-best notation system: stage directions. Brecht's various *Modellbücher,* which document his work with literary scripts, choreographic sketches, and staging instructions, are studies in a more general choreography of *gestus,* which again is designed to interrupt the stage. The *Modellbuch* for Brecht's staging of Sophocles' *Antigone* is one of the most pertinent examples of this project, for Antigone must speak selected stage directions aloud, one of the instances when actors actually do speak about themselves in the third person; the textual diegesis of the stage direction becomes the performed diegesis of a selected *gestus.* Upon first entering the scene, Antigone exclaims: "But Antigone, the child of Oedipus, went to collect with a jug/the dust with which to cover up the body of Polyneikes/which the raging Tyrant had thrown before the birds and dogs."[40] This stage direction, spoken in the third person and the narrative past tense, dissociates the actor from the role and infuses her with a narrative function; in addition, however, it serves to expose most blatantly the *gestus* of this scene, namely, Antigone's loyal attempt to bury her brother in the face of Creon's rage. *Antigone* thus becomes a play about one gesture—the gesture of burying a brother—and this isolated and diegetically evoked act becomes the *gestus* of the play.

For Brecht, stage directions are part of the larger narrative category of the fable, which likewise is directed against the theater. In fact Brecht claims that he has stage directions spoken aloud "in order to subordinate the [theatrical] representation to the fable" (17:1218), and thus, one might add, mimesis to diegesis. The fable is the sum of intertitles and includes important stage directions, such as the one describing Antigone burying her brother. A literary and textual principle, the fable is made to control the meaning of theatrical mimesis because it captures the *gestus,* or sequence of *gestūs,* on which a play is built. The "subordination of theatrical representation to the fable" is the consequence of Brecht's mistrust of the theater, and his theater reform is the product of a unique and productive encounter between anti-theatricalism and a desire to reform the modern stage.

Gestus is thus poised between a theatrical principle and an anti-theatrical one. It describes music, language, and acting on a stage and thus seems to be continuous with the theatricalization Wagner undertook in the name of gesture. At the same time, however, *gestus* signals a resistance to the theater: through it, Brecht seeks to work against the theatricality of actors and the totalizing effects of the pervasive theatricalization on which Wagner had based his own notion of gesture. In this sense, the term *gestus* epitomizes what happens when anti-theatricalism returns to the stage, namely, a conflictual struggle with and against every dimension of the theater, from actors to music and from text to dialogue. Indeed, one might conclude that no one has a greater claim to modernism in the theater than Brecht because he, more than anyone, managed to come to terms, as Nietzsche had demanded, with Wagner's theatricality.

Samuel Beckett: 7
Actors in Barrels and Gestures in the Text

Barrels

> Beckett does not want his actors to act. . . . When they try to act,
> he becomes very angry.[1]

Reported by Jean Martin, who played Lucky in the premiere of *En Attendant Godot* at the Théâtre de Babylon, the above observation sums up an impression that emerges from every production Beckett ever directed: Beckett was, as S. E. Gontarski put it, "repelled by mimesis." And this repulsion, or aversion, was caused primarily by the figure of the actor.[2] Beckett knew too much about the resistance he would encounter in his crusade against imitative acting to rely on directors and actors to implement it. Instead, as in the tradition of anti-theatrical drama at large, this crusade became a central feature of Beckett's plays. We can even find Yeats's fantasy of putting actors in barrels enacted most literally in *Endgame,* where half the cast is confined to ashcans; initially all we see of their gestures is fingers folded across the rim of the can in the very precise and geometrical manner Beckett specifies in his stage directions and in his own productions of the play.

Endgame is only the beginning of a series of such confinements, continued in *Happy Days* (1961), which embeds Winnie up to her waist in a mound; in *Play* (1962), which calls for nothing but three urns to be arranged so that "from each a head protrudes, the neck held fast in the urn's mouth," the heads being "almost part of urns";[3] and finally in *Not I* (1972), which features a figure whose name and function is restricted to only one body part: Mouth. Before we begin to speculate what message about the human condition is being communicated here, we must recognize that these plays participate in a modernist anti-theatricalism that is primarily directed against the integrity of actors and their freedom of movement. The increasing erasure of the actor's gestures leads to a theatrical genre, now often dismissed and overlooked, in which the actors' gestures disappear entirely: the radio play.[4] Beckett devoted considerable attention to this genre from the beginning of his dramatic career with *All That Fall* (1956) to its end with *Rough for Radio II* (broadcast on BBC Radio 3 in 1976). After World

War II the BBC played a central role for almost all careers in the postwar theater of Britain, including those of Osborne, Pinter, Orton, Stoppard, and Wesker.[5] For Beckett the use of this medium was not only an economic choice, but an anti-theatrical one as well, a means of reducing actors, as in Yeats's barrel-therapy, to nothing but their speech and voices.[6]

The radio play was not, however, the exclusive medium for Beckett's desire to control or even do away with the gestures of actors. His plays for radio have their counterpart in a second lineage, characterized by an increasing reliance on gestures. This lineage culminates in the genre of pantomime, most prominently represented by Beckett's *Act Without Words I* and *Act Without Words II*. The radio plays, which might be called "plays without gestures," are thus only half the story and so must be understood in conjunction with these "plays without words," composed entirely of gestures. Through these two genres Beckett achieves a separation between voice and gestures akin to Brecht's "separation of the elements." The bifurcation into radio plays and pantomime can be considered Beckett's own way of radically dissembling the *Gesamtkunstwerk* in a manner that has its equal only in John Cage's *EUROPERAS,* a work that breaks down the totality of the *Gesamtkunstwerk* into single components, such as light, orchestra, costume, aria, and set, and randomly assigns them parts from opera history.

It is in Beckett's pantomimes that the struggle against actors becomes visible because here, in contrast to the radio plays, this struggle is enacted in front of our eyes, on the stage, through the actors themselves. *Act Without Words I,* for example, presents an actor who is being subjected to various stimuli in the form of objects that are lowered to the stage from above and a whistle that encourages the actor to react to those stimuli. The objects — scissors, a carafe, cubes, a lasso — might help him reach a carafe labeled "Water" suspended three yards aboveground. The actor begins to devise and carry out strategies of reaching the carafe only when he is cued by the blast of a whistle. The play's resemblance to a laboratory experiment is no accident since at that time Beckett was reading a study in behaviorism, *The Mentality of Apes,* by the psychologist Wolfgang Köhler. In the process of trying to condition, control, and manipulate actors the director even becomes a kind of puppeteer or marionette player, manipulating objects on strings.[7] In this pure theater of object-marionettes the human actor is the only figure on the stage who is not yet attached to strings. This experiment in control can be seen as Beckett's own version of the symbolist program for a theater of marionettes. Beckett was even known to mention occasionally the romantic text from which most symbolist and modernist advocates of the marionette take their point of departure, namely, Kleist's *Über das Marionettentheater.*[8] Indeed, Alan Schneider saw Beckett as the ultimate puppet master. "Actors feel like impersonal or even disembodied puppets of his [Beckett's] will."[9]

The end of *Act Without Words I* puts a slightly different spin on the program of controlling actors. The more this human actor fails to reach the carafe, the more he hesitates to react to the next whistle blast. Toward the end, he even ceases to move altogether: "The carafe descends. . . . He does not move. The carafe descends further. . . . He does not move. . . . Whistle from above. He does not move" (206). Thus the play comes to a halt, if not to an end, with the actor's resistance to further manipulation. Beckett is here confronting the ideal of a theater of objects with a theater of the actor, and the actor fails. The implied consequence we might draw here is that this stubborn actor should be kicked off the stage, leaving behind a theater of nothing but objects on strings. The solution to the actor, it seems, is not simply to make actors move like marionettes but, as Craig had recommended, to have these object-marionettes replace actors altogether.

The split between plays without words and plays without gestures is the most pervasive feature of Beckett's entire dramatic oeuvre and can be located even in his first, unpublished play, *Eleutheria*, written at the same time as *Waiting for Godot*. Here the stage is divided into two areas; in the first unfolds the "main action" of the play, while in the other unfolds the "marginal action," a silent pantomime composed of the "vague movements of a single character."[10] While the split between words and gestures is spatialized in *Eleutheria*, it is contained in single actors in *Waiting for Godot*. In the opening scene, for example, Estragon replies to Vladimir's question "A ditch! Where?" with the remark "Over there" (*Complete*, 11). This reply is preceded, however, by a startling stage direction: "without gesture." The deictic utterance "Over there" needs to be grounded in a context; it can only work if the speaker accompanies it with a pointing gesture or a related nonverbal marker. Beckett's explicit removal of any such gesture from the stage not only empties Estragon's answer of its communicative function but also introduces a rupture between words and gestures that becomes increasingly central for his plays.[11] This rupture must be seen as one of the strategies with which Beckett attacks the integrity of the actor. The association of verbal and corporeal expression and the expectation that they together represent a character are challenged by this dissociation of dialogue from gestural expressivity. Because we can no longer see functioning on the stage the habitual coordination of verbal deixis and gestures, actors are split into separate means of expression—mouth and expressive body—breaking down the coordination of speech and gesture on which their mimesis depends.

The dissociation of speech from gestures does not mean that Beckett sought to undermine speech. On the contrary, Beckett's stage resonates with the ceaseless babble of narrators and raconteurs who tell jokes, remember dreams and memories, and recount thoughts and poems. Winnie, in *Happy Days,* even quotes the opening diegetic line of Yeats's *At the Hawk's Well,* "I call to the eye of the mind" (146). Other representations of storytelling range from Pozzo's speeches in *Waiting for Godot* to such late pieces as *Ohio Impromptu* (1981), which is devoted entirely to depicting the act of reading and listening to a story. The reader, R, reads aloud to a listener, L, who interrupts the narrative flow and directs the reader by means of small gestures to repeat lines or to continue reading. Another prominent narrative sequences consists of Krapp's recorded autobiographical stories in *Krapp's Last Tape* (1958). In the radio play *Cascando* a narrative voice tells a story that is endlessly interrupted, rewound, and fast-forwarded. In *Endgame* Hamm thinks of himself as a literary speaker and a poet and never ceases to tell stories, thus living in a universe of his own literary creation, like Prospero, whom he quotes when he says, "Our revels now are ended" (120). A stage direction makes sure that Hamm adopts a "narrative tone" (116) when he tells his main story, which lasts for about four pages and is taken up again later in the play. Even old Nagg is something of a storyteller, although his repertoire is restricted to telling jokes with a "Raconteur's voice" (102). All these figures are the remains of a literary and narrative theater.[12]

While most of these instances of narration do not constitute diegetic strategies in the sense used in this study, namely, a framing, controlling, and interrupting of the mimetic space, some plays do actually approximate such a type of diegesis. *Rough for Theater I* (late 1950s), for example, transfers the mutual dependence of Hamm and Clov to the relation between a crippled man and a blind man, the latter an embodiment of the radio play itself. In exchange for being pushed around by the blind man, the crippled man would have to describe, diegetically, the visible world: "Of course if you wish me to look about me I shall, and if you care to push me about I shall try to describe the scene, as we go along" (230). Not surprisingly, this cooperation, and the diegesis that would have resulted from it, never quite gets under way. However, other radio plays do employ more systematically what is only suggested in *Rough for Theater I.* Sometimes diegesis not only makes up for the lack of visual theatrical mimesis in the radio play but is directed toward the mimesis of sound. In *Embers* (1959), for example, Beckett employs a pathological talker who keeps describing not so much the visual setup of the scene that we cannot see but the sounds that we already hear. *Embers* thus presents what one might call a diegesis of the radio play, a doubling of the direct, mimetic sound and a commenting, framing, controlling descriptive voice speaking in the present tense. Beckett's narrators and radio voices may not describe, coopt, and control mimesis as consistently and systematically as their counterparts in the closet drama and in the diegetic theater of Yeats do, but Beckett does gather the remains of the diegetic theater, including its epic actors, narrative attendants, its Compères and Commères, as well as their desire to control actors and theatrical mimesis.[13]

But Beckett did not rest all his hopes for interrupting mimesis on the technique of diegesis. Instead, he intervened in a variety of ways in order not only to control human actors but to break them into isolated movements and gestures. It is this investment in single movements and gestures that betrays Beckett's debt to Yeats and to symbolist drama more generally. The assumption that everything in the work of art must be precisely the way it is and that everything is (equally) significant and signifying is expressed nowhere as vehemently as in symbolism, for symbolism, more than any other movement, relies on the symbolizing promise of material substrates, such as Hérodiade's hair or Igitur's gesture of opening the book of his ancestors. When this attempt to unleash the symbolic potential of material entities is brought into the theater, stage props and gestures bear at least the same weight as speech.[14] The symbolist theater, from Maeterlinck and Strindberg to Yeats, is therefore a quintessential theater of objects and isolated gestures, a theater in which objects and gestures compose an ensemble of primary signifiers on which the play relies and in which it invests much of its signifying energy.[15]

The task of turning objects and gestures into signifying entities can only be accomplished if the objects and gestures begin to represent more than just themselves, if they transcend their immediate mimetic relation to the world. Attacking, suspending, or foreclosing the self-sufficient presence of objects and actors—making objects and the actors' bodies talk—is therefore the prerequisite for achieving symbolism in the theater. For this reason, symbolism had to devise ways of controlling actors, whether in the text (Mallarmé), in the theater (Craig), or in both (Yeats).[16] Beckett inherits this symbolist project in that he too is invested in a theater of objects and a theater of gestures, an investment that led him to insist that everything must be staged precisely the way he wrote it and that the few selected stage props and isolated gestures be realized with utmost precision. This obsession was described by one of his assistants as, perhaps in contrast to Craig's rude tirades, a "polite dictatorship."[17] If today we are surprised that Beckett would go so far as to threaten lawsuits when directors did not respect his stage directions, as in the case of JoAnne Akalaitis's 1984 production of *Endgame* at the A.R.T., we have to remember that this symbolist heritage places all of its hopes on single, isolated objects and gestures.[18]

Gestures

If symbolism creates single gestures and objects charged with meaning and significance, Beckett takes the form of symbolism, namely the act of isolating objects and gestures, without the belief in their symbolist meaning. Beckett's own stagings at the Schiller Theater and elsewhere show that what occupied most of his attention as a director was ensuring that actors repeated identical gestures and words to the point where they might almost appear to be driven by a Freudian repetition compulsion.[19] In *Endgame* Beckett even introduced additional isolated gestures that had to be repeated with fidelity throughout the play, for example, the precise way in which Clov turns away from Hamm, and in the Schiller Theater staging of *Krapp's Last Tape* he instructed Krapp to repeat the exact same gesture of anxiously looking over his shoulder at several moments in the play.[20] These and many similar repetitions indicate that Beckett's plays draw on the symbolist investment in isolated gestures without believing in their revalatory promise.

But Beckett does not take the emptied symbolist form as an end in itself. He holds onto what is otherwise only a kind of by-product of symbolism, namely, an emphasis on isolated gestures and objects that dissolves the human actor. Beckett's choreography of isolated gestures is in the service of breaking the actor into single gestures. In order to perceive how Beckett's texts work against actors we therefore need a systematic analysis of what he does with gestures. In fact isolated gestures constitute the basic units with which Beckett constructs his theater, and it is through their analysis that we can observe how he takes apart the integrity of the human body. Linguists distinguish between emblematic, or signifying, gestures on the one hand and expressive, or nonsignifying, gestures on the other.[21] Emblematic gestures acquire meaning through modes of cultural encoding that are stable within the boundaries of specific geographic areas, thus enabling them to function like linguistic signs. Examples of emblematic gestures are the V sign and the thumbs-up. A second group of emblematic gestures is mimetic gestures, which derive their semantic value from abstracted imitations of recognizable actions. Expressive gestures, in contrast, cannot be easily described in terms of a clearly defined, if culturally restricted, meaning; they accompany speech, illustrating but also confusing the spoken message, and they are located at the margin of attention of speaker and listener alike.

Many of the gestures represented in Beckett's stage directions are part of this second group of gestures and belong to the domain of suggestive corporeality that occurs incessantly at the margin of our attention. In particular, Beckett singles out habitual, minor gestures to furnish his plays. He specifies that Clov scratches his belly (108), that Estragon fumbles in his pockets (63), that Krapp peels bananas (216), that A (in *Rough for Theatre*) rummages in his papers (244), and that Hamm keeps folding and unfolding his handkerchief (133). When Beckett's characters have hands and the ability to move them, the stage directions take great pains to specify such unremarkable gestures, again and again, especially those having to do with objects of everyday life, such as boots, hats, parasols, etc. From his early essay on Proust—originally intended as a comparison of Proust and Joyce—Beckett kept returning to the question of habit and the habitual gestures of everyday life.[22] What Beckett did in his plays, however, was to isolate such habitual gestures, to take them out of their context in order to play them off against the integrity of both the character and the actor.

Beckett's plays are filled with such isolated, habitual gestures, but also with habitual objects. *Endgame,* for example, has Hamm take his toque off and put it back on repeatedly throughout the play, and the play refers, even in its title, to a game, claiming that actors and objects are nothing but pawns in a chess endgame.[23] *Endgame* is in fact structured around such recurring objects and gestures. The play opens when Hamm removes his handkerchief, which had been covering his face like a second curtain. One by one, all of the objects in the play—gaffe, dog, whistle—are introduced by the player Clov, who manipulates them for Hamm; one by one, Hamm discards them at the end and concludes the play by covering his face once more with his handkerchief, thus bringing this endgame to a closure. While Hamm thinks of nothing but his stories and speeches, Clov, who has learned all his words from Hamm and does not particularly care for them, is the agent who interacts with the objects of the play, picking them up, bringing them to Hamm, and tidying up the room. In fact one might consider the dichotomy between Hamm, the raconteur, and Clov, the stage manager, to be one more version of the split between gestures and objects, on the one hand, and speech, on the other, that structures Beckett's plays on every level.

Once these expressive, habitual and ordinary gestures and objects are brought to the level of representation, they are no longer what they were: they are extracted from their context, isolated, and lifted to the center of attention. The ordinary, defined as that to which we usually pay no attention, is thus represented for the price of losing its constitutive feature. Hats and the gestures associated with them, for example, are no longer determined by cultural codes such as those associated with greeting an acquaintance or expressing respect, nor are they worn for the protection of the head. Instead, they are integrated into a set of constructed rules governing the play. The introductory scene of *Waiting for Godot* establishes a particular routine that organizes Vladimir's hat and the gestures of taking it off and putting it on, all described by a stage direction in a concise and distanced manner: "[He takes off his hat, peers inside, feels about inside it, shakes it, puts it on again]" (12 and 37). The same sequence and wording appears verbatim at different moments in the text, creating a pattern against which all its repetitions can be measured.

Beckett does not content himself with isolating particular sequences of gestures and objects through repetitions. He also subjects them to rules that are generated within the play. For example, Lucky's hat begins to work like a magic switch that can turn off Lucky's performances once they get out of hand. The self-generating nature of such functions is highlighted when Vladimir and Estragon find Lucky's hat lying on the floor. This surplus hat promptly initiates a happy game of substitution that could potentially go on forever: faced with one hat too many, Vladimir and Estragon let the three hats circulate between them without knowing when to stop. This scene is borrowed from the Marx Brother's *Duck Soup*.[24] In Beckett's hands, however, it is formalized and integrated into a self-sufficient game that is meticulously described in a stage direction: "[He takes off Lucky's hat, peers into it, shakes it, knocks on the crown, puts it on again]" (67). A little later the sequence is repeated in yet another variation: "[Vladimir takes off his hat (Lucky's), peers inside it, feels about inside it, shakes it, knocks on the crown, puts it on again]" (88). The stage direction organizing the circulation not only choreographs this act but takes great care to indicate whose hat is put on whose head by whom, providing a specificity certainly lost on any audience and only perceptible to the reader of the text.[25]

Stage Directions

What we can begin to fathom here is that Beckett was thinking as much about the reader of his stage directions as about the viewer of their enactment, that he was concerned not only with isolating single gestures and objects but also with the language of the stage direction.[26] This means that we must read Beckett's dramatic oeuvre through his stage directions.[27] Beckett takes the textual apparatus of the drama and, in particular, stage directions as seriously as they were taken in the tradition of the closet drama. The type of reading for stage directions I propose here tries to reverse the practice of directors, actors, and theorists who disregard stage directions as secondary and dispensable additions to the primary text. My reading for stage directions takes its cue from Beckett's pantomimes, which must be read exclusively through stage directions because stage directions are all they consist of. Isolated gestures are Beckett's second, not secondary, language — the counterpart, and often competitor, of dialogue.

The representation of something as transient as gesture is particularly difficult, and for this reason it is at the level of textual representation that the real struggle for isolating gestures, for seizing them from the actors and from their habitual context, takes place. Since there is no established notation system for representing gestures, stage directions must develop their own idiosyncratic strategies of appropriating the turbulent expressivity of the actor and of transcribing isolated gestures into language.[28] In response to this challenge, Beckett's stage directions try to capture gestures, a diegetic project that might be considered to be a continuation of, even an ekphrasis of, the mimetic agency of actors. One way of expanding the vocabulary of gestures is by means of figurative speech, using tropes such as metaphor or comparison to designate gestures in stage directions. Such comparative stage directions dictate that there should be "Gestures of Estragon like those of a spectator encouraging a pugilist" (18), that Vladimir be "Squirming like an aesthete" (39), and that Hamm engage in "attitudes of prayer" (119). They all derive their descriptive power from the work of analogy. Beckett's obsession with precise stage directions, however, made such figurative strategies unsatisfactory, and for this reason they diminished over the course of his career.

More common and pervasive is a strategy of relating gestures to the internal states to which they presumably give expression. In the beginning of *Act Without Words I,* for example, a series of neutral and mechanical descriptions of gestures suddenly leads to a characterization that relies on interiority: "He goes towards left wing . . . thinks better of it . . . turns aside" (203). In the middle of Beckett's neutral choreographic indications the description of an internal state of mind—"thinks better of it"—becomes the shorthand for the external gesture. Similarly, *Act Without Words II* inserts such a psychological reference into a series of otherwise external descriptions: "A, wearing shirt, crawls out of sack, halts, broods, prays, broods, gets on his feet, broods" (209). The internal state of brooding is taken to be expressed by a pose or gesture, just as crawling, praying, and getting up are.[29] "Broods," like "thinks better of it" or "[after reflection]" (97), substitutes the mechanical, or metaphorical, description of a gesture for the internal state by which it is caused and therefore utilizes human interiority and psychology for its project in description.[30]

That Beckett would use interiority as motivation despite his general rejection of psychology in the theater results from a general difficulty of representing expressive gestures. It is this difficulty that forces Beckett to take recourse in psychological motivation and interiority because the discourse of the passions provides stock phrases and general categories that are able to capture gestures in language. Gestures, here, are described according to the passions by which they are supposedly produced and that they therefore seem to represent.[31] The discourse of affects, passions, and other modes of interiority evolved as part of the rhetorical tradition, from Quintilian to Delsarte's system of gestures in the nineteenth century, and it found new confirmation in Darwin's *Expression of the Emotions in Man and Animals*, which reconsidered the theory of affect and the passions that had emerged in the eighteenth and nineteenth centuries. Even psychoanalysis, for all its theories of repression, displacement, and substitution, continues the attempt to read interiority into gestures, for example, in Freud's studies on hysteria.[32]

Beckett's reliance on this tradition creates a tension within his work, for his characters give the impression of being pawns, automatons, or behaviorist guinea pigs and do not possess a complex of repressions, desires, ideals, a formative past, and debilitating traumata associated with a full interiority. It was the absence or near absence of those interior features that led Beckett to demand that actors not "act" or "mime" in ways that would imitate human beings. But the very language through which Beckett isolates gestures in stage directions ties these gestures back to the expressive unity that is the actor. This twofold or counteractive strategy, which is as much an aesthetic choice as a rhetorical necessity, might be responsible for our sense that the characters in Beckett's plays have been split into speech and gesture and have been awkwardly stitched back together. This double structure gives rise to what Enoch Brater terms "absurd actors," not so much because these actors suffer from inhuman physical conditions but because they must act as if they had been dissociated and then halfheartedly fixed again.[33] Beckett's plays don't get rid of human experience, passions, and feelings; rather they use them in the confined space of the parenthesis. When one reads Beckett's stage directions, one realizes that in his universe the passions do exist after all, but they are passions in parentheses.

In no play are the various dimensions of my inquiry—the control of actors, the split between gestures and speech, the desire to isolate gestures, and the problem of their representation—foregrounded more clearly than in *Not I* (1972). The play presents the monologue of a speaker whose name, Mouth, indicates a disembodied voice that is directed toward a second figure, called Auditor, who repeats a single gesture four times.[34] Mouth speaks but cannot gesture because, according to Beckett's direction, only the actor's mouth is visible. Auditor, on the other hand, only gestures and never speaks. Because Auditor's gestures are only repetitions of the same movement, they constitute the same, negative response to the same sequence of questions in the text: "what?. .who?. .no! . .she?. . [*Pause and movement*]." It is in the introductory paragraph preceding the entire body of the text that this gesture is described in detail: "Movement: this consists in simple sideways raising of arms from sides and their falling back, in a gesture of helpless compassion. It lessens with each recurrence till scarcely perceptible at third. There is just enough pause to contain it as Mouth recovers from a vehement refusal to relinquish third person" (375). Movement here is reduced to a single gesture, which is removed from the text in which it occurs and isolated at the beginning but whose precise description nevertheless relates back to the passions of the actor: "a gesture of helpless compassion."

Because typical stage directions fail to prescribe precise movements and gestures and are habitually, even systematically, ignored by directors and actors, Beckett, like Wagner, had to intervene directly to assure their enactment in the theater. Brian Miller, the actor playing Auditor in the London premiere of *Not I*, reported in a letter that "there are four gestures indicated in the script for the Auditor but I don't do them now because they couldn't be seen, so Beckett worked out a final bowing of the head into hands on the final — 'she . . . she.'"[35] The substitution of one gesture (raising of arms and their falling back) for another (bowing the head into hands) happened, according to Miller, as part of a traditional process of staging: something in the text has to be changed because the original does not work on a particular stage. Given Beckett's obsession with the precise enactment of his stage directions, this flexibility might be surprising. What this anecdote indicates is that what is more important than the actual gesture is the requirement that it appear sufficiently isolated and thus repeatable.[36] Only then can Beckett assure the disassemblage of the actor, only then can he hope to successfully wrest gestures from the actor and use them as building blocks for his theater.

Interrupted Action

Gestures compose only half of Beckett's inventory; the other half is dialogue. After analyzing what Beckett does to and with gestures and their representation, we must ask how isolated gestures relate to the speech of his characters. We can begin this inquiry by continuing our analysis of *Not I*, for this play epitomizes the complexities not only of Beckett's stage directions but also of their interaction with dialogue. In a standard dramatic text the flow of the dialogue is interrupted by an inserted stage direction, separated from the primary text by parentheses or brackets. Through the layout of the page the stage directions thus always interrupt the dialogue. It is Beckett's strategy to transpose this typographical arrangement — this interruption — onto the stage and thus to make it visible for the audience in the theater. In *Not I*, Mouth stops talking precisely at the moment when Auditor begins to gesture. Instead of being performed simultaneously on the stage, gestures and speech interrupt one another. This interruption, I argue, replicates the experience of reading a play by transposing onto the stage the fact that in the regular layout of the dramatic text a stage direction always interrupts dialogue. Delighting in the textual interruption of speech by stage directions, Beckett turns the classicist argument against stage directions upside down. Corneille, in particular, had argued against the insertion of stage directions into the dramatic text because it interrupted the flow of speech. Beckett builds entire plays around that very effect. One could say that he is the first to capitalize on the fact that stage directions are bracketed from (written or printed) dialogue, and he is also the first to turn these brackets into a principle for the *mise en scène*. Like Brecht and Stein, Beckett recreates on the stage the experience of reading a dramatic text and thus demonstrates what it means for a play to address simultaneously a general reader and an audience in the theater. In this sense, Beckett's dramaturgy and *mise en scène* revolve around the experience of reading plays in a manner that takes stage directions to be as important as dialogue. Beckett's plays, like the tradition of the modernist closet drama and the diegetic theater of Yeats and Brecht, thus register the institutionalization of the dramatic text as literature to be read.

The sequential arrangement of gestures and speech—stage direction and direct speech—is not just an accidental feature of one text but a structuring principle of many of Beckett's plays. Moving back from *Not I*, we can perceive its effects in a slightly different form in the earlier and more traditional *Happy Days*. From the beginning the possibility of gesturing is constrained for Winnie by the fact that she is buried up to her waist in a mound.[37] Since her body's motion is restricted to hand movements, the gestures and movements that remain initiate a drama between body and speech. From Winnie's long introductory monologue onward, stage directions constantly interrupt the stuttering flow of words. However, Beckett also puts a new spin on this system of interruption: when Willie suddenly joins in the monologue, the constellation of speech interrupted by gesture is reversed: as soon as Willie begins to read, Winnie's gestures are frozen and interrupted, for the stage direction demands: "[arrests gesture as Willie reads]" (142). Here it is not gestures that interrupt the text but text that interrupts Winnie's gestures. This new constellation is continued over several pages and reappears throughout the text in different forms with slight variations. The different interrupted gestures—raising the head (four times), fanning (three times), rummaging in bag (one time), laying down glasses (one time), and putting a hat in a bag (one time)—mark moments when speech intrudes onto the gestures of the listener. This antagonistic relation between words and gestures is transformed only once into a relation of mutual reinforcement.[38] When Winnie resumes her monologue, she lets her parasol wander from one hand to the other in an apparently arbitrary manner, disconnected from the content of what she is saying. At one moment, however, when she is reflecting about "changing conditions," the word *changing,* although it has no relation to the parasol, triggers its change from one hand to the other, the stage direction reading "[She transfers parasol to left hand]" (153). This external parallelism only demonstrates the lack of an internal connection between gesture and speech, a humorous exception to the rule of mutual interruption.

We can trace this sequential and textual form back yet one step further, to *Waiting for Godot,* not so much to the original text as to Beckett's own 1975 staging at the Schiller Theater in Berlin. As we can see from his extensive rewritings documented in his notebooks and scripts, Beckett inserted into the text more than twenty interruptions—which he called *Wartestellen,* "places of waiting"—and twelve more extensive interruptions designated by the more traditional name *tableaux,* one of which refers to an actual painting, namely, *Zwei Männer betrachten den Mond,* by the romantic painter Caspar David Friedrich.[39] Some tableaux are already marked in the original published text, but in his 1975 staging Beckett increased their number substantially, imposing onto the play a much more developed version of the stop-and-go rhythm of gestures and speech that characterizes his later plays. It is as if in *Waiting for Godot* Beckett found it necessary to thematize what later would become the formal technique of interruption: places of waiting *(Wartestellen)* will take the place of waiting for Godot. Beckett's interruptions, like Stein's static ekphrasis, are thus directed against what since Aristotle had been the purpose of drama: the representation of action. It is a strategy that uses the dramatic text against the theater and stage directions against the integrity of actors. In this, Beckett draws on the anti-theatrical repertoire of the closet drama and of the modernist diegetic theater even though he may not share entirely all the anti-theatrical obsessions of his predecessors.

What I call Beckett's anti-theatricalism are the effects that have led some critics to claim that Beckett's oeuvre constitutes a retreat from politics, if not a return to *l'art pour l'art.* Indeed, Beckett's attacks on both the character and the actor, as well as the enclosed spaces in which so many of his plays take place, do suggest a retreat of the theater into some sort of theatrical closet, into a space closed off from the world of the audience. And it is true that Beckett was not a promoter of a political project comparable to German nationalism, Irish nationalism, or international socialism, nor of their theatrical counterparts, Bayreuth, the Abbey Theatre, or the Berliner Ensemble.

We owe it to Adorno's essay "Trying to Understand *Endgame*" that such a view of Beckett's theater as a retreat into an existential space of "closed doors" is only half the story. The other, more important half is that all of Beckett's strategies of interruption and retreat, everything I characterize as effects of his anti-theatrical impulse, are in fact responses to this world outside, if mostly in terms of resistance. Adorno sees in Beckett's theater—in his attack on the character, the individual, and the actor—a negative representation of this world.[40] But what, we must ask, does Beckett represent through such a negative attitude? Continuing the argument advanced in this book, it is possible to specify this negative relation as one directed against the theatrical politics of the thirties and forties, of which the Soviet agitprop spectacles and the Nuremberg rallies are only the two most conspicuous and well-known examples. Decades of public mass theater could only increase the suspicion of the theater's kinship to the public sphere; modernist stage fright, so to speak, had acquired a particular historical justification. From this point of view, Beckett's negative, anti-theatrical strategies, his interruption of the stage, the disintegration of actors and their senses, his diegetic control of the mimetic space, and his obsessive control of actors is not a formalistic turn against traditional theater but a response to a theatricalized mass politics. More particularly, we can assume that like Brecht and Yeats, Beckett distrusted the theater, its mode of representation and its seductive power, which he had seen at work in the decades before he turned toward the theater. Compared with Yeats's and Brecht's, Beckett's destruction of the theater is the most severe. After two decades of terrifyingly theatricalized mass politics, the attack on the theater had become an aesthetic, but also a historical, necessity.

Lucky Dancing

If Salomé's dance is the figure for poetic theater, for Mallarmé as well as for Yeats, then Beckett offers us his own dancer, Lucky from *Waiting for Godot,* as an indication of what has happened to the symbolist theater, the closet drama and the diegetic theater. Indeed, we can see Lucky's dance as a response to Yeats's "Plays for Dancers," to Mallarmé's textual dance, and even to Joyce's figure of the dancing master Maginni. Beckett was familiar with Yeats's "Plays for Dancers" and *Ulysses* alike, as he was with turn-of-the-century reforms in dance, in particular with Jacques-Dalcroze and his eurhythmics at Hellerau, a school Beckett visited repeatedly and to which he refers, ironically, as "Schule Dunkelbrau" in his *Dream of Fair Middling Women.* Having been instructed to dance for the amusement of Didi and Gogo, as well as of his master, Pozzo, Lucky fabricates a dance that is a complete failure, the bare remnants of a once glorious art. Pozzo muses: "He used to dance the farandole, the fling, the brawl, the jig, the fandango,

and even the hornpipe. He capered. For joy. Now that's the best he can do"
(39). Like Mallarmé or Joyce's Maginni, Pozzo here refers to an established
vocabulary of movement. However, Lucky's actual dance is a distortion of
these models to which Pozzo can refer conveniently by proper name; unlike the fandango and the fling, Lucky's dance does not have a name and
cannot be properly represented. As a consequence, Pozzo asks Vladimir
and Estragon, "Do you know what he calls it?" a remark that induces them
to come up with names that try to capture the nature of the dance: "Estragon: The Scapegoat's Agony. / Vladimir: The Hard Stool" (39). Unlike the
proper names of established dances, the names Vladimir and Estragon propose are metaphoric associations. Is Lucky, for Estragon, the scapegoat
and his dance the scapegoat's agony? Does Lucky impersonate a scapegoat
and the respective expression of agony?

The thematic but also symptomatic difficulty of naming Lucky's dance
led Beckett to an unusual number of revisions. Originally, Estragon's first
name for the dance was "La mort du canard" [the death of the duck], which
was later replaced with "la mort du lampiste" (the *lampiste* is the lowest em-
ployee of the railway system), which Beckett then translated into the final
"Scapegoat's Agony." Vladimir's name for the dance, "The Hard Stool,"
does not originally show up and is only later inserted to replace "Le cancer des Vieillards," which literally means "the cancer of old men." In yet
another version it is replaced again, this time by dancing "devant le buf-
fet" [in front of the buffet], an idiom that means "to starve."[41] Beckett here
seems to participate actively in the debate between Vladimir, Estragon,
and Pozzo about the nature and name of Lucky's dance, and he appears as
unable to solve its mystery as the audience he assembles on the stage.

Even though Pozzo, authoritative as always, responds to the two propo-
sitions made by Vladimir and Estragon with the remark, "The Net. He
thinks he's entangled in a net" (39), the question of Lucky's dance remains
unresolved on the level of interpretation and naming. Pozzo, presumably,
used to have absolute control over Lucky, but those days, if they ever existed, are long over. Lucky, although a truly theatrical performer in this
talent show and therefore the only figure in the play who is also an actor,
is a grotesque double of the ideal actor, who gestures only when told to.
And despite all of his control, Pozzo cannot turn Lucky's dance into anything like Yeats's climactic dances or Craig's impersonal "art of the theatre."
Lucky thus anticipates a series of failed performers that populate Beckett's
stage, including all those mimes who refuse to be trained and who refuse
to perform.

As we ponder the utter failure of Lucky's dance and the different failures
it brings with it—the failure of description, of naming, of interpretation,

of imitation, of actors' training and of performance — we cannot but take it as an indication that Beckett knew the limits of the desire to control actors on the level of actor's training, of dramaturgy, and of stage directions. If Salomé's dance is the figure for the power of poetic theater and the glory of its textual diegesis, then Lucky's dance might be taken to be the figure for a theater struck by a radicalized anti-theatricalism. Indeed the audience, Vladimir and Estragon, will end up almost beating this dancer to death. Such an allegorical reading might be at odds with the critique of the human figure advanced by the anti-theatrical theater, but then again, Lucky is a figure already undone or else a figure in the process of breaking down.

Epilogue

It is tempting to regard what is generally called postmodernism as the ultimate triumph of theatricalism over the modernist anti-theatrical impulse. And yet, a cursory look at the dramatic literature of the last decades reveals the continuing persistence of many features that characterize the modernist diegetic theater. Peter Handke, for example, bases entire plays on the collision between diegesis and mimesis, most clearly so in his most well known play, *Kaspar* (1968), in which an offstage voice controls the scene and its human actors. Richard Foreman's play *Pandering of the Masses: A Misrepresentation* (1975) also employs an offstage voice, whose purpose resides in a similar combination of commentary and control. Peter Weiss's celebrated *Marat/Sade* (1964) installs an intermediary commentator-narrator, borrowed from Brecht, to whom Weiss acknowledges a direct influence. But Weiss's play is also related to Yeats's musicians and attendants in that this narrator-commentator frames the mimetic space of the play and conditions its reception. Suzan-Lori Parks's *America Play* (1990–93) demands "A great hole, In the middle of nowhere. The hole is an exact replica of the Great Hole of History," without giving us any indication how such a hole might be represented on a stage. And Heiner Müller's *Hamletmaschine* (1977) enacts the confrontation between Hamlet and Gertrude through a figure called "the player of Hamlet," who describes meticulously his own actions and Gertrude's reaction in an entirely diegetic manner: "Now I bind your hands . . . . Now I tear up the bridal veil. Now you have to cry. Now I smear on the pieces of your dress the earth my father has become."[1] As in the plays of Gertrude Stein, there are no stage directions specifying either the *dramatis personae* or their mimetic actions on the stage. The total disregard these texts show not only for the requirements of the stage but also for mimetic, theatrical representation more generally seems to place them in the modernist anti-theatrical tradition. And yet, they operate on the stage with astonishing ease. Has the theater, after decades of anti-theatrical, diegetic theater, learned to accommodate the modernist resistance to theatrical representation?

One reason why diegesis no longer seems to effect a resistance to the

theater is registered in Robert Wilson's *The Day Before: death, destruction &*
Detroit III (1999), which "stages" extracts from Umberto Eco's novel *The*
Island of the Day Before by having an actor (Fiona Shaw) read aloud from
the book and thus describe what is simultaneously represented, albeit in
an imaginative manner, on the stage. Novels have been turned into dramatic texts for a long time, with particular frequency in the nineteenth century, but Wilson brings the novel onto the stage without any adaptation,
thus merging diegetic theater, the closet drama, and stage directions into
a theater that circumvents the dramatic text entirely. If even a novel can
be accommodated by the theater, then no dramatic text, no matter how
novelistic its stage directions, can ever hope to resist the theater. Perhaps
after a century of attacks the dramatic text no longer has the absolute authority it once had, and so the strategies of the modernist closet drama—
mixing stage direction and direct speech (Mallarmé, Stein, Joyce); refus-
ing to assign speech to specific *dramatis personae* (Mallarmé, Stein); narrative
stage directions (Joyce)—no longer appear to be viable anti-theatrical devices.[2] And an audience used to supertitles in opera and subtitles in foreign-
language theater is not likely to be stunned when it sees Brechtian text written across the stage.

The fate of the closet drama and also of diegetic theater is perhaps
best exemplified in the work of the Wooster Group, which has in fact
staged closet dramas such as Stein's *Dr. Faustus Lights the Lights* (1998–99).
Unlike Thomson, the Wooster Group did not feel the need to transform
Stein's original text into a libretto, to distinguish between stage directions
and direct speech, or to turn the play into some more personal or human
drama. They took the play as it was, with its full anti-theatrical force. They
were able to do this because, in contrast to Thomson and Grosser, they
were already in possession of a *mise en scène* directed against the integrity
of human impersonation. It is not Stein's anti-theatrical text that brings
about the depersonalization of the stage but rather what could be more
broadly called the technological mediation or mediatization of the theater.
Through sound loops and various types of manipulation, the actors' voices
are estranged and dissociated from the speaking bodies; and video monitors not only double these bodies but hide them at least partially, replacing the live actors with temporally and spatially estranged images of themselves. Often the duplicating voices and gestures are not even the actors'
own. Thus mediated, their performance is not directed exclusively or even
primarily at the audience. Instead, these so-called actors keep their eyes
on monitors through which they remain in contact with their mediatized
doubles as well as with the video engineers responsible for their transmis-
sion, located somewhere beyond the horizon of the audience. The appara-

tus of reproduction thus mediates not only the actors' corporeal presence but also the audience's relation to the stage, for the audience almost begins to resemble that of a crowd attending the shooting of a film.[3] Like many contemporary theater companies, the Wooster Group uses sound and film technology not just to alter the theater but to evacuate its very core: the presence of live performers on a stage.[4]

All of these features adhere to Walter Benjamin's analysis of the destruction of (theatrical) aura through reproducible mediatization. As Philip Auslander has argued, extending and modifying Benjamin's argument, this pervasive mediatization means that we can no longer define theater and performance art through a concept of pure, live presence based on the unchallenged presence of the live human actor on a stage; instead many forms of contemporary theater and performance present a mixture of mediatization and liveness.[5] This development has profound implications for the fate of modernist anti-theatricalism. On a stage fractured by monitors and sound technology, material mimesis is no longer the governing mode of theatrical representation; in this sense the mediatized stage makes obsolete the modernist call for a resistance to the "personal," "auratic," and "mimetic" theater. The "live present" and "thereness" that worried Stein have been broken apart; Brecht's separation of the elements has been completed beyond his wildest hope; speech and acting body are more dissociated than in Yeats's separation of mimesis and diegesis. We might even go so far as to say that the mediatized stage is in fact the continuation of diegetic theater by other, technological means, that our contemporary stage has fully absorbed textual resistance and diegesis into its own technological repertoire.

The fact that the mediatized stage was capable of absorbing both diegetic theater and the closet drama allows us to draw two conclusions: First, it shows the extent to which the mediatized stage continues a modernist anti-theatrical impulse through technological means. Second, it allows us to use the contemporary stage as a lens through which to look back at modernist anti-theatricalism. From such a vantage point, the convergence between the closet drama and the mediatized stage suggests that the closet drama and the diegetic theater are themselves part of a history of mediatization. Indeed, text and diegetic speech are devices through which theatrical representation is estranged, controlled, framed, fragmented, and fundamentally questioned in its material integrity; and through textual or diegetic mediation the liveness and presence of the human actor, and with it the aura of the theater, is under attack. Moreover, text achieves this anti-auratic mediatization precisely by virtue of being, like film and sound technology, reproducible. It may not seem entirely accurate to align text with modes of audio and video reproduction, and it is true that textual description and diegesis do not constitute a recording in the same sense that film and audio recording do. Nevertheless, text translates the space of the stage and its actors into a nonvisual, abstracted, and highly codified medium; altering what it transcribes, it transposes a live event into a fixed medium just as audio and video reproductions do. As Benjamin notes, text was the first fully reproducible medium, and the system of printed literature constitutes a domain of art detached from its auratic origin. Like the new media, text therefore represents the intrusion of the reproducible into the auratic theater. The closet drama and Brecht's use of text on stage, as well as the privileging of text over theatrical representation, thus can be understood to be devices directed against the theatrical aura. The closet drama is an anti-auratic art form in the age of textual reproducability.

The structural similarity between text and technological mediatization also emerges when one considers the reception of the closet drama and of text on stage, which attracted the critique of theater enthusiasts such as Craig and Artaud and were used in the anti-theatrical tradition for that reason. Upon its introduction, the technology of writing caused anxieties about reproducibility comparable to those associated with the new media today.[6] The convergence between the closet drama and the mediatized stage can be seen most clearly in the work of Brecht and Beckett, both of whom translated the anti-auratic effects of radio and film into different forms of textual and diegetic mediation. We can speculate, then, that diegetic speech and text constituted a conscious and strategic use of mediatization against the liveness of the theater, in particular the type of liveness grounded in the presence of human actors and human audiences.[7]

In order to understand the transformation of a modernist anti-theatricalism we must look not only at the role of the live human actor in current practices of *mise en scène* but also at the other component of modernist anti-theatricalism, namely, its resistance to the theater's collaborative production and collective reception. For while the mediatized stage suggests some continuation of modernist anti-theatricalism, it remains to be seen whether contemporary theater subscribes to all the values of modernist anti-theatricalism. And indeed, rather than reducing collaboration, as many modernist directors had tried to do, most directors in the second half of the twentieth century celebrated the value of collaboration. The first wave of such valued collaborations can be detected in early avant-garde performances, such as dadaism, which pitted collaboration and improvisation against the single, isolated artist figure favored by the closet drama and the director's theater. By virtue of forming collective movements, the avant-garde generally had a more active stake in collaboration; this dedication to collaboration is in fact one of the reasons why it subscribed to the value of theatricality in the first place. A second wave of collaboration began in the sixties, most passionately practiced by the Living Theater. Here the value of collaboration was not only that it destroyed the myth of the isolated artist, still so dominant in high modernism and in particular in the anti-theatrical tradition, but also that it promised to serve as a model for building communities and new forms of living. While the political investment in collaboration has perhaps decreased, contemporary groups such as the Wooster Group or the Elevator Repair Service still value the collaborative process of creation, even if they do not hope to derive from it a transformation of everyday life.[8]

One can see a similar shift away from modernist anti-theatricalism in the theater's attitude toward collective reception, the assembled audience. Perhaps because the theater is no longer the dominant art form, the audience no longer seems a potentially unruly public. One might even suspect that the underlying idea of the *theatrum mundi* as a political model has been replaced by what Guy Debord called "the spectacle," which is derived, despite its name, from the idea of the image, and not the theater. So while contemporary theater continues the modernist mediation of the living actor, it has by and large abandoned the modernist ambivalence about collaborative production and collective reception.

The closet drama has not had a continual genre history. It has appeared and disappeared depending on both the history of writing and the history of the theater. And so one might speculate that the mediatized stage may yet breed a new form of textual resistance. This resistance would not be a text's resistance to theatrical impersonation, collaborative production, and collective reception, but the resistance of one form of mediation (and mediatization) to another. But what sort of textual mediation would be capable of responding to, let alone resisting, the mediatized stage? And what value would motivate such a resistance?

Notes

Introduction

1. The newer medium film here exposes an anxiety that is particular to the older medium theater.

2. Barish, *Antitheatrical Prejudice*. Within this frame of moral prejudice one can find various subforms, such as the fear that the stage might be a space of rule breaking, that the theater actually attracts whores and pickpockets, a fear that emerges in many Elizabethan tracts and extends all the way to Hitchcock's teasing bait of the actor, and more particularly the stage diva, as murderer.

3. At the end of his history of anti-theatricalism as prejudice, Barish himself notices the presence of anti-theatricalism within the theater and hesitantly attributes to it a more productive role. Nevertheless, Barish seems disturbed by this internalized anti-theatricalism and refers to it as a temporary extremism that will give way to a return to more traditional, and therefore less anti-theatrical, types of theater: "After the disturbances of the nonsense theaters . . . and the disruptive maneuvers of fringe and underground groups, the dominant sources of theatrical energy seem still to be the familiar, traditional ones: representation of the observed and the actual, intelligible configurations of character, narrative coherence, meaningful patterns of action" (464).

4. Scheppard, *Modernism—Dada—Postmodernism*. The shift within the field of modernism away from using the term modernism

in the singular is also testified to by the annual "New Modernisms" conference.

5. Some scholars have reacted to the consecration of a small canon of high modernism by declaring that modernism should be used only as a period marker, with no consecrating or otherwise charged meaning to it. Indeed, such a view is appealing because it promises to "solve" in one stroke all the difficult questions we have been asking about modernism. This approach is problematic, however, because the very act of creating *one* period—including *one* period that would house a plurality of modernisms—relies on some form of unity, even if, in a second step, this unity is questioned and broken into different strands. What this means for the study of modernism is not that we have to go back to simply repeating and perpetuating the small canon of high modernism; our hypostasized unity of modernism does not have to be that of the modernists or their earliest theorists. But it does means that the fantasy of modernism as a pure period marker is ultimately only the counterpart to the attempt to hold onto the small canon of high modernism. What we should do, in my view, is take into account the fact and the manner in which modernists consecrated a particular work of art and the effects of this consecration on those phenomena within modernism that could not, or did not want to, submit to it. In the last analysis the notions of one modernism and of a multitude of modernisms are just two ways of

stating the same problem from opposite points of departure, and they are both valid as long as their dependence on one another is kept in mind. It is in this spirit that I speak about a specific tradition within modernism, namely, anti-theatrical modernism, relate to it a pro-theatrical modernism, and then go on to show how these two strands interact.

6. Friedrich Nietzsche, "Der Fall Wagner," in *Richard Wagner in Bayreuth, Der Fall Wagner, Nietzsche contra Wagner,* 117; hereafter cited in the text as "Fall." Unless otherwise noted, translations are mine.

7. See esp. Michael Fried's reviews from the 1960s, now collected in *Art and Objecthood.*

8. Fried, "Art and Objecthood," 19.

9. In "Art and Objecthood" Michael Fried writes: "Exactly how the movies escape theater is a difficult question, and there is no doubt but that a phenomenology of the cinema that concentrated on the similarities and differences between it and stage drama—e.g. that in the movies the actors are not physically present, that the screen is not experienced as a kind of object existing in the specific physical relation to us—would be rewarding ("Art and Objecthood," reprinted in Fried, *Art and Objecthood,* 171).

10. Walter Benjamin, "Das Kunstwerk im Zeitalter seiner technischen Reproduzierbarkeit," in Benjamin, *Illuminationen,* 150 (originally published in French in 1935).

11. Adorno, *Philosophie der neuen Musik,* 150.

12. Adorno, *Ästhetische Theorie,* 181.

13. Adorno, "Versuch das Endspiel zu verstehen."

14. This latent anti-theatricalism might also explain Adorno's interest in and admiration of Hugo von Hofmannsthal, the writer of lyrical closet dramas, which has surprised many commentators.

15. Roach, *Player's Passion.* See also Worthen, *Idea of the Actor.*

16. Following a semiotic vocabulary, Anne

Ubersfeld *(Lire le téâtre II)* and others have observed that the theater is bound to the iconic rather than the symbolic sign without discussing the consequences of this circumstance for the tradition of anti-theatricalism.

17. One example is Umberto Eco's *Limits of Interpretation,* 101–10. Erika Fischer-Lichte devised a semiotic model that takes this process of transformation as a double or dialectical one in which the actor's body is transformed into a sign and the textual character is transformed into a body (Fischer-Lichte, *Show and the Gaze of Theater,* 294). Anne Ubersfeld emphasizes the tension between the presence of live actors and the imperative of turning them into signs (Ubersfeld, *Lire le théâtre II,* 36–37).

18. Eco, *Theory of Semiotics,* 217.

19. Lawrence, *Sea and Sardinia,* 201–2.

20. Fuchs, *Death of Character.* Marco de Marinis sees in the twentieth century a tradition of an "actor's theater" [*teatro d'attore*] that emerges in response to the director's theater. This "actor's theater" can be seen as a reaction to the modernist critique of the actor (De Marinis, *In cerca dell' attore*).

21. The term *theatricalism* has been used by, among others, Harold B. Segel in *Twentieth Century Russian Drama* and Elinor Fuchs in *Death of Character.*

22. This celebration of theatricalism could be compared, perhaps, to the baroque *theatrum mundi,* whose importance for expressionism was first recognized by Walter Benjamin in his *Ursprung des deutschen Trauerspiels.*

23. Fuchs, *Die Schaubühne der Zukunft.*

24. Erika Fischer-Lichte considers Fuchs's notion of the re-theatricalization of the theater as the central maxim of early-twentieth-century theater reform (see Fischer-Lichte, *Geschichte des Dramas;* see also her more recent *Show and the Gaze of Theater*). While Fischer-Lichte emphasizes the manner in which the re-theatricalization is directed against older forms of theater, such as psychological or illusionist theater (ibid.,

115 ff.), I am particularly interested in its relation to anti-theatricalism.

25. "Tutto è teatrale quando ha valore" (Marinetti, *Teoria e invenzione futurista,* 117).

26. Peter Bürger's classic argument in *Theorie der Avantgarde* holds that the avant-garde tried to overcome the separation of art and life, while modernism holds onto the bourgeois institution of art. While I do not agree with all aspects of Bürger's theory, the perspective offered by a genealogy of theatricality allows us to recast some elements of Bürger's distinction between high modernism and the historical avant-garde in terms of anti-theatricalism and pro-theatricalism.

27. Surprisingly, the category of the theater has been absent from a whole range of seminal studies on the avant-garde, from Renato Poggioli through Peter Bürger to Richard Murphy. Marjorie Perloff is one of the few critics to have consistently connected the tradition of literary modernism to that of the theatrical avant-garde. Perloff discusses the tensions between the literary and other media in her study on futurism, *Futurist Moment;* in her attention to Cage's poetry in performance *(Poetics of Indeterminacy);* and in her book *Radical Artifice.* The other exception is Manfredo Tafuri's *Sphere and the Labyrinth.* Otherwise, only more local studies on futurism and dadaism or analyses devoted specifically to avant-garde theater, such as Richard Schechner's theory of performance, pay attention to the avant-garde's obsession with the theater (see Aronson, *American Avant-garde Theatre;* Berghaus, *Italian Futurist Theatre;* Meltzer, *Dada and Surrealist Performance;* Jelavich, *Munich and Theatrical Modernism;* Segel, *Turn-of-the-Century Cabaret;* Calinescu, *Faces of Modernity;* and Schechner, *Performance Theory).*

28. One example is Davis, "Post-Performancism." Bonnie Marranca's essay "Performance/Art/Theatre," while also critical of Fried, is an ex-ample of a theater criticism that does not fall easily into the theatricalism/anti-theatricalism polarization and instead thinks critically about theater and performance.

29. Vendler, *Yeats's Vision and the Later Plays;* Winters, *Poetry of W. B. Yeats.*

30. Derrida, *La dissémination.* A somewhat similar effect of Derrida's insistence on writing appears in his reading of Artaud, whose fantasy of a text-free theater he reads as an impossible project realized only in the form of writing (Derrida, *L'écriture et la différence).* While de Man notices the pressures that are put on literary modernism by such figures as Antonin Artaud, he does not see that the weapon with which Artaud attacks literary modernism is *theatricality,* a term precisely calibrated to exposing modernism's aversion to the theater (de Man, *Blindness and Insight,* 161–62).

31. Patrice Pavis, "Towards a Semiology of Mise-en-Scène?" in *Languages of the Stage,* 131–61; Ubersfeld, *Lire le théâtre I.*

32. Continuing the observation made by Andreas Huyssen that Adorno's critique of Wagner is a critique of what we call postmodernism (Huyssen, *After the Great Divide,* 42), one might say that the feature postmodernism shares with Wagner's phantasmagorias is a belief in the value of theatricality.

33. Adorno, *Ästhetische Theorie;* Jameson, "Reflections on the Brecht-Lukács Debate." Lukács charges modernism with solipsism in *Wider den mißverstandenen Realismus,* 28.

34. This tradition of a director's theater, from Craig through Appia to Robert Wilson, tends to stylize Wagner as a hero of directorial control, a man capable of uniting the functions of composer, poet, stage director, scene designer, acting coach, and theorist of the *Gesamtkunstwerk.*

35. Fried, *Absorption and Theatricality;* idem, *Art and Objecthood.*

36. Fried discusses the difference between being a reader and being a member

of an audience in his *Absorption and Theatricality.*

37. Habermas, *Strukturwandel der Öffentlichkeit,* 88. This idea of the theater as a training ground for political action was applied by Augusto Boal and his concept of the forum theater.

38. Sennett, *Fall of Public Man.*

39. Rousseau, *Lettre à M. d'Alembert.*

40. Benjamin, *Illuminationen,* 169.

41. Williams, *Politics of Modernism.*

42. Richard Wagner, "Das Kunstwerk der Zukunft," in *Gesammelte Schriften und Dichtungen,* 3:132.

43. My analysis of the closet drama and its relation to the theater is a continuation of Benjamin Bennett's analysis of the relation between dramatic literature and the theater to which it remains tied (Bennett, *Theater as Problem*). I argue that this tie must be expanded to the closet drama, even though the closet drama rejects the theater.

44. Lukács, *Entwicklungsgeschichte des modernen Dramas.*

45. The point of reference for arguments in favor of reading drama is always Shakespeare. Even a recent collection of essays entitled *Reading Plays: Interpretation and Reception,* edited by Hanna Scolnicov and Peter Holland, takes Shakespeare as the paradigm for the act of reading drama.

46. Alan Richardson *(Mental Theater)* and Jane Ruth Heller *(Coleridge, Lamb, Hazlitt, and the Reader of Drama)* both point out the importance of Shakespeare idolatry for the romantic closet drama. In general, studies on romanticism are the only ones that pay attention to the closet drama. See also Simpson, *Closet Performances.* The continuation of this genre in modernism has received little attention.

47. One reason why Greek tragedy and Shakespeare were seen as reading drama early on has to do with the relation between the closet drama and poetry. Up until the nineteenth century almost all intentional, as opposed to retrospectively categorized, closet

dramas were poetic dramas, and they were tragedies. Poetic, or verse, drama was pushed in the direction of the closet drama when prose began to win the favor of theatergoing publics, and poetic drama, usually tragedy, was therefore more likely to be read. The history of the poetic drama and the history of the closet drama no longer ran on parallel tracks when prose drama and comedy began to appear in the genre of the closet drama as well, as they did in the case of the prose comedies of Alfred de Musset, which were not intended for the stage.

48. Friedrich Nietzsche recognized that the new dramatic genre Plato invented could be seen as a precursor of the novel (Nietzsche, *Die Geburt der Tragödie,* 112), an argument that Bakhtin would make later (*Dialogic Imagination,* 22), without attributing it to Nietzsche. Nietzsche's view of the novel as a mixture of tragedy and comedy in fact puts Bakhtin's theory of the novel in a nutshell, describing as a "cynical" approach to the limits of style and genre (122) what Bakhtin would describe as irony. Benjamin sees in Plato's dramatic form a precursor to the German *Trauerspiel* (Benjamin, *Ursprung des deutschen Trauerspiels,* 94). Martha Nussbaum refers to Plato's dialogues as "antitragic theater" (Nussbaum, *Fragility of Goodness,* 122ff.), without, however, reflecting on their resistance to the stage, which becomes visible when one recognizes Plato's dialogues as closet dramas.

49. Aristotle, *Poetics* 1447b. All references to Aristotle are to this edition.

50. Jonas Barish and other commentators have stressed the contradictory nature of Plato's generic choice, a contradiction typical among those philosophers who use theatrical terminology and therefore must keep the actual theater at a distance.

51. Hofmannsthal, *Sämtliche Werke,* 377.

52. Segel, *Body Ascendant;* Fischer-Lichte, *Show and the Gaze of Theater,* 63.

53. Hofmannsthal noted on a draft of *Das Kleine Welttheater,* "verse of a puppet play that has been driven through water" (Hofmannsthal, *Sämtliche Werke,* 593 n. 3), and he even planned to have this play performed by a group of marionette players (619 n. 619). At the same, he speculated about having his play *Der Weiße Fächer* performed by the shadow theater of Victor Mannheimer (642 n. 2).

54. In a similar vein, Michael Simpson has described the strategic politics of romantic closet drama in *Closet Performances.* Valeria Wagner offers an account of the confluence of drama and political action and suggests what a politics of inaction would look like in *Bound to Act.*

55. One theorist who advanced such a view was Deleuze, in his *Différence et répétition,* which was acclaimed by Michel Foucault as a new *theatrum philosophicum* (Foucault, "Theatrum Philosophicum").

56. See Butler, *Gender Trouble;* and idem, *Bodies That Matter.* See also McKenzie, *Perform or Else.*

57. Sedgwick, *Epistemology of the Closet.*

58. Brecht, *Gesammelte Werke,* 17:991–92. Unless otherwise noted, all references to Brecht are to this edition.

59. As Julie Stone Peters *(Congreve, the Drama, and the Printed Word)* has demonstrated, one cannot speak of a strong alliance between theater, drama, and print before the late seventeenth century. I seek to trace the effects of this alliance in modern drama, where it finally comes to full fruition.

60. Wolfgang Iser's notion of the implied reader *(Der Akt des Lesens)* has not yet been put to systematic use in the study of dramatic literature. One exception is Benjamin Bennett, who constructs the figure of a "virtual reader," who watches a theatrical performance in light of the dramatic text (Bennett, *Theater as Problem,* 151).

61. Henderson, *Changing Drama.*

62. *Mrs. Warren's Profession* was censored in 1893, *Salomé* one year earlier, but both appeared in print, the one in *Plays Pleasant and Unpleasant* (1898), the other in an elaborate edition with the celebrated drawings by Beardsley.

63. Two important legal changes occurred at the Bern Convention in 1885 and through the American Copyright Act 1891.

64. The relation between film scripts and film is in a similarly transitional period today. Even though film scripts are included in the printed works of some select authors, they usually are not printed for a general readership and are made available only after the films have come out. One might add that film scripts still are not being taught at Harvard, Yale, and Columbia, or at least they are not being taught as literature. Moreover, we still have to wait for the emergence of what then could be called closet film scripts.

65. *The British Library Statistics,* for example, lumps together poetry and drama and therefore does not furnish any usable data on the publication of drama (Eliot, *Some Patterns and Trends in British Publishing, 1800–1919*).

66. For a good account of print culture as it pertains to drama, see Stephens, *Profession of the Playwright.*

67. Plato, *Plato's Republic.*

68. Gérard Genette even quotes a translation of the *Poetics* to back up the claim that Aristotle uses the term *diegesis* (Genette, *Figures of Literary Discourse,* 128), referring to the first section of the *Poetics,* where Aristotle in fact uses primarily the term ἀπαγγελία, or *apaggelia,* except in a few cases (1456b, 1459b) that carry no terminological weight. The text in which Aristotle uses *diegesis* mostly critically is the *Rhetoric,* where he questions the usefulness of diegesis in political speeches.

69. At one point Aristotle says: "Περὶ δὲ τῆς διηγηματικῆς καὶ ἐν μέτρῳ μιμητικῆς" [with regard to narrative and verse mimesis] (*Poetics* 1459a 16), thus subsuming diegesis under mimesis.

70. Issacharoff, *Discourse as Performance*, 55ff.

71. William Worthen makes a similar observation, arguing that poetic theater implies a competition between dramatic text and theatrical space (Worthen, *Modern Drama and the Rhetoric of the Theater*).

72. I would like to acknowledge a debt here to Evlyn Gould's fascinating study, *Virtual Theater from Diderot to Mallarmé*. Taking her point of departure from Plato, Gould traces the tradition of a "virtual theater," centered on idealist and romantic philosophy, ranging from Diderot through Hugo, Stendhal, and Flaubert to Mallarmé. I consider this tradition a precursor to the tradition of modernist antitheatrical drama and theater that I study here.

73. The most important and most balanced analysis of stage directions was undertaken by Marvin Carlson in "The Status of Stage Directions." Considering stage directions as a secondary text is a dogma that has been promoted by almost everyone, mostly tacitly but on occasion overtly. Issacharoff, one of the few theorists to have given stage directions some attention, recognizes their importance but still sees them as "virtual performance" mediating text that is bound to disappear in a theatrical production, thus repeating what earlier critics considered to be the reason for the secondary importance of stage directions (see Issacharoff, "Inscribed Performance," 94; see also idem, *Discourse as Performance*, 49). Other studies devoted to an analysis of stage directions are Andrzej Ceymowa's "Defense of Stage Directions"; and Patricia A. Suchy's "When Words Collide").

74. In 1999 the *New Yorker* cunningly came up with a similar program for the oeuvre of O'Neill, presenting a collage of those stage directions that, because of their psychological specificity, were impossible to represent accurately onstage.

75. There is an Anglo-American tradition of literary theory that arrives at the comparable conclusion that language depends on gestures and cannot be cut off from them. This tradition is represented by Kenneth Burke and by Blackmur, *Language as Gesture*.

76. I am less concerned here with anthropological studies of gestures or the tradition of phenomenology, from Merleau-Ponty to Vilém Flusser, which are not interested in gestures' contentious relation to writing but tend to see gestures as part of a phenomenology of the practices of the body (see Flusser, *Gesten*).

Chapter 1 Richard Wagner

1. Friedrich Nietzsche, "Der Fall Wagner," in *Richard Wagner in Bayreuth, Der Fall Wagner, Nietzsche contra Wagner*, 88.

2. Adorno, "Wagners Aktualität," 548.

3. Adorno, "Versuch über Wagner," 32; hereafter cited in the text as "Versuch."

4. Nietzsche, *Die Geburt der Tragödie*.

5. Herbert Blau shows the extent to which the relation between performance and audience is the driving force behind various kinds of theater reform (Blau, *Audience*). Nietzsche might be considered one of the earliest modernists to rebel against the audience as such, envisioning a fully participatory ritual.

6. Wagner, *Oper und Drama*, 19. Unless otherwise noted, all references to *Oper und Drama* are to this edition and cited as *Oper*.

7. I do not know whether Nietzsche was aware of the fact that the expression *hocus-pocus* itself is a gestural one, denoting the ceremony of transubstantiation as an acronym of *hic est eius corpus meum*.

8. Cf. Nietzsche, "Der Fall Wagner," 102.

9. Adorno's borrowing from Nietzsche's anti-theatrical polemic might seem surprising given that Adorno never ceased to critique Nietzsche's own classicist understanding of musical form and continued to have an ambiguous relation to the nineteenth-century phi-

losopher. It is particularly symptomatic that Adorno would distance himself from Nietzsche's musical aesthetics thirty years later in a new essay entitled "Wagners Aktualität," 547.

10. Rampley, *Nietzsche, Aesthetics, and Modernity,* 227. Mathew Rampley discusses the affinity between Nietzsche's and Adorno's critique of Wagner and mentions different attacks on Wagner's reliance on gesture. As Rampley points out, Nietzsche is at his most antimodernist and, one could add, at his most classicist in his critique of Wagner (225 ff.).

11. We can relate this claim to the insight on the part of theater semiotics, developed most convincingly by Patrice Pavis, that it is impossible to form hypotactic or syntactic structures and hierarchies in the mime's art of gesture (Pavis, *Languages of the Stage,* 53 ff.).

12. Of course, this is not true in the case of explicit attempts to create a spatial, gestural syntax, as it governs those sign languages that are not based on phonetic languages. One example of such a "genuinely" gestural syntax is American Sign Language.

13. Giorgio Agamben, whose understanding of gesture is derived from Benjamin and Brecht, seeks to align gesture with the cinema. Nevertheless, most of the terms Agamben associates with gesture, such as *interruption* and *suspendedness,* in particular the notion of a "means without an end," are not at odds with the theater. In fact Agamben refers to Mallarmé's "Mimique" as well as to Beckett's *Nacht und Träume,* thus transporting gesture back into the realm of theatrical writing (Agamben, *Means without End,* 54 ff.). In an earlier essay, "Kommerell, or On Gesture" (1991), Agamben examines both the theory of the gestural origin of language and the theatricality of gesture as they appear in the work of Benjamin (Agamben, *Potentialities*).

14. Leitmotif composition has at times had powerful practitioners in film music.

In particular the great Italian film composer E. Morricone, in his collaboration with the director Sergio Leone, employed leitmotifs with astonishing impact and power in *Once Upon a Time in the West.*

15. For a more detailed reading of *Philosophie der neuen Musik,* see my "Polyphonous Gestures."

16. Said, *Musical Elaborations;* Goehr, *Quest for Voice.*

17. Mann, "Versuch über das Theater."

18. Anette Ingenhoff lists several types of narration in the *Ring,* dividing them primarily into narratives about a scene's prehistory and narratives that repeat scenes from within the *Ring* itself, usually from previous parts of the cycle. Both types of narration point beyond the immediate scene and thus do not lead to diegetic doubling (Ingenhoff, *Drama oder Epos?* 123 ff.).

19. Hilda Meldrum Brown also critiques the simplistic opposition between drama and epic (Brown, *Leitmotiv and Drama,* 43 ff.). I agree with her assessment that Wagner's leitmotif should not be considered to be simply an epic device and that in general Brecht's polemical notion of epic theater, along with Thomas Mann's defense of the novel, has led to a simplistic opposition between drama and epic. Often, when Wagner himself speaks about drama, he really means theatrical representation, and what Brecht critiques in Wagner is Wagner's use of theatricality, not his dramaturgy. The only tradition that has paid attention to this issue of theatricality is the anti-theatrical tradition from Nietzsche to Adorno. A critical reconstruction of Wagner's theory and practice thus should take its point of departure from this tradition, without, of course, simply adopting its ideological or polemical assumptions.

20. One of the few exceptions is Herbert Lindenberger's *Opera,* which details the struggle not only between different arts but also between different modes of representation.

21. In *Richard Wagner, Fritz Lang, and the Nibelungen* David Levin shows the ways in which the epic scope of the *Ring* kept expanding, forcing Wagner to introduce more and more narrative elements into the artwork even as he planned to bring the entire myth onto the stage. Eventually, the expanding scope, according to Levin, made it impossible to realize the *Gesamtkunstwerk*'s project of theatrical presentation *(Darstellung)*. I agree with this description, and with Levin's critique of Abbate's attempt to see in the use of narration a compromise on Wagner's part (39 ff.). I would only emphasize here that Wagner's desire for total theatrical representation, even if this desire remained unfulfilled, meant that he tried to draw narration into the sphere of the theater. Unlike the diegetic tradition, which uses narration to control the theater, Wagner hoped to integrate narration into the theater.

22. Wagner, *Gesammelte Schriften und Dichtungen,* 9:196. All references to Wagner's oeuvre, with the exception of those to *Oper und Drama,* are to this edition.

23. "Über Schauspieler und Sänger" (9:261–65). In his landmark study, to which this chapter is much indebted, Herbert Lindenberger mentions Wagner's fascination with acting and foregrounds the "performative values" that inform Wagner's work (61).

24. Friedrich Kittler observes that Wagner's orientation toward dramatic action led to a radical increase in stage directions. Despite this observation, Kittler insists on the privileged position of breathing in the "data-stream" of Wagner's operas (Kittler, "World-Breath: On Wagner's Media Technology," in Levin, *Opera through Other Eyes,* 218). I argue, on the contrary, that by means of his aesthetics of gesture Wagner actually tries to subject all other arts, or data-streams, to the visible language of gestures.

25. This attempt to contrast "German" acting with "French" affectation is a common topos in the history of German theater, employed frequently, for example, by Gottsched and Lessing.

26. One of the first totalizing codifications of gestures, not so much for acting as for pictorial representation, was proposed by Charles Le Brun in the seventeenth century. Le Brun provided a complete taxonomy of gestures that not only dominated French painting for centuries but also found its way into manuals for *tableaux vivants,* pantomime, and acting. His system of codification was organized, as were many of the systems that followed, by considering specific gestures as expressions for specific emotions; the gestures became readable in terms of the emotion they expressed (Le Brun, *L'expression des passions et autres conférences*).

27. Meisel, *Realizations.*

28. Lacoue-Labarthe mentions Wagner's Rousseauist conception of the origin of poetry and language in *Musica ficta,* 49.

29. In his devoted faithfulness to Wagner, Hans Pfitzner replicates Wagner's gestural terminology and discusses the coordination of the corporeal gesture, "szenisch-leibliche Geste," with the gesture of music, "musikalische Geste" (Pfitzner, *Werk und Widergabe,* 96).

30. Lacoue-Labarthe sees this alliance of orchestral music and the stage as a step toward a fictive music, *musica ficta,* that also entails an intimate relation to the theater (Lacoue-Labarthe, *Musica ficta,* 14).

31. Here my argument can be related to Lydia Goehr's inspiring analysis of Wagner's "quest for voice" (Goehr, *Quest for Voice*). Goehr's analysis runs parallel to mine in that she too emphasizes Wagner's quest for expressivity and the fact that he turns to the debate about the origin of language. While Goehr foregrounds Rousseau and the role of the voice in that debate, I emphasize gesture, which occupies a similarly originary role in the writings of Rousseau but also of Condillac, Herder, or Warburton.

32. Wagner's contemporary Julian Schmidt,

for example, complained, "Er redet blos noch in Bildern, die nichts bestimmtes ausdrücken, z.B. 'das Auge des Gehörs'" [He only speaks in images, which no longer express anything, for example, "the eye of hearing"] (quoted in the preface to *Oper and Drama,* 93).

33. Baudelaire saw in the *Lohengrin* overture the enactment of analogies and crossings of sounds, colors, and ideas, arguing that it "would be really surprising . . . that sound could not suggest color, that color could not convey a melody, things having been expressed by reciprocal analogy" (Baudelaire, *Richard Wagner et "Tannhäuser" à Paris,* 199). Kandinsky comments on and applies this synaesthetic aspect of Wagner's text to his own theory of art. In addition, he recognizes Wagner's attempt to give up absolute music and to mobilize the rhythmic dimension of movement (Kandinsky, *Essays über Kunst und Künstler,* 55). However, Kandinsky argues that the relation between music and character achieved by the leitmotif is only a mechanical reproduction and therefore an external coordination of the different dimensions in stage art (56). His call for an "internal" relation is meant to initiate a pursuit of Wagner's ideal with radicalized means.

34. In a suggestive argument Herbert Lindenberger relates Wagner's oeuvre to the emergence of philology in nineteenth-century Germany (Lindenberger, *Opera in History,* 138–39). Continuing this line of thought, I would argue that Wagner's theory of alliteration, which is oriented toward Middle High German poetry and the *Edda* epos, can be seen as an attempt to "aestheticize" philology and transform it into a poetic practice.

35. Slavoj Zizek interprets the *Gesamtkunstwerk* as an attempt of aesthetic totalization, which he relates to political totalization (Zizek, *Sublime Object of Ideology*). My account of the intersection of the aesthetic and political dimensions constitutive for gesture can be seen as part of this politico-aesthetic understanding of Wagner.

36. Friedrich Kittler considers the project of a total work of art in terms of media technology as an aesthetics that tries to speak to as many senses as possible, combining as many forms of art as possible, allowing for as many different acts of perception as possible, trying to send a maximum of data on all sensory channels (Kittler, "World-Breath," 232ff.).

37. Wagner writes: "Da ich das deutsche Wesen in seinen idealsten Anlagen aufzusuchen hatte, mußte mir die unmittelbar betheiligte Künstlerschaft hierfür näher stehen, als das sogenannte Publikum" [Because I had to search for the most ideal forms of German nature, it was only natural that I found the artists involved in the work of art closer to this ideal than the so-called public] (9:382).

38. Richard Wagner, "Beethoven," in *Gesammelte Schriften und Dichtungen,* vol. 9.

39. In a letter to Cosima Wagner, Houston Stewart Chamberlain extends Wagner's vision of a spectacle without actors (Pretzsch, *Cosima Wagner und Houston Stewart Chamberlain,* 146). Friedrich Kittler ("World-Breath") refers to this passage in the context of finding in Wagner an anticipation of film (186). Indeed, in some late comments Wagner likens the opera of the future to the dream vision evoked by a magic lantern.

40. Nietzsche, *Unzeitgemäße Betrachtungen,* 318.

41. We have to turn to Horkheimer and Adorno's *Dialektik der Aufklärung* to find in Adorno's thought a critical discussion of the association of Jews and actors, an association that constitutes one of the most established anti-Semitic and anti-theatrical topoi. Adorno relates the conjunction of these two prejudices to a larger anxiety within civilization: because civilization depends on the overcoming of

crude, literal mimesis, civilization needs mimetic scapegoats through which it can reenact its always fragile sense of having overcome this primitive mimesis: "the social ban of actors and gypsies . . . is the prerequisite of civilization" (190). For the anti-Semitic imagination, Jews become the ciphers of this vulgar mimesis in that they come to stand, in the eyes of "civilization," for mimesis and in particular for "undisciplined mimicry" (191). In a particularly interesting turn of his argument, Adorno sees in fascism's anti-Semitic obsession with this allegedly Jewish mimesis an occasion to release fascism's own repressed desire to mimic by mimicking what it takes to be "typically" Jewish gestures. Fascism thus channels its own mimetic repression into the obsessive repetition of the anti-Semitic repertoire.

42. See also Weiner, "Reading the Ideal."

43. For a detailed analysis of these and other anti-Semitic topoi see Weiner, *Richard Wagner and the Anti-Semitic Imagination.*

44. Wagner, *Siegfried,* 668–69.

45. Here I differ somewhat from Marc Weiner's reading of this scene ("Reading the Ideal"), to which I am otherwise indebted. Even though Wagner critiques deception, he depends, theoretically and practically, on the art of acting and on what he calls "Nachahmungstrieb." The critique of actors and mimesis in Mime is not, therefore, indicative of an anti-mimetic or anti-theatrical doctrine; on the contrary, it is Wagner's attempt to come to terms with his own reliance on actors and theatrical representation. Wagner's anti-Semitism, which entails anti-theatrical topoi and also, as Weiner shows, a way of talking about superficial and external imitation of "authentic" German culture (66), makes it difficult for Wagner to distinguish, within the sphere of mimesis and acting, between the "good" German actor and the bad "Jewish" one. What Weiner

considers to be an "ironic" critique of mimesis via mimesis (79) points, I think, to a tension within Wagner's theory and practice centered on his reliance on gesture.

46. Peter Kivy, in *Sound and Semblance,* provides a detailed account of the way in which the questions of representation, illustration, and program music are intertwined with the kinds of musical language and notation systems used. My remarks on the notation of the *Gesamtkunstwerk* can be seen as a note to this larger project. See also De Marinis, *In cerca dell' attore,* 73–100.

47. As a good Wagnerian, Hans Pfitzner, in *Werk und Wiedergabe,* also reads specific gestures into the score of the orchestra in *Tannhäuser* (90) and insists on a faithful adherence to Wagner's stage directions, which are mostly, as he acknowledges, un-naturalistic (91). He complains, for example, about two singers who disregarded Wagner's stage directions in *Lohengrin* (51–53).

48. Shaw, *Perfect Wagnerite,* 129.

49. Wagner's understanding of gesture as the language of the unsayable itself is part of melodrama as theorized, for example, by Peter Brooks in *The Melodramatic Imagination.*

50. Carl Dahlhaus, in *Richard Wagners Musikdramen,* notices these correspondences, without, however, reflecting on their pictorial status and their function in the notation systems of the *Gesamtkunstwerk* (166). Dahlhaus misses the significance of this connection between gesture and musical notation because he considers gestures in Wagner's works to be of secondary importance (even though he admits that they are part of Wagner's composition): "Scenic representation, gesture, is not to the same degree a component of the work as music or language is, even though Wagner also 'composes' them" (229–300). Dahlhaus here comes close to recognizing the central importance of gestures, as a link between music and theatrical representation through the

iconic quality of musical notation, but at the same moment dismisses them as secondary.

51. This separation, as well as the idea of the interpretative translation of the authorial text into a *mise en scène,* formulated by Adolphe Appia *(Texts on Theatre),* sounds unspectacular to us now because it became the widely acknowledged doctrine in theater hermeneutics and semiotics, whose sharpest proponent, Patrice Pavis *(Languages of the Stage),* formulated his semiotics of the stage precisely in Appia's tradition and terminology.

52. Jacques-Dalcroze, *Jacques-Dalcroze Method of Eurhythmics.*

53. For a survey of Wagner's reception on the part of the avant-garde, see Baxmann, "Verbindung der Künste und Verknüpfung der Sinne."

54. Bourdieu argues in *Rules of Art* that in the late nineteenth century theatricality became a value comparable to what the formalists called "literariness" (138).

Chapter 2 Stéphane Mallarmé

1. This chronology is based on Mallarmé, *Correspondance.* Unless otherwise noted, all quotations from the correspondence are from this edition and identified as *Correspondance.* See also Mondor, *La vie de Mallarmé.*

2. Although French symbolism is often considered to be an aesthetics for poetry that was later transferred to the theater, it was a theatrical aesthetics to begin with, albeit one designed to evade the physical presence of the actors and objects onstage.

3. At the same time, Mallarmé wrote the unpublished *Ouverture ancienne* (1866), which he later prefaced with the direction *"(Incantation)* (P 137)" and which he referred to as a "musical overture" (*Correspondance,* 1:207). During the final two years of his life Mallarmé continued to experiment with two new outlines and changed the generic description of the "poem" to *Les noces d'Hérodiade, Mystère* (unless otherwise noted, all

references to the unpublished parts of *Hérodiade* are to the edition by Gardner Davies, hereafter cited as *Noces*). In 1886 he envisioned a tripartite scheme, and in 1898 a division into five parts both replacing the *Ouverture* with a *Prélude* and adding a finale and a *Cantique de Saint Jean.*

4. This earliest version, which was never published, survives as a 1968 copy in the album of Ellen Linzee Prout (see Mallarmé, *Oeuvres complètes,* 1221). The published version no longer contains stage directions.

5. Françoise Meltzer's *Salome and the Dance of Writing* discusses the fascinating history of Salomé adaptations.

6. This point has been observed by Haskell Block in *Mallarmé and the Symbolist Drama* and by Mary Lewis Shaw in *Performance in the Texts of Mallarmé.* The dialogue itself has a sort of classical origin in the heroine-nurse and heroine-servant dialogues of French theater in Racine and Corneille.

7. Mallarmé, *Les interviews de Mallarmé,* 60, 61.

8. In *Virtual Theater from Diderot to Mallarmé* Evlyn Gould argues that Hérodiade "fictionalizes" herself and observes that Saint Jean only speaks about himself (146). Dominique Fisher also mentions that Hérodiade's body becomes an artifact (Fisher, *Staging of Language and Language(s) of the Stage,* 42). Frantisek Deak notices the scenic imagination of this dialogue and the centrality of the three gestures of the nurse (Deak, *Symbolist Theater,* 75). In addition to these analyses I tease out the anti-theatrical attitude at work in this isolation of Hérodiade from her environment. According to my reading, *Hérodiade* is not so much a drama about self-consciousness as a drama about self-creation or self-fashioning, a project that implies Hérodiade's desire to control her imaginary theatrical representation.

9. Peter Szondi observes in *Das lyrische Drama des Fin de siècle* the implicit re-

jection of the physical in *Hérodiade* and speaks of a tendency to dematerialize, concluding that *Hérodiade* was written for an imaginary theater (77). My reading follows his, but I emphasize the extent to which *Hérodiade* is written against the theater and constitutes a writing back to the theater.

10. Mary Lewis Shaw suggest a similar view of the status of these texts in *Performance in the Texts of Mallarmé*, 118.

11. Only in this sense is it possible to follow Edmund Wilson's attempt to find in symbolism and in the symbolist protagonist of Villiers de L'Isle-Adam's closet drama *Axel*, on which *Igitur* is in part modeled, a figure of symbolist modernism (Wilson, *Axel's Castle*).

12. In fact all of Mallarmé's plays are centered on and named after such half-fabulous protagonists, from Hérodiade through Faune (the protagonist of Mallarmé's second poetic closet drama) to Igitur.

13. Mallarmé, *Igitur, Divagations, Un coup de dés,* 188. Unless otherwise noted, all references to Mallarmé's prose texts are to this edition.

14. Cf. Heller, *Coleridge, Lamb, Hazlitt, and the Reader of Drama.*

15. Mallarmé to Armand Renaud, in Mallarmé, *Oeuvres complètes,* 712.

16. Paraphrasing Mallarmé's observation that "the world was determined to end up in a book," Kristeva observed that Mallarmé's *Livre* could be considered a paradigm for symbolist theater in that it was determined not to end up as spectacle (Kristeva, *La révolution du langage poétique,* 562). For a detailed study of the relation between the history of the book and the history of the theater see Peters, *Theater of the Book.*

17. Mallarmé, *Igitur, Divagation, Un coup de dés,* 274.

18. This schematic history was first proposed by Peter Bürger in 1974 and is still useful in its understanding of symbolism and aestheticism (Bürger, *Theorie der Avantgarde*). I do not agree, therefore, with those who consider

symbolism to be the first avant-garde. Such a classification focuses too narrowly on a few formal features of symbolism and disregards the relation of symbolism to the institution of art and the social class that supports it.

19. Sartre, *Mallarmé.*

20. Johnson, *World of Difference,* 57ff.

21. This description is based on Scherer, *Le "Livre" de Mallarmé,* sheet 195A, which numbers the individual sheets and adds letters to them.

22. In *Performance in the Texts of Mallarmé* Mary Lewis Shaw uses the term *ritual art* to describe Mallarmé's art and considers him a precursor of the avant-garde primitivists. I emphasize the difference between Mallarmé's ceremony and an avant-garde search for ritual, for they fulfill different functions: Mallarmé's ceremony seeks to preserve the integrity and autonomy of art, while the avant-garde ritual attacks precisely this autonomy; and while for Mallarmé ceremony would elevate art to the highest autonomy, the ritualists hoped to create objects and practices that would critique and circumvent the institution of art altogether.

23. One could consider the *Livre* and its enactment to be an example of what Michael Kirby calls "non-matrixed performance," which refers to a type of performer who refuses to act or represent (Kirby, *Formalist Theatre,* 3ff.). Jacques Scherer hinted at the fact that the operator does not act—"il ne joue pas *Le Livre* et ne l'écrit pas; il le présente" (Scherer, *Le "Livre" de Mallarmé,* 69)—without, however, embedding this observation in its larger anti-theatrical context.

24. The content of the reading, that which is being read, is governed by the permutations and sequencing of sheets of paper in a manner that anticipates similar techniques in the group OULIPO and, in particular, Queneau's permutative novel *La vie mode d'emploi.*

25. Scherer, *Le "Livre" de Mallarmé,* 43ff.

26. Haskall M. Block was one of the first to

see in the *Livre* a response to Wagner's *Gesamtkunstwerk* (Block, *Mallarmé and the Symbolist Drama*, 79).

27. "Vous avez à subir un sortilège, pour l'accomplissement de quoi ce n'est trop d'aucun moyen d'enchantement impliqué par la magie musicale, afin de violenter votre raison aux prises avec un simulacre" ("Crayonné au théâtre," in Mallarmé, *Igitur, Divagations, Un coup de dés*, 170. Unless otherwise noted, all references to "Crayonné au théâtre," are to this edition).

28. Jean Pol Madau relates Mallarmé's understanding of music and rhythm to Nietzsche's conception of a Dionysiac music as well as to a Wagnerian understanding of myth (Madau, "Language, Myth, Musique"). Madau himself, however, uses Lévi-Strauss's structural analysis of myth and projects such an understanding of myth back to Wagner. Mallarmé does not propose such a critical analysis of myth in Wagner and therefore distances himself from the bombastic and mind-numbing type of Dionysiac ritual, searching instead for a modernist, impersonal, and controlled experience.

29. Lacoue-Labarthe has called Mallarmé's text a "deconstruction" of Wagner (Lacoue-Labarthe, *Musica ficta*, n. 17), a description that responds not so much to the so-called ambiguities of Mallarmé's text as to the fact that Mallarmé critiques the *Gesamtkunstwerk* while trying to preserve some of its traits.

30. Mallarmé was the first modernist to do so, but he could look back to a long history of visual writing, from medieval illumination to baroque lyric, such as the one by Herbert.

31. In a compelling study, Elinor Fuchs speaks of the "death of character" as a general feature of twentieth-century drama and theater (Fuchs, *Death of Character*). The texts of Mallarmé and indeed the entire anti-theatrical tradition I discuss show that this "death of character" is a direct result of the anti-theatrical thrust of modern theater,

in particular the critique of actors and impersonation.

32. Critics such as Janine Langhan *(Hegel and Mallarmé)* have repeatedly called attention to Mallarmé's use of the words *idea* and *ideality* and constructed a genealogy to Hegel and idealism. I argue that the notion of idea, for Mallarmé, plays a role in the depersonalization of the dancer and that idealism becomes instrumentalized in Mallarmé's discourse to disengage the performance on stage from its individual corporeality. Mallarmé's idealism is therefore the idealism of the symbolist theater.

33. Mallarmé, "Crise de vers," in *Poésies*, 243.

34. The tradition of critics who have subscribed to Mallarmé's own values includes Philippe Sollers, Jacques Derrida, and more recently Mary Lewis Shaw, Timothy Clark, and Dominique Fisher.

35. Mary Lewis Shaw *(Performance in the Texts of Mallarmé)* mentions these theatrical references and distinguishes between the different myths that make up the *Livre*. Mallarmé comes back to the circus in a short piece on a dancing bear called *Un spectacle interrompu*, which continues Mallarmé's technique of isolating and freezing single gestures and postures.

36. This interest in the parerga of the theater is one instance of Mallarmé's dedication to a Kantian notion of functionless beauty, which for Kant is represented in arabesques and other nonmimetic ornaments. Barbara Johnson discussed the importance of arabesque in Mallarmé's poetry in *Défigurations du langage poétique*, 175ff.

37. Barbara Johnson, "'Les Fleurs du Mal Armé': Some Reflections on Intertextuality" and "Mallarmé as Mother," both in *World of Difference*.

38. A good overview of the emergence of the field of writing on dance is provided by Jane Desmond's collection *Meaning in Motion*. Mallarmé occupies a central position in this history, for

it was he who turned the ballet and theater review into a literary genre. It is not surprising, therefore, that the most innovative examples of writing on dance can be found in the Mallarméian tradition, for example, in the work of his most committed British admirer, Arthur Symons. Even the celebrated dance reviews of Edwin Denby *(Dance Writings and Poetry)* can be seen as part of this tradition, a genealogy that is confirmed by his occasional poems on dancers.

39. Cf. Benjamin, *Charles Baudelaire,* 33 ff.

40. For an extended discussion of the status of the theater in relation to the other arts, see Bourdieu, *Rules of Art.*

41. "A savoir que la danseuse *n'est pas une femme qui danse,* pour ces motifs juxtaposés qu'elle *n'est pas une femme,* mais une métaphore résumant un des aspects élémentaires de notre forme, glaive, coupe, fleur, etc., *et qu'elle ne danse pas,* suggérant, par le prodige de raccourcis ou d'élans, avec une écriture corporelle ce qu'il faudrait des paragraphes en prose dialoguée autant que descriptive, pour exprimer, dans la rédaction: poème dégagé de tout appareil du scribe" (Mallarmé's emphasis).

42. "Quand s'isole pour le regard un signe de l'éparse beauté générale, fleur, onde, nuée et bijou, etc."

43. "Se demander devant tout pas, chaque attitude si étranges, ces pointes et taquetés, allongés ou ballons. 'Que peut signifier ceci.'"

44. Each of these terms does nothing but specify and prescribe a particular sequence of movements: *taqueté* is a dance *sur les pointes* consisting of quick, little steps in which the points strike the floor sharply in a staccato manner; *allongé* is the extending or stretching of the leg, as, for example, in the *arabesque allongée;* and *ballons* is the light, elastic quality in jumping in which the dancer bounds up from the floor, pauses a moment in the air, and descends lightly and softly, only to rebound into the air, resembling the smooth bouncing of a

ball. These definitions are taken from Grant, *Technical Manual and Dictionary of Classical Ballet,* 93, 45.

45. "Évoquer, dans une ombre exprès, l'objet tu, par des mots allusifs, jamais directs, se réduisant à du silence égal, comporte tentative proche de créer" ("Grands faits," in Mallarmé, *Igitur, Divagations, Un coup de dés,* 304).

46. Lisa Bixensteine Safford points out the pictorial quality of Mallarmé's notion of hieroglyphics and relates it to Degas's paintings of dancers (Safford, "Mallarmé's Influence on Degas's Aesthetics of Dance in His Late Period").

47. Philippe Sollers introduces the formula of text as theater and theater as text in his essay "Literature and Totality," in Bloom, *Stéphane Mallarmé.* Mary Lewis Shaw continues this tradition in her article "Concrete and Abstract Poetry." For her, the two lines of the chiasmus, however, describe concrete and abstract art, respectively; concrete poetry, in the insistence on its own materiality, sees the world as text, while abstract poetry, deprived of reference, understands the text as world. I try to consider both moments as converging in Mallarmé's phantasm of gestural writing. Timothy Clark also follows Mallarmé's and Derrida's equation of gesture and writing (Clark, "Being in Mime"). Finally, Patrice Pavis carries this literary and philosophical tradition of considering theater as text into theater studies, considering the theater as a "performance text" (Pavis, "Towards a Semiology of Mise-en-Scène?").

48. Fredric Jameson comes to a similar conclusion, observing, "It is certain that de Man's form of deconstruction can be seen as a last-minute rescue operation and a salvaging of the aesthetic—even a defense and valorization of literary study and a privileging of specifically literary language" (Jameson, *Postmodernism,* 251). My analysis approaches this nexus of ideas through the notion of antitheatricalism, which contributes, I

argue, to this desire to preserve the aesthetic sphere.

49. In a landmark study that situates Mallarmé in the context of the modernist theater, Haskall Block observes that the overture is an imaginative set design, without, however, identifying the struggle between diegesis and theatrical mimesis implied in this strategy (Block, *Mallarmé and the Symbolist Drama,* 13). It is because of his investment in demonstrating Mallarmé's significance for the theater that Block overstates the extent to which Mallarmé's texts are geared toward the theater, for example, when he says that Hérodiade "almost cries out for stage representation." I would maintain that Mallarmé needs the concept of the theater in order to defy it. This anti-theatrical element is lost in most studies devoted to proving the close tie between Mallarmé and the theater. In an insightful and important study, *Symbolist Theater,* Frantisek Deak uses the term *conceptual theater* (58 ff.) to describe Mallarmé's use of theatricality. With this term Deak refers to the performance of the *Livre,* which includes a "mise-en-scène," "acting," and "self-transformation" (90). While the existence of a reader in a library setting certainly introduces a "personal" element into the reading, I would insist that the reading, however choreographed it may be, keeps its distance from a theater that proceeds by "embodiment" (92). Deak comes close to recognizing the anti-theatrical thrust of Mallarmé's writings but dismisses it ultimately as only a "seemingly" antitheatrical tendency (86). Deak thus argues for the sometimes neglected theatrical element in Mallarmé by overemphasizing its theatricality and by downplaying its anti-theatricality.

50. A notable exception to this rule is Evelyn Gould's *Virtual Theater from Diderot to Mallarmé,* which situates Mallarmé in a different but highly relevant tradition of skepticism about the theater, namely, a half-philosophical half-literary tradition centered on the theater not as an actual but as an imaginary entity.

51. Nichola Anne Haxell discusses the disappearance of Loie Fuller's body amidst her veils and emphasizes Fuller's influence on symbolist aesthetics (Haxell, "Le Serpent qui Danse"). Following the denaturalized aesthetics of symbolism, Fuller's performances were set on a stage with little decoration and electric lighting, turning her into the icon of French symbolism, inspiring such writers as Paul Adam, Rodenbach, Lucini, and Valéry to issue poetic responses to her depersonalized dance but also inspiring pictorial representation from symbolism to art nouveau that equally emphasized the disappearance of her body amidst her gestures and veils. Paul Adam, for example, not only saw in her *Danse serpentine* the realization of a symbolist aesthetics of the stage; like Mallarmé, he related her dance directly to Wagner's aesthetics. A Wagnerian herself, Loie Fuller used, for example, Wagner's "Ride of the Valkyries" for her famous *Danse de feu* in 1896, and when Craig saw Loie Fuller in 1906, he immediately recognized in her dance the suggestive aesthetics of Wagner.

52. "La scène libre, au gré de fictions, exaltée du jeu d'un voile avec attitudes et gestes, devient le très pur résultat."

53. For the same reason, perhaps, dancers and choreographers, such as Martha Graham, Jerome Robbins, George Balanchine, and Nijinski, adopted Mallarmé's closet dramas for dance. Ruth Matilda Mésavage, for example, called Nijinski's *L'Après-midi d'un Faune* an "incarnation de l'image poétique évoquée par Mallarmé" (Mésavage, "Écriture, danse, et mondes imaginaires," 66).

Chapter 3 James Joyce

1. Hegel, *Vorlesungen über Ästhetik III.*
2. Bakhtin, *Dialogic Imagination.*
3. Franco Moretti, *Modern Epic.* Peter Brooks gives a different version of such

a sublation narrative when he argues that nineteenth-century melodrama was continued in a more "complex" form in the nineteenth-century novel (Brooks, *Melodramatic Imagination,* 109; see also Mendelson, "Encyclopedic Narrative").

4. Other examples could be added here, for example, Virginia Woolf's last novel, *Between the Acts* (1941), which also inserts dramatic sections into an otherwise narrative structure. Jan Kott is one of the few critics to have indicated this path, observing that "'The Night of the Walpurgis' from *Ulysses* is written not by accident in dialogue, and it is in reality the greatest drama of the theatre of cruelty and of the absurd" (Kott, *Theatre Notebook,* 261). Relating "Circe" to Artaud's theater of cruelty does not explain, however, the puzzling existence of this dramatic text in the middle of a novel, especially since the theater of cruelty attacks most obsessively the role of dialogue and by extension the "dominance" of the dramatic text over the other mimetic art forms at work in the theater. Thematic correspondences between "Circe" and the theater of cruelty, such as the ritualistic element and an interest in hallucinatory processes—after all, Artaud had put Strindberg's *Dream Play* on the playbill for his Théâtre Alfred Jarry—thus should not distract from the generic and formal differences between these two projects.

5. Bakhtin never acknowledged that his dialogism was in fact a dramatic model. As Marvin Carlson argues, Bakhtin seems to have derived his understanding of drama as "monologic" from the German romantic theory of tragedy (Carlson, "Theater and Dialogism," in Reinelt and Roach, *Critical Theory and Performance,* 313–23).

6. Szondi, *Theorie des modernen Dramas.*

7. My analysis can be related to Joseph Litvak's *Caught in the Act,* which has been paradigmatic for the study of theatricality in the novel. A more re-

cent and equally excellent study that combines an analysis of narrative and theatricality is Alan Ackerman's *Portable Theater.* This perspective has received only occasional attention, most prominently at moments when the novel was being confronted with other genres, such as the theater or film. Sergei Eisenstein's essay on Dickens and Griffith stands as one of the paradigmatic studies in this field (see Eisenstein, "Dickens, Griffith, and the Film Today," in *Film Form*).

8. Joyce, *Poems and Shorter Writings.*

9. Joyce, *Critical Writings,* 39.

10. R. G. Hampson speaks of "Circe" as a "textual memory" for the entire *Ulysses* (Hampson, "Tofts Cumbersome Whirligig," 171). Michael Seidel observes that "Circe is, indeed, the interior of *Ulysses.* It is the interior of the city, the interior of the mind, and the interior of the novel" (Seidel, *Epic Geography,* 217). Hélène Cixous recognized that "Circe" puts the entire *Ulysses* on a stage (Cixous, "At Circe's, or the Self-Opener").

11. Erika Fischer-Lichte uses the term *theatricality* to describe turn-of-the-century theater reform at large in *Geschichte des Dramas.*

12. Because of his narrative paradigm, Gérard Genette does not actually mention stage directions in his study. See Genette, *Paratexts.* Cf. Wales, "Bloom Passes Through Several Walls," in which Katie Wales places Joyce's stage directions in the context of late-nineteenth-century drama and its increasing attention to stage directions. This history of the stage direction, however, demands explanation, which I try to provide by referring to the emergence of modern drama as reading drama and the affinity of modern drama to the closet drama.

13. Patrice Pavis and Keir Elam express their distrust of stage directions in, respectively, "From Text to Performance" and "Much Ado About Doing Things with Words (and Other Means):

Some Problems in the Pragmatics of Theatre and Drama," in Issacharoff and Jones, *Performing Texts,* 86–100 and 39–58. John Searle states his position in "Logical Status of Fictional Discourse."

14. Herring, *Joyce's Notes and Early Drafts from Ulysses,* 211–12; the single and double curly brackets indicate two levels of insertion, and the horizontal lines indicate deletions.

15. Joyce, *Ulysses,* 353. Unless otherwise noted, all quotations from *Ulysses* are from this edition.

16. R. G. Hampson also points out that the early draft of "Circe" is "closer to narrative and that the manuscript shifts increasingly towards the dramatic form" (Hampson, "Tofts Cumberson Whirligig," 149). Hampson argues that Joyce increasingly moves away from the dramatic form toward a "self-conscious theatricality" (156).

17. Patrick McCarthy mentions the narrative voice of the stage directions controlling the narrative point of view and views the dramatic structure in terms of a narrative experiment, a "narration masquerading as drama" (McCarthy, "Non-Dramatic Illusion in 'Circe,'" 24, 25).

18. Vladimir Nabokov called "Circe" an "authorial hallucination" (Nabokov, *Lectures on Literature,* 352). With regard to the Bella-Bello transformation and Bloom's sex change, some critics consider "Circe" a script for performance and therefore would have to "play" these characters as transvestites. Since "Circe" only imagines a scene, however, this necessity is suspended, and we cannot decide what really happens—our frame is a stage that is not real.

19. I would like to thank David Kurnick for helping me to think through this and many other problems pertaining to this chapter.

20. Much critical attention has been paid to the way Joyce represents corporeality. Evelyne Grossman, links, for example, the presentation of the body in *Ulysses* to its presentation in Artaud (Grossman, *Artaud/Joyce*).

21. These transformations follow a particular pattern, namely, the commodification of persons and the personification of objects: Bella herself is for sale, and her accessories—her fan and boot—become dramatic characters to be worshipped by Leopold Bloom. The setting of this chapter in Dublin's red-light district suggests that these commodified persons and personified objects are fetishes in a Marxist as well as a Freudian sense, as Fredric Jameson has pointed out, while also arguing that *Ulysses* exposes the limits of such processes. This limit is set by the fact that both personified objects and commodified and also reified persons appear as imaginary *dramatis personae;* their ultimate status, a status attributed to them by Marx himself, is that of the theater, what Debord would later call the spectacle (Jameson, "Ulysses in History." See also Moretti's analysis of consumer culture and modernism in *Modern Epic,* 123 ff.). Jacques Derrida has pointed out Marx's use of a theatrical vocabulary when describing the nature of commodities (Derrida, *Specters of Marx,* 125 ff.).

22. It is more than a simple irony that J. L. Austin's theory, which explicitly excludes all fictional and theatrical utterances, has been one of the most widely used paradigms to investigate speech in the theater (see Austin, *How to Do Things with Words*). Since most of Austin's examples rely not only on social institutions but also on social or even religious rituals—baptism, marriage, contracts—the expanded field of theatricality and performativity has easily incorporated into a performance-studies paradigm precisely such situations as the ones analyzed by Austin. While some proponents of this terminology would be advised to develop sharper distinctions between different forms of ritual, ceremony, and social

institutions, it would be wrong merely to deplore this absorption of Austin by performance studies as a "category" mistake between theater and world, for it sheds light on a blindness on Austin's part to the interaction between speech acts and the ritualistic character of most of what he calls the "context" of an utterance.

23. Too great is the temptation to consider "Circe"'s hallucinations as an "acting out" of repressed desires, the representation of the unconscious of, alternatively, Leopold Bloom, Stephen Dedalus, or James Joyce himself. Needless to say, in trying to explain "Circe" with reference to any of these three figures one encounters insurmountable difficulties and contradictions because "Circe"'s exuberant theatricality cannot be determined by the subjectivity of author or protagonists, no matter how many repressions one endows them with. Michel Rabaté takes a more differentiated view and speaks of the hallucinatory and gestural "Circe" as the "textual unconscious" of the novel (Rabaté, *James Joyce,* 76).

24. David Hayman discussed the extent to which Joyce was interested in Mallarmé at various stages of his career. Most of Joyce's knowledge of Mallarmé was probably funneled through Arthur Symons (Hayman, *Joyce et Mallarmé;* see also Atheron, *Book at the Wake*).

25. In his recent study on the romantic closet drama, *Closet Performances,* Michael Simpson also links this genre to Eve Sedgwick's project of an epistemology of the closet drama.

26. In *Time and Western Man,* Wyndham Lewis dismisses *Ulysses* because of its theatricality and speaks of Joyce's "stage Jew (Bloom), a stage Irishman (Mulligan), or a stage Anglo-Saxon (Haines)" (94).

27. Marguerite Harkness recognizes the central role of gesture in "Circe" and underlines the relation between rhythm and visibility (Harkness, "Gesture in 'Circe,'" 17).

28. The most influential notation system for dance was designed by Raoul Anger Feuillet about 1700. His notation method formalizes primarily the positions and movements of the feet and the posture of the whole body, a notation that appears to the eye of the observer as a veritable arabesque. The system of choreography devised around 1850 by Friedrich Albert Zorn tried to expand this notation to represent positions for hands and other, more differentiated gestures and postures. According to his method, some of the commands, such as "Balancé!" or "Ronde!" can be represented in not only the patterns they form on the floor but also the gestures and postures that go along with them. The Benesh movement notation similarly tries to capture the entire body in its choreography. For this purpose, Benesh devised a system in the mid-twentieth century dividing the human body into five parts, so that every kind of gesture and posture could be transcribed onto the five lines of the notation system, taken from musical notation.

29. Fritz Zenn has pointed out that "Circe"'s interest in verbs of movement is often characterized by a lack of co-ordination (Zenn, "'Circe' as Harking Back in Provective Arrangement").

30. The stage direction also alludes to a popular song, "My Head is Simply Swirling," and the sequence "weaving, unweaving" can be seen as related to Walter Pater's aesthetics.

31. The word *arabesque* itself is a romantic term and comes from Arabic script; it is, at it origin, both shape and text.

32. In a recent study, *Gestural Politics,* Christy L. Burns has used the term *gesture* to describe the parodic strategies of Joyce.

33. Robert McAlmon, "Mr. Joyce directs an Irish word ballet," in Beckett et al., *Our Exagmination Round his Factification for Incamination of Work in Progress,* 106.

34. Christy Burnes even argues that Joyce was influenced by Jacques-Dalcroze,

although there is little more than circumstantial evidence for this interesting speculation (Burnes, *Gestural Politics*, 25).

35. These two traditions, the search for a universal or even perfect language and the search for an original language are two sides of the same coin. Umberto Eco, for example, has traced the lineage of the search for the perfect language from Genesis through Dante to Raimond Lull, the cabala and Leibniz to Esperanto (Eco, *La ricerca della lingua perfetta nella cultura europea*). They all try to overcome the trauma of Babel through systems, whether rational or mystical. The search for the origin tries to undercut the trauma of Babel through a quasi-natural language, whether of gestures, sounds, or other primitive signs, and supposedly can do without code and interpretation.

36. Hugo von Hofmannstal, for example, turned from prose to drama and opera in order to overcome literature's exclusive reliance on language.

37. L. H. Platt relates "Circe"'s ritualistic elements to the Irish Literary Theatre and its revivalist national mythology (Platt, "Ulysses 15 and the Irish Literary Theatre").

38. Stephan Heath discusses *Ulysses* in conjunction with Marcel Jousse in "Joyce in Language." Concentrating on the chapter "Oxen of the Sun," he relates Joyce's concern with the origin of language to Jousse's system and to the notion of a gestural language in *Finnegans Wake*. Lorraine Weir also reconstructs Jousse's argument about the origin of language and applies it to *Finnegans Wake*, without, however, engaging in a discussion of its gestural aesthetics (Weir, "Choreography of Gesture").

39. Colum and Colum, *Our Friend James Joyce*, 130–31.

40. Laurent Milesi discusses the relation between Vico's model of hieroglyphics and Jousse's adaptation of the origin of language debate in *Finnegans Wake*, describing them by means of a deconstructive notion of *écriture* (Milesi, "Vico . . . Jousse: Joyce . . . Langue").

41. Jousse, *L'anthropologie du geste*, 88.

42. Joyce, *Finnegans Wake*, 468.

43. Bergson, "Laughter."

44. In *Stephen Hero* Stephen observes: "There should be an art of gesture, . . . Yes? Of course I don't mean an art of gesture in the sense that the locution professor understands the word. For him a gesture is an emphasis. I mean a rhythm" (184). Jackson Cope follows Stephen's insistence on the rhythmic quality of an art of gesture, placing it in the context of Plato's dialogue on the origin of language but also in the context of Mallarmé's interest in rhythm (see Cope, "Rhythmic Gesture").

45. Steven Connor, in "Jigajiga . . . Yummyyum . . . Pfuiiiiiii . . . Bbbbblllllllblbl-blbloschb! 'Circe's' Ventriloquy," reconstructs the Aristotelian tradition of understanding the first entelechy as the autonomy of objects to express themselves and thus discusses the different languages of objects in "Circe."

46. St. Augustine first differentiated among natural, artificial, and conventional signs, so that the elements of the sacraments could be considered natural, rather than conventional or arbitrary, signs for Christ's body and blood. And Irenaeus established the doctrine that they not only signified body and blood but "became" body and blood, so that the priest no longer quoted Jesus but uttered the words *Hoc est corpus meum* — *Hic est sanguis meus* as Christ, *in persona Christi*. Duns Scotus emphasized the central importance of the gestures involved in the sacraments, and he therefore differentiated between the material objects involved in the transubstantiation, *materia remota*, and the gestures of the priest, *materia prossima*. Bread and wine, as well as the gesture of holding them up, are material components that are transformed during the sacrament; the one cannot be conceived of without the other. For an authoritative

account of the history and present state of Catholic dogma, see Cardinal Joseph Ratzinger and Johann Auer's *Dogmatic Theology,* the authoritative synopsis by two of the present-day hard-liners in the Vatican establishment.

47. The *Rubaiyat* includes a glorification of the drinking of wine, which has surprised many commentators. The claim is that Mohammed's prohibition of wine was due to an accident and that if God placed love of wine into human nature, he must have wanted us to drink it.

48. Dujardin, *The Bays Are Sere and Interior Monologue,* 100, 113.

49. Barkentin, *James Joyce's "Ulysses" in Nighttown.*

50. The only attempt to re-create a parallel structure between the two is made in the final scene, when Stephen's mother appears only to Stephen, while the other figures present in the brothel see Stephen fighting an invisible apparition with his ashplant. Here the authors of the dramatic script indicate, again in square brackets, that the hallucinatory nature of the scene applies only to Stephen, while the other characters remain at the "reality" level.

51. The only time Joyce indicates an act of pantomime in "Circe" occurs within a stage direction saying that "people" are casting "pantomime stones" at Leopold Bloom (Joyce, *Ulysses,* 100). Acts of pantomime are added at least three times (34, 74, 119), while Joyce's indication of the pantomime stoning is elided in the dramatized version.

Chapter 4 Gertrude Stein

1. In her excellent study *"They Watch Me as They Watch This"* Jane Bowers argues that *Four Saints* became an opera only through Thomson's music and observes that the text can be described as a "counter-text," a text that counters its performance (43). It is the purpose of my argument to specify the ways in which the text of *Four Saints in Three Acts* must be changed in order to be

staged, but also to describe the extent to which this "counter-text" also depends on the theater and the notion of the stageable text from which it departs so decidedly.

2. Stein, *Last Operas and Plays,* xl. All references to *Four Saints in Three Acts* and to Stein's essay "Plays" are to this edition.

3. Foremost among the critics to have foregrounded this culture is Ian Watt in *Rise of the Novel.*

4. Ackerman, *Portable Theater,* xii.

5. Bourdieu, *Rules of Art.*

6. Marjorie Perloff, in her classic study *The Poetics of Indeterminacy,* aligns Stein's repetition with surrealism (108).

7. The possibility of such a critique of theatricalism outside the theater testifies to the dissociation of theater as an art form and theatricality as a general value. This dissociation is confirmed by the fact that Fried's particular formulations against theater have found an unlikely echo, as Philip Auslander has pointed out, on the part of performance studies, which is eager to distance itself from theater studies (this echo is one instance of protheatricalism and anti-theatricalism's sharing a critique of real existing theater) (Auslander, *From Acting to Performance,* 49ff.). Advancing a related argument, I will not defend the theater against Fried's attack, as is frequently done, but will argue that his explicitly modernist anti-theatricalism is a late version of modernism's resistance to the theater.

8. Fried, "Art and Objecthood," 21.

9. See Bowers, *"They Watch Me as They Watch This,"* 133: "Stein tries to minimize the intervention of the actor, to oppose his dynamism and, in a sense, to prevent him from acting."

10. In his notebooks, which are full of observations about the theater and dramatic fragments, Franz Kafka makes a similar observation about the act of readings plays with one's finger on the list of *dramatis personae.*

11. It is Stein's reform of the dramatic text that determines her in a tradition that Marc Robinson has called the "other American drama."

12. Stein, *Geography and Plays,* 298, 300, 301.

13. Stein, *How to Write,* 239.

14. Virgil Thomson even went so far as to posit a correspondence between Stein's version of the textual portrait and the opera, both of which, according to him, depend on such essential "characterization" (Tommasini, *Virgil Thomson's Musical Portraits,* 15). In fact, Thomson was so taken with Stein's textual portraits that he readily transposed her technique into music and composed almost 150 such musical portraits, for which the person to be depicted had to sit as for a painted portrait (23).

15. Daniel Albright's interesting account of *Four Saints in Three Acts* as an "antinarrative" model of theater could therefore be slightly modified to include forms of descriptive narrative (Albright, "Opera with No Acts," 578).

16. Meisel, *Realizations.*

17. Jane Bowers discusses Stein's break with the time of narration and opposes it to the effect of seamless flow Stein's writings aspire to (Bowers, *Gertrude Stein,* 133–34). Such a seamless flow, I would argue, ultimately ends up converging with the *stasis* of ekphrasis.

18. Thomson, *Virgil Thomson,* 171.

19. Elinor Fuchs takes Stein's notion of the landscape play and constructs a tradition of static landscape plays from Maeterlinck through Heiner Müller to Robert Wilson (Fuchs, *Death of Character,* 96 ff.).

20. At least from the perspective of drama and theater Stein is situated squarely within a modernist, and not a postmodernist tradition, as some critics such as Ellen Berry have argued. In the history of the theater the postmodern is associated with performance and with a tradition that seeks to eliminate the dramatic text. Not only does Stein insist on the dramatic text but the dramatic text derives its energy from a modernist anti-theatricalism (see Berry, *Curved Thought and Textual Wandering*).

21. Bonnie Marranca has continued this Steinian tradition of placing static image over dramatic action and coined the term *theater of images* (Marranca, *Theater of Images*).

22. Stein had of course promoted this view of her work and also written *Three Painters,* on Cézanne, Picasso, and Matisse.

23. Ryan, *Gertrude Stein's Theatre of the Absolute,* 163–64.

24. Benjamin K. Bennett has used the phrase *Cubism of time* to describe Strindberg and Ibsen (Bennett, "Strindberg and Ibsen").

25. Stein, *Everybody's Autobiography,* 48, 98, 111, 193, 194, 283.

26. Gertrude Stein to Mabel Dodge, 1913, quoted in Bowers, *Gertrude Stein,* 107.

27. Thomson, *Virgil Thomson Reader,* 56.

28. Ibid., 54.

29. Maurice Grosser, scenario included with compact sound disk of Stein's *Four Saints in Three Acts,* 7.

30. Michael J. Hoffman observed that Compère and Commère are "really confidantes to speak some of the lines of narration" (Hoffman, *Gertrude Stein,* 82).

31. Virgil Thomson, libretto included with Stein's *Four Saints in Three Acts.*

32. Michael Kaufmann situates Stein's oeuvre, and *Tender Buttons* in particular, in a history of "meta-textual" writings "that show the effects of print's repetition and codification on language" (Kaufmann, *Textual Bodies,* 16). My analysis, by extension, situates Stein's plays in the particular context of textual theater.

33. Thomson, *Virgil Thomson Reader,* 55.

34. In a related vein Daniel Albright observes that "it is as if Stein were not so much writing a play as making a preliminary sketch for one" (Albright, "Opera with No Acts," 582). However, he then proceeds to claim that the narrative of the play never gets told without realizing that there is a narra-

tive that gets told, namely, the narrative of preparing a play. Cf. Andrej Wirth's "Gertrude Stein und ihre Kritik der dramatischen Vernunft," whose thesis is that in *Four Saints in Three Acts* the metalanguage of theater becomes the object language of the play.

35. This interest in the process of production has been pointed out with various degrees of specificity by different critics, in particular by Bonnie Marranca in her introduction to Stein, *Last Operas and Plays,* viii–ix.

36. Here I disagree with Jane Bowers, who argues in *"They Watch Me as They Watch This"* that Thomson's libretto "obscured its [Stein's text's] purpose and meaning . . . by ignoring the improvisational illusion that Stein created" (60). Since the improvisational nature applies not only to the process of writing but also to the process of staging, the metatheatrical discussion between Compère and Commère carries the improvisation to the stage.

37. Meg Albrinck makes a related argument, observing that the adaptation by Grosser violates the "fluidity" and "free play" of the original libretto, thus discounting "the powerful female vision of the 1927 version by positioning the women, specifically Saint Therese, as objects of the male gaze" ("How can a sister see Saint Therese suitably," 1). Again I would argue that this is true, though not because of some heterosexual fantasy on the part of Grosser (an unlikely proposition, given that Grosser was Thomson's lover), but because the theater subjects the textual, resistant closet drama to the more general visibility of the theater.

38. One of the prominent readings along the lines of Kristeva's and Cixous's *écriture feminine* is Marianne DeKoven's *A Different Language.* A more recent and very compelling example is Lisa Ruddick's *Reading Gertrude Stein.*

39. Johnson, *World of Difference,* 25 ff.

40. Watson, *Prepare for Saints.*

41. Cf. Douglas, *Terrible Honesty,* 117.

Chapter 5 William Butler Yeats

1. Yeats, *Autobiography,* 215.

2. One can turn to the work of Arthur Symons in order to trace the influence of Mallarmé's theatrical writings in the English-speaking world. Early in his career, Symons started to imitate the technique of Mallarmé's theater-texts in a series of poems on dancers and, more specifically, in poetic ballet reviews published in such literary journals as *Sketch.* In addition, his aesthetic treatises on dance and the other arts, collected as *Studies in the Seven Arts* (1906), include passages that sound like domesticated versions of Mallarmé's theater-texts: "and the dancer, with her gesture, all pure symbol, evokes, from her mere beautiful motion, idea. . . ; and her rhythm reveals to you the soul of her imagined being" (Symons, *Studies in the Seven Arts,* 391). These isolated gestures of dancers, fractured syntax, and depersonalized dances evoking nothing but an abstract notion of beauty are taken directly from Mallarmé's more elegant texts. Finally, it was Arthur Symons who wrote the most authoritative summary of Wagner's theory, "The Idea of Richard Wagner" (1905), also collected in *Studies in the Seven Arts,* in which he faithfully underlined Wagner's insistence on the theatricality of the mime and even mentioned Wagner's obscure theory of gesture, in particular the functional kinship between gesture and orchestra in the expression of the so-called unsayable (264). Symons was thus responsible for transmitting the cultural context of Mallarmé and French symbolism, including their surprising celebration of Wagner, to England.

3. Such an attitude is a familiar topos in eighteenth-century theater reform, especially in Gottsched, who instructed actors to gesture only while reciting their lines in order to keep gestures in their subservient position to language.

4. In 1906 Yeats disapprovingly singled out an actor who "gesticulates wildly,"

thus breaking up the rhythm of the line (Yeats, *Explorations,* 214).

5. In the reconstructed origin of Greek theater it is a messenger who first addresses the chorus and thus initiates a short scene, or *epeisodion,* of dialogue in iambic meter before the chorus continues its lyrical recitation. This messenger is, according to Wolfgang Schadewaldt and others, the first actor, whose name, *hypokrites,* originally means "answerer" before it begins to imply illusionist impersonation and then finally our "hypocritical" deception (Schadewaldt, *Die griechische Tragödie*).

6. Yeats alienated the acting couple Willie and Frank Fay, who had helped found the Irish National Theater but had tried in vain to convince Yeats to produce more "popular" and less "literary" plays (Yeats, *Explorations,* 108).

7. Yeats, *Variorum Edition.* Unless otherwise noted, all references to Yeats's dramatic oeuvre are to this edition.

8. We may be reminded here of Henry James's *The Real Thing* (1891), a short story in which an impoverished aristocratic couple hired to pose for a painting is ultimately replaced by a charwoman and a street vendor who are better at representing the attributes of aristocracy than the aristocrats themselves. There can be no doubt that James relished this argument about the absurd success of impersonation in this story, which was written in the middle of his troubled engagement with the theater. A few years later he would phrase the same intuition more explicitly: "I may have been meant for the Drama—God Knows—but I certainly wasn't meant for the Theatre" (James, *Letters,* 226).

9. See Karen Dorn's discussion of how Yeats's theory of the "Mask and the Antithetical Self" may have influenced the ending of *The Player Queen* (Dorn, *Players and Painted Stage,* 58–60).

10. Yvor Winters, the most reliably antitheatrical critic, also refuses to consider Yeats's plays as pieces of dramatic literature; but then again, he also refuses to consider Yeats's poems as adequate pieces of lyrical poetry (see Winters, *Poetry of W. B. Yeats*). Helen Vendler calls Yeats's plays "dramatized lyric" (Vendler, *Yeats's Vision and the Later Plays,* 140). This position is endlessly replayed in the opposition between readers of Yeats's lyrical poetry and those historians of the Irish drama movement, who feel compelled to praise his plays excessively.

11. Here I disagree with Katherine Worth, who reads this scene as a universal playacting: "By the end of the play, the theatrical mode has become universal; there are no non-actors, only different degrees of skill and self-consciousness in performance" (Worth, *Irish Drama of Europe from Yeats to Beckett,* 156). If there is universal playacting at the end, this universality exists by virtue of having banished any "real" player and having transformed all the "real" players into dancers, who no longer impersonate.

12. Frank Kermode traces Yeats's use of dance to the *fin-de-siècle*'s obsession with the female body (see Kermode, *Romantic Image*).

13. Here I am indebted to William Worthen's essential work on Yeats. Worthen also sees in Yeats an attempt to transpose poetry onto the theater, creating what he then defines as poetic theater (see Worthen, *Modern Drama and the Rhetoric of the Theater*). My notion of diegetic theater takes its point of departure from Worthen's notion of poetic theater in order to place Yeats in the tradition of anti-theatricalism.

14. James Flannery sees in Yeats's work in the theater an endorsement of actors (Flannery, *W. B. Yeats and the Idea of a Theatre,* 191ff.).

15. If Yvor Winters *(Poetry of W. B. Yeats)* could have overcome his deeply rooted prejudice against all things theatrical, which led him to ignore Yeats's dramatic work even when he was attacking the poet, he might have seen in

Yeats's turn to the theater a much closer analogy to Mallarmé's aesthetics of suggestion than in the more rigid and decodable system that perhaps governs Yeats's poetry.

16. W. B. Yeats, introduction to Pound and Fenollosa, *Classic Nôh Theatre of Japan,* 159, hereafter cited as *Classic Nôh.*

17. See Sekine, "Yeats and the Noh," 160. While Sekine is insightful in his assessment of Yeats's lack of intimacy with Nôh, he at times does not do justice to Yeats's literary and theatrical ambitions. Sekine's comments on Yeats's use of the Noh musicians is particularly interesting: Sekine describes these musicians who interact with the players on the main stage as a combination of Nôh musicians *(hayashikata),* who comment on the play through music, and the Greek chorus, which interacts with the individual players (156).

18. Yeats proved weak in his knowledge of Nôh on other fronts as well, mistaking, for example, Japanese dancers for Chinese ones in his poem *Nineteen Hundred Nineteen:* "When Loie Fuller's Chinese dancers enwound/A shining web, a floating ribbon of cloth" (*Collected Poems,* 208).

19. Despite the significance of the Nôh theater for Yeats's new understanding of theater, it is difficult to identify which elements may have been borrowed from what he took to be the Nôh tradition. Massaru Sekine and Christopher Murray *(Yeats and the Noh)* highlight the superficiality of Yeats's knowledge. The distance between Yeats's *At the Hawk's Well* and Nôh theater is demonstrated most clearly, perhaps, by the fact that the play had to be entirely rewritten so that it would at least resemble Nôh theater when it was finally performed in Japan. Akhtar Qamber mentions this Nôh version, while at the same time trying to establish the Nôh-qualities of Yeats's "Plays for Dancers" (Qamber, *Yeats and the Noh,* 78). In fact the retranslation of *At the Hawk's Well* into Nôh proved

to be an inspiring experience for the adapters. At least in the most famous of the several readaptations, the adapters took several liberties not allowed by the rigid Nôh tradition and introduced, for example, a moving and disjointed chorus. Thematic comparisons between Nôh and Yeats's plays give us little more than a few abstract topoi and character constellations. Richard Taylor, for example, points out a certain similarity between *At the Hawk's Well* and *Kami No Yoro* (Sustenance of age), by Motokiyo Zeami, as well as certain formal correspondences, such as the removal of the protagonist during the climactic scene (Taylor, *Drama of W. B. Yeats,* 120, 131).

20. Eric Bentley has pointed out the selective character of Yeats's interest in the Nôh theater: "Yeats's dance plays are as distinct from their Japanese prototypes as from Western drama. The Noh play can become anything you want to make it. Brecht's Noh plays—*Der Jasager* and *Der Neinsager*—are utterly different in spirit from Yeats's" (Bentley, *In Search of Theater,* 302).

21. Yeats also might have noted an antigestural argument in his reading of Nietzsche's *Der Fall Wagner.* Frances Nesbitt Oppel discusses at length Nietzsche's influence on Yeats and remarks on Yeats's reading of *Der Fall Wagner* in 1903 (Oppel, *Mask and Tragedy,* 1).

22. Paul de Man, "The Rhetoric of Temporality," in *Blindness and Insight.*

23. Writers from Mallarmé to Yeats inherit this understanding of the symbol from what Tzvetan Todorov calls the "syntheticism" of the romantic symbol (Todorov, *Theories of the Symbol,* 184). Todorov shows how the notion of the symbol, from St. Augustine to Freud, oscillates between the romantic understanding described here and the notion of the symbol as conventional sign, which he sees at work, somewhat mistakenly I believe, in Freud's system of symbols.

24. Craig's harsh polemic against actors did not keep him from idolizing individual actors such as Eleonora Duse, whose "natural" style he praised for its economy in contrast to the melodramatic style of her rival Sarah Bernhardt.

25. In her insightful study *The Plays of W. B. Yeats* Sylvia Ellis observes, for example, that Craig's father, a famous actor, decorated his house *à la japonaiserie* and liked his wife to dress in a kimono (90).

26. The first play to feature Craig's screens was *The Hour Glass*, written in 1903.

27. Craig, *On The Art of the Theatre*, 61–62.

28. Katherine Worth mentions Beckett's attachment to *At the Hawk's Well* (*Irish Drama of Europe from Yeats to Beckett*, 256). Anthony Roche, in his *Contemporary Irish Drama*, observes that Beckett copied the entire opening passage in his notebook but then used only the first line in the published version of *Happy Days* (25).

29. Frank Kermode, in his study *Romantic Image*, aligns Yeats's notion of the image with romanticism and the imagists.

30. Michael Issacharoff introduced this terminology in *Discourse as Performance*, 211–24. See also his article "Stage Codes" in Issacharoff and Jones, *Performing Texts*.

31. While Yeats's use of diegetic attendants and musicians placed at the back of the stage corresponds to Nôh theater, it is remarkable that when it comes to the dramaturgy of the play, he reverts to the basic techniques of the so-called well-made play. The characters' past, motivations, and desires are revealed indirectly through dialogue, avoiding the direct introduction of characters to the audience—the players' singing "I am so-and-so, I have come to do so-and-so"—that is the mark of Nôh theater. We might say, then, that Yeats retains elements of the Western dramaturgy when it comes to structuring an exposition or a dramatic climax even as he also adopts diegetic musicians and stylized gestures from the Nôh theater. (At the same time he does not,

for example, adhere to the use of masks in the Nôh theater, where only women, ghosts, and gods wear masks, while neither male characters, musicians, attendants, nor the chorus do.)

32. Yeats explains: "I had begun it with an ordinary stage scene in the mind's eye, curtained walls, a window and door at back, a curtained door at left. I now changed the stage directions and wrote songs for the unfolding and folding of the curtain that it might be played in a studio or a drawing-room like my dance plays" (*Collected Plays*, 364).

33. In the introduction to Pound's edition of Nôh theater, Yeats writes: "The players wear masks and found their movements upon those of puppets: the most famous of all Japanese dramatists composed entirely for puppets" (*Classic Nôh*, 158).

34. Wilde's *Salomé* is one of the many bridges between French and British symbolism. Written in French, it received its first staging by the symbolist director Lugne-Poe. Arthur Symons could not resist writing a long piece, "Dance of the Daughters of Herodias" (in Symons, *Poems*, 2:36), on the Salomé material, which had captivated so many of his symbolist predecessors.

35. Ellis observes that Salomé is situated in the fifteenth phase of Yeats's system presented in his text *A Vision* (Ellis, *Plays of W. B. Yeats*, 66).

36. Frank Kermode comments on the connection between *A Full Moon in March* and *Salomé* (Kermode, *Romantic Image*, 89).

37. Françoise Meltzer, in her study *Salome and the Dance of Writing*, has reconstructed the intricate intertextuality and different modes of adaptation that characterize the history of the Salomé story from the Bible via Flaubert and Mallarmé, using the notion of ekphrasis to describe how the poetic strategies of transcribing dance are affected by their object and thus acquire qualities of the dance themselves.

38. Denis Donoghue discusses Yeats's

understanding of fable in "Yeats's Theater" in Bloom, *William Butler Yeats,* 160.

Chapter 6 Bertolt Brecht

1. Peter Szondi uses the term *epic theater* as a characterization of theater as such (Szondi, *Theorie des modernen Dramas*). Other dramatic critics acknowledge Brecht's status by defining the theater that came after him as post-Brechtian theater. Hans-Thies Lehmann, for example, calls "post-dramatic" a tradition of theater that leaves the horizon of epic theater (Lehmann, *Postdramatisches Theater*).

2. I will reiterate what some critics have already pointed out, namely, that the translation of Brecht's *Verfremdungs-effect* as "alienation effect" is a severe and also ideological mistake that derives from a cold-war association of Brecht with dogmatic communism. Martin Esslin's work on Brecht, for all its merits, is one of the origins of this misunderstanding (see Esslin, *Brecht, a Choice of Evils*). Brecht's term *Ver-fremdung* has in fact nothing to do with Marx's *Entfremdung,* which has been correctly translated as "alienation," as in "alienation from nature" or "alien-ated labor." Brecht's *Verfremdung,* in contrast, must be translated as "es-trangement," which implies making something that is familiar unfamiliar, or strange, a term Brecht inherits from the Russian formalists' *ostranenje.* It is true that Brecht did think about "alien-ation" [*Entfremdung*], but this term is at all times distinct in its meaning from the German *Verfremdung.*

3. Reinelt, for example, adopts Brecht's method for feminist theory (see Reinelt, *After Brecht*). See also Dia-mond, *Unmaking Mimesis.*

4. Jameson, *Brecht and Method.*

5. All references to Brecht's work are to Brecht, *Gesammelte Werke.*

6. Ibid., 17:991–92.

7. Friedrich Nietzsche, "Der Fall Wagner," in *Richard Wagner in Bayreuth, Der Fall Wagner, Nietzsche contra Wagner,* 119.

8. Martin Esslin in his seminal 1959 study on Brecht, *Brecht, a Choice of Evils,* and many after him consider Brecht's critique too narrowly as a reaction against naturalism and expressionism (110ff.).

9. For a more extended discussion of this hierarchy, see Bourdieu, *Rules of Art.*

10. Decades later the Doors would take up as one of their lead songs "Show me the way to the next whiskey bar," testifying perhaps to the fact that the strategy of critical thematization had failed.

11. At the same time, the separation of the elements would solve the ancient rivalry among the different arts. Once the arts are fundamentally indepen-dent of one another there is no longer a question of creating a hierarchy among them.

12. In the reception history of Wagner's operas critics have foregrounded either these operas' lack of organic unity, as did Nietzsche and Adorno, or their melting-pot effect, as did Brecht and Weill. Cf. Richard Klein's reading of modernist critiques of Wagner, from Adorno to Thomas Mann, through the lens of Nietzsche (Klein, *Solidarität mit Metaphysik?* 275ff.).

13. Brook, *Empty Space,* 9.

14. Brecht, *Stücke 2,* 520. Translation taken from, Bertolt Brecht, "'The Rise and Fall of the City of Mahagonny' and 'The Seven Deadly Sins,'" edited by John Willett and Ralph Manheim, translated by W. H. Auden and Chester Kallman (New York: Arcade, 1996) 21.

15. It is striking that the most important anti-naturalist plays, such as Maeter-linck's *Pélléas et Mélissande* and Wilde's *Salomé,* survive only as part of the opera repertoire and that Stein's dra-matic texts are performed mostly in Thompson's opera versions. By the same token, one is tempted to say that the only way for Yeats's "Plays for Dancers" to establish themselves in a performance repertoire would have been for Yeats to collaborate with a more gifted composer.

16. Rather than being a turning point in Brecht's oeuvre, as the "Plays for Dancers" were for Yeats, *Der Jasager* (1930) marks the end of the collaboration between Brecht and Kurt Weill, which had included *The Three Penny Opera, Man Equals Man,* and *The Rise and Fall of the City of Mahagonny.*

17. In adapting Nôh dramaturgy but not Nôh theatricality, Brecht is closer to Pound than to Yeats, since Pound too was more interested in Nôh dramaturgy. In contrast to Brecht, Pound never developed a reform of the theater that would enable him to adapt Nôh theater.

18. The mimetic repertoire of *Taniko* includes, for example, a boy's putting his head on his master's lap and being carried across the stage by pilgrims, who hurl him down a mountain, and finally a god who actually fells two small trees with an ax. By the sixteenth century the taste of the Nôh public had apparently changed and demanded more mimetic action than the classical Nôh plays of the fourteenth century.

19. John Fuegi argues that Brecht exploited Elizabeth Hauptmann by not crediting her enough for her collaboration (Fuegi, *Brecht and Company*).

20. Brecht's use of the chorus is even further removed from the Nôh chorus than Yeats's musicians. In *Der Jasager* the chorus stands for the "thousand" eyes and lives of the party and thus introduces a point of view that is dissociated from the fate of the individual who must be sacrificed for the greater good.

21. Brecht, *Der Jasager und Der Neinsager,* 7; all references to *Der Jasager* and *Taniko* are to this edition. This similarity does not extend to the register of language. *Taniko,* like all Nôh plays, uses an extremely stylized language full of references to contemporary poetry and saturated with repetitions. It is a language that even contemporary court audiences had difficulty understanding. Brecht's language, in contrast, may be stylized, but it is not removed from

spoken German. Needless to say, it is not a language for an aristocracy.

22. Yeats had avoided this aspect of Nôh dramaturgy, relying exclusively on the chorus to provide explanatory and diegetic commentary. Yeats extended the reach of the commenting musicians also in his later plays, such as *A Full Moon in March.*

23. States, *Pleasures of the Play,* 111.

24. In his compelling analysis of Brecht, Austin E. Quigley writes that "reality-reproducing mimesis thus goes the same way as empathy" (Quigley, *Modern Stage and Other Worlds,* 153), foregrounding the way in which Brecht forces the audience to assume multiple perspectives. My analysis of Brecht's technique of dividing and framing theatrical mimesis by means of diegesis can be seen as yet one more version of Brecht's attempt to make it impossible to assume a single, "transcendental perspective" (154).

25. Reiner Steinweg and, following him, Fredric Jameson have pointed out that the *Lehrstücke* do not demand an audience. Steinweg's work, in particular, has been important to understanding the centrality of the *Lehrstücke* for Brecht (Steinweg, *Das Lehrstück;* idem, *Lehrstück und episches Theater;* Jameson, *Brecht and Method*).

26. Brecht's mistrust of the theater is, for example, what separates him from Erwin Piscator, who tried to increase the theatricality of the stage by including, in a dadaist manner, as many sign systems, media, and arts as possible. For an analysis of Piscator's political theater, see, e.g., Bryant-Bertail, "*The Good Soldier Schweik* as Dialectical Theater."

27. Jameson recognizes a more general principle of allegory at work in Brecht's oeuvre, especially in the "radical insufficiency of the representation itself" (*Brecht and Method,* 122). My discussion of the *subscriptio* in *Mahagonny* can be seen as an extension of Jameson's understanding of Brecht.

28. Benjamin, *Versuche über Brecht,* 22.

29. Dieter Wöhrle pursues this trajectory further and discusses Brecht's radio plays and his contribution to film (Wöhrle, *Bertolt Brecht's medienästhetische Versuche*). Dietrich Scheunemann ("Montage in Theater and Film") has pointed out in detail the influence of montage on Brecht.

30. Borrowing from Benjamin, Susan Sontag has pointed out the difference between continuous space in theater and discontinuous space in film (Sontag, "Film and Theatre").

31. A good account of this connection between gesture, bearing, and character is given in Schmidt, "Ethics of Gesture."

32. This emphasis on presenting only selected pieces of reality makes for the spare and diminished quality of many of Brecht's plays and has frequently provided the occasion to denounce their pedagogical impetus. But as Fredric Jameson has shown, Brecht's sparseness is not the same as the didactic simplicity of course books in Marxist history. Brecht does not offer solutions but presents situations that are first analyzed by actors and must then be analyzed and evaluated again by the audience. Augusto Boal recognized that Brecht's call for critical analysis was addressed to the actor and the audience alike and turned this insight into a practice of performance in which different members of the audience were invited to perform various versions and solutions of a given dramatic situation (Boal, *Theatre of the Oppressed in Europe*). These participatory models, which do not preach dogma but suggest problems, are no more than the extension of Brecht's own didactic *Lehrstücke* written for the interactive and participatory training of actors.

33. Here my analysis comes close to that of Patrice Pavis, who discusses Brecht's *gestus* as a link between the iconic system of gesture and the symbolic system of the arbitrary sign (Pavis, *Languages of the Stage,* 47). Mostly, however, Pavis refers to *gestus* as a "signal" emitted by the actor (41, 44). By concentrating on the semiology of *gestus,* Pavis does not consider, as I do, *gestus* as a compromise between mimesis and diegesis and hence in a formal manner as a combination of mimesis's iconicity and diegesis's arbitrary signs.

34. Quigley, *Modern Stage and Other Worlds,* 149 ff.

35. Gilbert, *Bertolt Brecht's Striving for Reason,* 11. While Brecht overcame his habit of "conducting" Wagner's *Tristan und Isolde* in his study, Weill, much to Brecht's chagrin, acknowledged the "strongest detachment from Wagner (but not at all a rejection)" (Weill, *Musik und Theater,* 302). Although Weill joined Brecht in seeking to "destroy the notion of music drama" (302), he was more aware than Brecht that Wagner was the single most dominant model for a genuinely theatrical music available in the early twentieth century. It was Weill, then, who made the definition of gestural music compatible with Wagner's operas, emphasizing its grounding in dramatic action and more specifically in the movements of the body. This debt runs counter to the more overt differences, most prominently Weill's commitment to the number opera, which must be seen as the opposite of Wagner's *opera seria* and its technique of transition and endless melody. In particular, Weill continued to consider Wagner's operas to be the "purest theater music" (248).

36. Weill, *Musik und Theater,* 53.

37. The musical *gestus* is thus a particular instance of Weill's more general opposition to Wagner's operas, to which he nevertheless remained attached throughout his life. Herbert Lindenberger has outlined how Weill's number opera is directed against Wagner's music drama (Lindenberger, *Opera in History,* 191–239).

38. Even as Weill tries to use music to control and notate theatrical mimesis, he turns music itself into a theatri-

cal, and gestural, entity by proposing that the orchestra be moved onto the stage. This decision to expose the gestures of music is directed explicitly against Wagner's famous strategy of hiding the orchestra in a pit. For Weill, music becomes one of the arts competing for the space of the stage, interrupting and framing other arts, such as acting, scenery, or writing, and it ceases to merely amplify theatrical action from behind, or below, the scene. In his desire to expose music Weill follows Stravinsky's dedication to the spectacle of absolute music, for Stravinsky insisted that "one sees music. An experienced eye follows and judges, sometimes unconsciously, the performer's last gesture" (Stravinsky, *Poetics of Music in the Form of Six Lessons,* 171). Vera Stegmann discusses Stravinsky's affinity with Brecht and Weill and their interest in the visible gestures of making music in Stegmann, "An Opera For Three Pennies, A Violin For Ten Francs." Stravinsky and Weill introduced to modernism a conception of theatrical and gestural music that shaped an entire music tradition in the twentieth century, from Cage through Stockhausen to Kagel, a tradition that integrated the theatricality of musical performance into the structure of composition. Along similar lines, Edward Said discussed the irreducible performance character in figures such as Toscanini and Glenn Gould (Said, *Musical Elaborations;* cf. Sennett, *Fall of Public Man;* Goehr, *Quest for Voice*).

39. Hans-Georg Werner discusses Brecht's notion of *gestus* in relation to his lyrical poetry in "Gestische Lyrik."

40. Brecht and Neher, *Antigonemodell 1948,* 19.

Chapter 7 Samuel Beckett

1. Jean Martin, quoted in Worton, "*Waiting for Godot* and *Endgame,*" 67.

2. Gontarski, *Intent of Undoing in Samuel Beckett's Dramatic Texts,* 1.

3. Beckett, *Complete Dramatic Works,* 307.

All references to Beckett's dramatic oeuvre are to this edition.

4. William Worthen, Ruby Cohn, and others have devoted attention to the significance of the radio play for Beckett's dramatic oeuvre (see Cohn, *Just Play*).

5. The BBC was an institution and a medium that allowed this generation of playwrights to circumvent the apparatus and industry of the stage. At the same time, however, it forced them to conceive of a theater entirely without visual gestures and movement. An important part of postwar British theater was thus born from voices transmitted over the radio, a circumstance that certainly contributed to the conversational and discursive quality of these playwrights. Here we can find at least one important factor in the emergence of what John Russel Brown detailed as the "theatre language" of postwar British theater, in particular in the plays of Arden, Osborne, Pinter, and Wesker, all of which he traces back to the single-handed influence of *Waiting of Godot.* For Beckett shares with these playwrights an unusual dedication to the radio play (see Brown, *Study of Arden, Osborne, Pinter, and Wesker*).

6. My attempts to trace Beckett's antitheatricalism in his work against mimesis, against character, and against the actor, as well as in Beckett's stage directions, at times parallels William Worthen's excellent argument about "scripted bodies" in Yeats and Beckett (see Worthen, *Modern Drama and the Rhetoric of the Theater*).

7. I would like to thank Matt Laufer for stimulating discussions concerning this and other points pertaining to this chapter.

8. Knowlson, *Damned to Fame,* 558.

9. Schneider, "Any Way You Like, Alan," 35.

10. Beckett, *Eleutheria,* 5.

11. See also McMulligan, "Samuel Beckett as Director," 197.

12. S. E. Gontarski argues that Beckett's

prose is theatrical, considering those texts, such as *Company,* that were written as narrative prose texts but were later adapted to the stage. *Company,* therefore, is an "androgynous" work (Gontarski, "*Company* for Company," 193). Ruby Cohn has argued that Beckett's characters are "fictionalizers" (*Just Play,* 76), characters who define themselves in acts of fictionalization. Similarly, H. Porter Abbott has argued that in *Ohio Impromptu* "reading itself is theatrical" (Abbott, "Reading as Theatre," 5).

13. William Worthen *(Modern Drama and the Rhetoric of the Theater)* has pointed to the significance of stage directions in Beckett's oeuvre, in particular their relation to the stage. My own reading advances this understanding by embedding it in the history of antitheatricalism and by specifying the manner in which Beckett pits diegesis against mimesis.

14. Objects were central plot devices and means of expressions before symbolism—the handkerchief in Othello or the macaroons in *A Doll's House,* for example, as Austin Quigley demonstrates in his exemplary reading of the play (Quigley, *Modern Stage and other Worlds*). Symbolism, I argue, takes such uses of objects to an extreme and expands the ways in which they contribute to the signifying structure of the play.

15. Symbolism is not the first theater of gestures. The entire comic tradition, beginning with Greek comedy, relies on (often obscene) gestures, a tradition continued by the gestural commedia dell'arte and all varieties of physical comedy and slapstick. Also, medieval passion plays rely on liturgical and other gestures endowed with religious symbolism. Both traditions are central for the European avant-garde, in particular for Artaud's theater of symbolic gestures, modeled, even if in an orientalist fashion, on the gestural Balinese theater.

16. Shivaun O'Casey remarked in an inter-

view that she recognized the influence of her idol Craig in Beckett's theater (O'Casey, *Women in Beckett,* 29).

17. Haerdter, *Samuel Beckett inszeniert das "Endspiel,"* 103.

18. My intention is not to endorse Beckett's attitude toward the stagings of his plays but merely to outline the tradition and logic behind it. Beckett's control fantasy does not only have to do with a power struggle between author and director; it is embedded in a symbolist heritage that includes an entirely new understanding of stage directions.

19. In his seminal essay on *Endgame,* Adorno mentions repetition compulsion as a description of Beckett's characters ("Versuch das Endspiel zu verstehen," 313).

20. Oppenheim, *Directing Beckett,* 106.

21. Morris et al., *Gestures, Their Origins and Distribution,* xx.

22. There is a heterogeneous group of scholars concerned with the study of the ordinary. Michel de Certeau, for example, in his *Arts de faire* combines a Wittgensteinian study of ordinary language with Bourdieu's work, while Henri Lefebvre's *Critique de la vie quotidienne* considers the ordinary from a Marxist perspective. Freud, in his *Psychopathologie des Alltagslebens,* directs attention to the neglected gestures of the ordinary, most of which would be classified as expressive gestures.

23. *Endgame* thus participates in the tradition of works of art referring to chess, from various medieval works to Caroll's *Through the Looking-Glass* and Nabokov's *The Real Life of Sebastian Knight.*

24. The relation between Beckett's characters and different figures of slapstick comedy has been pointed out repeatedly, for example, by Norman Berlin in " Tragic Pleasure of Waiting for Godot."

25. Such scenes mark the moments of highest formalization in Beckett's art; they also mark the moments in which Beckett's plays embrace the mathematical possibilities of games, a features

that also surfaces in his narrative prose. Beckett's first major novel, *Molloy,* for example, written one year before *Waiting for Godot,* also contains gestures that put an object into circulation. The first-person narrator invents a complicated system of sixteen circulating pebbles by first taking them from his pockets one by one, sucking on them, and putting them into the next pocket. Even more so than the characters in *Waiting for Godot,* the narrator is concerned with keeping track of the stones and the probability of recurrence, permutation, and distribution.

26. Katharine Worth notes Beckett's reliance on stage directions, observing, "He uses stage-directions as a sculptor uses tools" (Worth, "The Space and the Sound in Beckett's Theatre," 185).

27. Charles R. Lyons emphasized the importance of the written text for Beckett and wondered to what extent his dramatic texts are "prose fiction enclosed in a theatrical conceit" (Lyons, "Beckett's Fundamental Theatre," 80).

28. Among the various attempts to create a notation system for gestures, Oskar Schlemmer's system of corporeal notation deserves particular attention since it not only served to describe Schlemmer's new gestural ballet, called *Triadisches Ballet,* but also influenced some of his famous paintings and therefore became an aesthetic principle. Its complex nature, however, prevented its more general distribution and application.

29. The gesture of praying constitutes, strictly speaking, yet another class of gestures: ritual and ceremonial gestures. Ritual gestures, more than any other set of gestures, are not only symbolic in the linguistic sense, i.e., gestures with a definite semantic structure; they are also symbolic in a ritualistic or even theological sense.

30. Ruby Cohn similarly argues that Beckett's plays try to "avoid soliloquy" (*Just Play,* 58), at least to the extent that soliloquies function to externalize

the speakers' internal thoughts and passions.

31. A comparable inversion can be seen in Delsarte's system of gestures. For Delsarte, not only are gestures produced and effected by specific passions but, conversely, when they are enacted they produce these respective passions in the agent. Most theories of affect and expression posit a principle of expression that determines the correlation between affect and gesture. The German philosopher Ludwig Klages, for example, calls the principle that organizes this correlation the principle of expression, *Ausdrucksprinzip* (Klages, *Grundlegung der Wissenschaft vom Ausdruck*). Other systems assume such a principle in a more tacit manner.

32. The main assumption for Freud and Breuer's case studies of hysteria is that the hysteric gestures are not directly correlated to certain affects and interior states. The analyst has to establish anew the "broken" connection between the corporeal gesture and the hidden trauma that is encrypted in the body (see Freud and Breuer, *Studien über Hysterie*).

33. Brater, "'Absurd' Actor in the Theatre of the Absurd," 207.

34. Anna McMulligan mentions the separation of speech and movement in *Waiting for Godot* in McMulligan, "Samuel Beckett as Director," 197.

35. Pountney, *Theatre of Shadows,* 189.

36. Paul J. Smith and Nic. Van der Toorn mention the difference between seeing the possible result of stage directions in a performance and reading them in the text. This difference leads them to the analysis of a "plus-value esthétique" (Smith and Van der Toorn, "Le Discours Didascalique dans *En Attendant Godot* et *Pas,*" 115). I argue that Beckett not only exploited the aesthetic value derived from the act of reading stage directions but also used this experience as a structuring principle for his plays. See also James Knowlson's detailed analysis of Beckett's notebooks,

which bear witness to the fact that Beckett frequently changed his own stage directions (Knowlson, "Beckett as Director").

37. Marie-Claude Hubert examines the nature of the truncated body in *Happy Days* and other plays in "Corps et voix dans le théâtre de Beckett a partir des années soixante," 46.

38. Colin Duckworth (*Angles of Darkness*, 74) has called this technique "contra-punctal," a useful term if one keeps in mind that the logic behind it is textual (the speech–stage direction sequence) and that its purpose is the mutual interruption of speech and gesture.

39. McMillan and Fehsenfeld, *Beckett in the Theatre*, 119.

40. More differentiated than Adorno's negative dialectics is Austin Quigley's Wittgensteinian approach. Quigley takes modern drama to be an investigation of the world, an epistemological tool that must be related to our world even if the world presented in a play no longer resembles our own (Quigley, *Modern Stage and Other Worlds*, 52).

41. Driven by the same desire, Beckett even intervened in the German translation, changing names once more: Estragon's "Scapegoat's Agony" becomes "Der Tod des armen Schluckers," which literally means "death of the beggar," and Vladimir's "Hard Stool" is retranslated to approximate the original French as "Krebsgeschwür der Greise," meaning "the tumors of old men" (*Warten auf Godot*, 55–56).

Epilogue

1. Müller, *Mauser*, 91.

2. This trend is supported from another side as well: when every drama is also read, taught, and circulated as text, printed drama no longer signifies a particular resistance to the theater.

3. Philip Auslander reports, for example, that Willem Dafoe sees a similarity between film acting and his acting as a member of the Wooster Group (Auslander, *Liveness*, 29).

4. Heiner Müller declared, for example, "I am not that interested in the theater" (quoted in Theweleit, *Heiner Müller*, 52). Theweleit also speaks of Müller's "Gestus des Nicht-Theater-Machens" (39). Similar sentiments can be found, for example, among the members of Elevator Repair Service (ERS), one of the newer New York companies. These declarations are particularly striking when one remembers that these companies tend to present performances that are nonetheless based on "classical" dramatic texts, such as *Phaedre*, the 2001 production of the Wooster Group, or *The Bacchae*, the 2000 production of ERS.

5. Analyzing theater in a fundamental way, we have to say that even the purest theatrical performance participates in some forms of repetition and iterability. The idea of a singular, unrepeatable event is the back formation of this fundamental form of iterability as it has been outlined by Jacques Derrida (*Limited Inc.*) and extended by Judith Butler (*Gender Trouble*). In this sense, the new recording media have only made apparent what has always been the case: there is no such thing as a unique event. Every event refers to previous events, some forms of trained behavior, forms of rehearsal, and so forth. In fact it was thanks to this general feature of iterability that both textual and spoken diegesis, as well as the new media, were able to invade theatrical performance in the first place.

6. This opposition can be fathomed from Plato's *Phaedrus* and its anxiety about writing as a secondary, recoded form of speech. Here I differ from Philip Auslander's *Liveness* (52ff.), to which this epilogue is otherwise much indebted. The difference between writing and other recorded media is only one of degree, since all recordings change what they record. Although a written description may be more indirect, it nevertheless constitutes a form of re-creation in a fixed medium. This is the

quality that alone matters here, for it means that a live event is invaded by something fixed, repeatable, something that has a copyright, and so forth.

7. From this vantage point, a particular dynamic of textual modernism begins to emerge: for all its withdrawal from the theater and from a theatrical vision of the public, the closet drama did not withdraw from the marketplace. On the contrary, it chose a potential mass market over the ritualist auratic form of the theater. This dynamic takes a particularly interesting form in the case of Mallarmé's *Livre*. Besides the ritual-ist reading envisioned by Mallarmé, the *Livre* was to be available for mass distribution, which would also serve to pay for the ritualist reading open only to a select coterie. The double vision of the *Livre,* at once mass-produced and unique, widely distributed and exclu-sive, testifies to this choice, while at the same time indicating Mallarmé's resistance to abandoning the auratic theater entirely.

8. For an extended discussion of The Wooster Group, see David Savran's excellent *Breaking the Rules.*

Bibliography

Abbott, H. Porter. "Reading as Theatre: Understanding Defamiliarization in Beckett's Art." *Modern Drama* 34 (March 1991): 5–22.

Ackerman, Alan L., Jr. *The Portable Theater: American Literature and the Nineteenth-Century Stage*. Baltimore: Johns Hopkins University Press, 1999.

Adorno, Theodor W. *Ästhetische Theorie*. Frankfurt am Main: Suhrkamp, 1970.

———. *Philosophie der neuen Musik*. 1949. Reprint, Frankfurt am Main: Suhrkamp, 1978.

———. "Versuch das Endspiel zu verstehen." In *Noten zur Literatur*. Frankfurt am Main: Suhrkamp, 1974.

———. "Versuch über Wagner." In *Die musikalischen Monographien,* 7–148. 1952. Reprint, Frankfurt am Main: Suhrkamp, 1971.

———. "Wagners Aktualität." In Theodor W. Adorno, *Gesammelte Schriften,* edited by Rolf Tiedemann, 16:543–64. 1964. Reprint, Frankfurt am Main: Suhrkamp, 1997.

Agamben, Giorgio. *Means without End: Notes on Politics*. Minneapolis: University of Minnesota Press, 2000.

———. *Potentialities: Collected Essays in Philosophy*. Stanford: Stanford University Press, 1999.

Albright, Daniel. "An Opera with No Acts: Four Saints in Three Acts." *Southern Review* 33, no. 3 (1999): 594–604.

Albrinck, Meg. "'How can a sister see Saint Therese suitably': Difficulties of Staging Gertrude Stein's *Four Saints in Three Acts*." *Women's Studies: An Interdisciplinary Journal* 25, no. 1 (1995): 1–22.

Appia, Adolphe. *Texts on Theatre*. Edited by Richard C. Beacham. London: Routledge, 1993.

Aristotle. *Poetics*. Edited by Stephen Halliwell. Cambridge: Harvard University Press, 1995.

Aronson, Arnold. *American Avant-garde Theatre: A History*. London: Routledge, 2000.

Atheron, James. *The Book at the Wake*. New York: Paul Appel, 1959.

Auslander, Philip. *From Acting to Performance: Essays in Modernism and Postmodernism*. London: Routledge, 1997.

———. *Liveness: Performance in a Mediatized World*. London: Routledge, 1999.

Austin, J. L. *How to Do Things with Words*. Cambridge: Harvard University Press, 1962.

Bakhtin, M. M. *The Dialogic Imagination*. Edited by Michael Holquist. Translated by Caryl Emerson and Michael Holquist. Austin: University of Texas Press, 1981.

Barish, Jonas. *The Antitheatrical Prejudice*. Berkeley: University of California Press, 1981.

Barkentin, Marjorie. *James Joyce's "Ulysses" in Nighttown*. Dramatized and transposed by Marjorie Barkentin under the supervision of Padraic Colum. New York: Random House, 1958.

Baudelaire, Charles. *Richard Wagner et "Tannhäuser" à Paris*. Introduction by Robert Kopp. Paris: Belles Lettres, 1994.

Baxmann, Inge. "Verbindung der Künste und Verknüpfung der Sinne: Zur Wagner-Rezeption der Avantgarde in Frankreich." In *Von Wagner zum Wagnérisme*, edited by Annegret Fauser and Manuela Schwartz, 513–34. Leipzig: Leipziger Universitätsverlag, 1999.

Beckett, Samuel. *The Complete Dramatic Works*. London: Faber & Faber, 1986.

———. *Eleutheria*. Translated by Barbara Wright. London: Faber & Faber, 1996.

———. *Warten auf Godot, En attendant Godot, Waiting for Godot*. Translated by Elmar Tophoven. Preface by Joachim Kaiser. Frankfurt am Main: Suhrkamp, 1971.

Beckett, Samuel, et al. *Our Exagmination Round his Factification for Incamination of Work in Progress*. With letters of protest by G. V. Slingsby and Vladimir Dixon. London: Faber & Faber, 1929.

Benjamin, Walter. *Charles Baudelaire: Ein Lyriker im Zeitalter der Hochkapitalismus*. 1969. Reprint, Frankfurt am Main: Suhrkamp, 1974.

———. *Illuminationen*. 1955. Reprint, Frankfurt am Main: Suhrkamp, 1977.

———. *Ursprung des deutschen Trauerspiels*. Frankfurt am Main: Suhrkamp, 1955.

———. *Versuche über Brecht*. 1955. Reprint, Frankfurt am Main: Suhrkamp, 1971.

Bennett, Benjamin K. "Strindberg and Ibsen: Towards a Cubism of Time in Drama." In *Modernism in European Drama: Ibsen, Strindberg, Pirandello, Beckett*, edited by Frederick J. Marker and Christopher Innes, 69–91. Toronto: University of Toronto Press, 1998.

———. *Theater as Problem: Modern Drama and Its Place in Literature*. Ithaca: Cornell University Press, 1990.

Bentley, Eric. *In Search of Theater*. New York: Vintage Books, 1954.

Berghaus, Günther. *Italian Futurist Theatre, 1909–1944*. Oxford: Clarendon, 1998.

Bergson, Henri. "Laughter." In *Comedy*, edited by Wylie Sypher, 59–190. Baltimore: Johns Hopkins University Press, 1980.

Berlin, Norman. "The Tragic Pleasure of Waiting for Godot." In *Beckett at 80 / Beckett in Context*, edited by Enoch Brater, 46–63. Oxford: Oxford University Press, 1986.

Berry, Ellen E. *Curved Thought and Textual Wandering: Gertrude Stein's Postmodernism.* Ann Arbor: University of Michigan Press, 1992.

Blackmur, R. P. *Language as Gesture: Essays in Poetry.* New York: Harcourt, Brace, 1952.

Blau, Herbert. *The Audience.* Baltimore: Johns Hopkins University Press, 1990.

Block, Haskall M. *Mallarmé and the Symbolist Drama.* Detroit: Wayne State University Press, 1963.

Bloom, Harold, ed. *Stéphane Mallarmé.* New York: Chelsea House, 1987.

———. *William Butler Yeats.* New York: Chelsea House, 1986.

Boal, Augusto. *The Theatre of the Oppressed in Europe: Forum Theatre.* London: Pluto, 1979.

Bourdieu, Pierre. *The Rules of Art: Genesis and Structure of the Literary Field.* Translated by Susan Emanuel. Stanford: Stanford University Press, 1995.

Bowers, Jane Palatini. *Gertrude Stein.* New York: St. Martin's, 1993.

———. *"They Watch Me as They Watch This": Gertrude Stein's Metadrama.* Philadelphia: University of Pennsylvania Press, 1991.

Brater, Enoch. "The 'Absurd' Actor in the Theatre of Samuel Beckett." *Educational Theatre Journal* 27 (1975): 197–207.

Brecht, Bertolt. *Der Jasager und Der Neinsager: Vorlagen, Fassungen, Materialien.* Frankfurt am Main: Suhrkamp, 1966.

———. *Gesammelte Werke.* 20 vols. Frankfurt am Main: Suhrkamp, 1967.

———. *"The Rise and Fall of the City of Mahagonny" and "The Seven Deadly Sins."* Edited by John Willett and Ralph Manheim. Translated by W. H. Auden and Chester Kallman. New York: Arcade, 1996.

Brecht, Bertolt, and Caspar Neher. *Antigonemodell 1948.* Berlin: Gebrüder Weiss, 1949.

Brook, Peter. *The Empty Space.* New York: Atheneum, 1968.

Brooks, Peter. *The Melodramatic Imagination: Balzac, Henry James, Melodrama, and the Mode of Excess.* New York: Columbia University Press, 1984.

Brown, Hilda Meldrum. *Leitmotiv and Drama: Wagner, Brecht, and the Limits of "Epic" Theatre.* Oxford: Clarendon; New York: Oxford University Press, 1991.

Brown, John Russel. *Theater Language: A Study of Arden, Osborne, Pinter, and Wesker.* New York: Taplinger, 1972.

Bryant-Bertail, Sarah. "*The Good Soldier Schweik* as Dialectical Theater." In *The Performance of Power: Theatrical Discourse and Politics,* edited by Sue-Ellen Case and Janelle Reinelt, 19–40. Iowa City: University of Iowa Press, 1991.

Bürger, Peter. *Theorie der Avantgarde.* Frankfurt am Main: Suhrkamp, 1974.

Burns, Christy L. *Gestural Politics: Stereotype and Parody in Joyce.* Albany: State University of New York Press, 2000.

Butler, Judith. *Bodies That Matter: On the Discursive Limits of "Sex."* London: Routledge, 1993.

———. *Gender Trouble: Feminism and the Subversion of Identity.* London: Routledge, 1990.

Calinescu, Matei. *Faces of Modernity: Avant-Garde, Decadence, Kitsch.* Bloomington: Indiana University Press, 1977.

Carlson, Marvin. "The Status of Stage Directions." *Studies in the Literary Imagination* 24 (fall 1991): 37–48.

Cavell, Stanley. *In Quest of the Ordinary: Lines of Skepticism and Romanticism.* Chicago: University of Chicago Press, 1988.

Certeau, Michel de. *Arts de faire: The Practice of Everyday Life.* Translated by Steven Rendall. Berkeley: University of California Press, 1984.

Ceymowa, Andrzej. "Defense of Stage Directions: Some Remarks on Language in Modern Drama." *Studia Anglica Posnaniensia: An International Review of English Studies* (Poznan, Poland) 13 (1981): 191–203.

Cixous, Hélène. "At Circe's, or the Self-Opener." *Boundary 2: A Journal of Postmodern Literature* 3 (1975): 387–97.

Clark, Timothy. "Being in Mime: Heidegger and Derrida on the Ontology of Literary Language." *Modern Language Notes* 101, no. 5 (1986): 1003–21.

Cohn, Dorrit. *Transparent Minds: Narrative Modes for Presenting Consciousness in Fiction.* Princeton: Princeton University Press, 1978.

Cohn, Ruby. *Just Play: Beckett's Theater.* Princeton: Princeton University Press, 1980.

Colum, Mary Maguire, and Padraic Colum. *Our Friend James Joyce.* Garden City, N.Y.: Doubleday, 1958.

Connor, Steven. "Jigajiga . . . Yummyyum . . . Pfuiiiiiii . . . Bbbbblllllllblbl-blbloschb! 'Circe's' Ventriloquy." In *Reading Joyce's "Circe,"* edited by Andrew Gibson, 93–142. Amsterdam: Rodopi, 1994.

Cope, Jackson I. "The Rhythmic Gesture: Image and Aesthetic in Joyce's *Ulysses.*" *ELH* 29 (March 1962): 67–89.

Craig, Edward Gordon. *On the Art of the Theatre.* 1911. Reprint, London: Heinemann, 1980.

Dahlhaus, Carl. *Richard Wagners Musikdramen.* Stuttgart: Reclam, 1996.

Darwin, Charles. *The Expression of the Emotions in Man and Animals.* Vol. 23 of *The Work of Charles Darwin.* Edited by Francis Darwin. London: William Pickering, 1989.

Davis, Douglas. "Post-Performancism." *Artforum* 20 (1981): 31–39.

Deak, Frantisek. *Symbolist Theater: The Formation of an Avant-Garde.* Baltimore: Johns Hopkins University Press, 1993.

Debord, Guy. *Society of the Spectacle.* Detroit: Black & Red, 1977.

DeKoven, Marianne. *A Different Language: Gertrude Stein's Experimental Writing.* Madison: University of Wisconsin Press, 1983.

Delaumosne, Abbé. *The Art of Oratory: System of Delsarte.* Translated by Angelique Arnaud. New York: E. S. Werner, 1884.

Deleuze, Gilles. *Différence et répétition.* Paris: Presses Universitaires de France, 1968.

De Man, Paul. *Blindness and Insight: Essays in the Rhetoric of Contemporary Criticism.* Minneapolis: University of Minneapolis Press, 1983.

De Marinis, Marco. *In cerca dell' attore: Un bilancio del Novecento teatrale.* Rome: Bulzoni, 2000.

Denby, Edwin. *Dance Writings and Poetry.* Edited by Robert Cornfield. New Haven: Yale University Press, 1998.

Derrida, Jacques. *La dissémination.* Paris: Éditions du Seuil, 1972.

———. *L'écriture et la différence.* Paris: Éditions du Seuil, 1967.

———. *Limited Inc.* Translated by Samuel Weber. Baltimore: Johns Hopkins University Press, 1988.

———. *Specters of Marx: The State of the Debt, the Work of Mourning, and the New International.* Translated by Peggy Kamuf with an introduction by Bernd Magnus and Stephen Cullenberg. New York: Routledge, 1994.

Desmond, Jane C., ed. *Meaning in Motion: New Cultural Studies of Dance.* Durham: Duke University Press, 1997.

Diamond, Elin. *Unmaking Mimesis: Essays on Feminism and Theater.* London: Routledge, 1997.

Donoghue, Denis. *The Third Voice: Modern British and American Verse Drama.* Princeton: Princeton University Press, 1959.

Dorn, Karen. *Players and Painted Stage: The Theatre of W. B. Yeats.* Sussex: Harvester, 1984.

Douglas, Ann. *Terrible Honesty: Mongrel Manhattan in the 1920s.* New York: Farrar, Straus, & Giroux, 1995.

Duckworth, Colin. *Angles of Darkness: Dramatic Effect in Beckett and Ionesco.* London: George Allen & Unwin, 1972.

Dujardin, Edouard. *The Bays Are Sere and Interior Monologue.* 1931. Reprint, London: Libris, 1991.

Eco, Umberto. *The Limits of Interpretation.* Bloomington: Indiana University Press, 1990.

———. *La ricerca della lingua perfetta nella cultura europea.* Bari: Editori Lateraza, 1993.

———. *A Theory of Semiotics.* Bloomington: Indiana University Press, 1976.

Eisenstein, Sergei. *Film Form: Essays in Film Theory.* Edited and translated by Jay Leyda. San Diego: Harcourt, Brace, 1977.

Eliot, Simon. *Some Patterns and Trends in British Publishing, 1800–1919.* London: Bibliographical Society, 1994.

Eliot, T. S. *Poetry and Drama.* London: Faber & Faber, 1951.

Ellis, Sylvia C. *The Plays of W. B. Yeats: Yeats and the Dancer.* New York: St. Martin's, 1995.

Esslin, Martin. *Brecht, a Choice of Evils: A Critical Study of the Man, His Work, and His Opinions.* 1959. Reprint, London: Methuen, 1980.

Fischer-Lichte, Erika. *Geschichte des Dramas: Epochen der Identität auf dem Theater von der Antike bis zur Gegenwart.* Vol. 2, *Von der Romantik bis zur Gegenwart.* Tübingen: Francke, 1990.

————. *The Show and the Gaze of Theatre: A European Perspective.* Iowa City: University of Iowa Press, 1997.

Fisher, Dominique. *Staging of Language and Language(s) of the Stage: Mallarmé's Poème Critique and Artaud's Poetry-Minus-Text.* New York: Peter Lang, 1994.

Flannery, James W. *W. B. Yeats and the Idea of a Theatre: The Early Abbey Theatre in Theory and Practice.* New Haven: Yale University Press, 1976.

Flusser, Vilèm. *Gesten: Versuch einer Phänomenologie.* Frankfurt am Main: Fischer, 1995.

Foucault, Michel. "Theatrum Philosophicum." Translated by Donald F. Bouchard and Sherry Simon. In *Language, Counter-Memory, Practice,* edited by Donald F. Bouchard, 165–96. Ithaca: Cornell University Press, 1977.

Freud, Sigmund. *Psychopathologie des Alltagslebens.* Berlin: S. Karger, 1912.

Freud, Sigmund, and Joseph Breuer. *Studien über Hysterie.* Leipzig: Franz Deuticke, 1916.

Fried, Michael. *Absorption and Theatricality: Painting and Beholder in the Age of Diderot.* Chicago: University of Chicago Press, 1980.

————. "Art and Objecthood." *Artforum* 5, no. 10 (1967): 12–23.

————. *Art and Objecthood: Essays and Reviews.* Chicago: University of Chicago Press, 1998.

Fuchs, Elinor. *The Death of Character: Perspectives on Theater after Modernism.* Bloomington: Indiana University Press, 1996.

Fuchs, Georg. *Die Schaubühne der Zukunft.* Berlin: Schuster & Loeffler, 1905.

Fuegi, John. *Brecht and Company: Sex, Politics, and the Making of the Modern Drama.* New York: Grove, 1994.

Genette, Gérard. *Figures of Literary Discourse.* Translated by Alan Sheridan. New York: Columbia University Press, 1982.

————. *Paratexts: Thresholds of Interpretation.* Translated by Jane E. Lewin. Cambridge: Cambridge University Press, 1987.

Gilbert, Michel. *Bertolt Brecht's Striving for Reason, Even in Music: A Critical Assessment.* New York: Peter Lang, 1988.

Goehr, Lydia. *The Quest for Voice: Music, Politics, and the Limits of Philosophy.* Berkeley: University of California Press, 1998.

Gontarski, S. E. "*Company* for Company: Androgyny and Theatricality in Samuel Beckett's Prose." In *Beckett's Later Fiction and Drama: Texts for Company,* edited by James Acheson and Kateryna Arthur, 193–202. London: Macmillan, 1987.

————. *The Intent of Undoing in Samuel Beckett's Dramatic Texts.* Bloomington: Indiana University Press, 1985.

Gould, Evlyn. *Virtual Theater from Diderot to Mallarmé.* Baltimore: Johns Hopkins University Press, 1989.

Grant, Gail. *Technical Manual and Dictionary of Classical Ballet.* New York: Dover, 1967.

Grossman, Evelyne. *Artaud/Joyce: Le corps et le texte*. Paris: Editions Nathan, 1996.

Habermas, Jürgen. *Strukturwandel der Öffentlichkeit: Untersuchungen zu einer Kategoire der bürgerlichen Gesellschaft*. 1962. Reprint, Frankfurt am Main: Suhrkamp, 1990.

Haerdter, Michael. *Samuel Beckett inszeniert das "Endspiel."* Frankfurt am Main: Suhrkamp, 1967.

Hampson, R. G. "'Tofts Cumbersome Whirligig': Hallucinations, Theatricality, and Mnemotechnic in V.A.19 and the First Edition Text of 'Circe.'" In *Reading Joyce's "Circe,"* edited by Andrew Gibson, 143–78. Amsterdam: Rodopi, 1994.

Harkness, Marguerite. "Gesture in 'Circe.'" In *Joyce and Paris, 1902 . . . 1920–1940 . . . 1975: Papers from the Fifth International James Joyce Symposium,* edited by J. Aubert and M. Jolas, 17–19. Paris: Editions du C.N.R.S, 1979.

Haxell, Nichola Anne. "Le Serpent qui Danse: Woman as Dancer in the Works of Baudelaire, Mallarmé, and Colette." *Romance Studies* 19 (1991): 117–24.

Hayman, David. *Joyce et Mallarmé*. 2 vols. Paris: Lettres Modernes, 1956.

Heath, Stephan. "Joyce in Language." In *James Joyce: New Perspectives,* edited by Colin MacCabe, 129–48. Bloomington: Indiana University Press, 1982.

Hegel, G. W. F. *Vorlesungen über Ästhetik III*. Frankfurt am Main: Suhrkamp, 1986.

Heller, Jane Ruth. *Coleridge, Lamb, Hazlitt, and the Reader of Drama*. Columbia: University of Missouri Press, 1990.

Henderson, Archibald. *The Changing Drama*. New York: Henry Holt, 1914.

Herring, Phillip E., ed. *Joyce's Notes and Early Drafts from Ulysses: Selections from the Buffalo Collection*. Charlottesville: University Press of Virginia, 1977.

Hitchcock, Alfred. *Stage Fright*. 110 min. Great Britain, 1950.

Hoffman, Michael J. *Gertrude Stein*. Boston: Twayne, 1976.

Hofmannsthal, Hugo von. *Sämtliche Werke*. Critical edition. 38 vols. Frankfurt am Main: Hochstift, 1982.

Horkheimer, Max, and Theodor W. Adorno. *Dialektik der Aufklärung: Philosophische Fragmente*. Frankfurt am Main: Fischer, 1969.

Hubert, Marie-Claude. "Corps et voix dans le théâtre de Beckett a partir des années soixante." *Cahiers de L'Association Internationale des Études Françaises,* 1994.

Huyssen, Andreas. *After the Great Divide: Modernism, Mass Culture, Postmodernism*. Bloomington: Indiana University Press, 1986.

Ingenhoff, Anette. *Drama oder Epos? Richard Wagners Gattungstheorie des musikalischen Dramas*. Tübingen: Niemeyer, 1987.

Iser, Wolfgang. *Der Akt des Lesens: Theorie ästhetischer Wirkung*. Munich: W. Fink, 1976.

Issacharoff, Michael. *Discourse as Performance*. Stanford: Stanford University Press, 1989.

————. "Inscribed Performance." In *Rivista di Litterature Moderne e Comparate* (Pisa) 39 (1986): 93–106.

Issacharoff, Michael, and Robin F. Jones, eds. *Performing Texts.* Philadelphia: University of Pennsylvania Press, 1988.

Jacques-Dalcroze, Émile. *The Jacques-Dalcroze Method of Eurhythmics.* New York: H. W. Gray, 1920.

James, Henry. *The Letters of Henry James.* Edited by Percy Lubbock. Vol. 1. New York: Octagon Books, 1970.

Jameson, Fredric. *Brecht and Method.* New York: Verso, 1998.

————. *Postmodernism, or The Cultural Logic of Late Capitalism.* Durham: Duke University Press, 1991.

————. "Reflections on the Brecht-Lukács Debate." In *The Ideologies of Theory: Essays, 1971–1986,* vol. 2, *The Syntax of History,* 133–47. Minneapolis: University of Minnesota Press, 1989.

————. "Ulysses in History." In *James Joyce: A Collection of Critical Essays,* edited by Mary T. Reynold, 145–58. Englewood Cliffs, N.J.: Simon & Schuster, 1993.

Jelavich, Peter. *Munich and Theatrical Modernism: Politics, Playwriting, and Performance, 1890–1914.* Cambridge: Harvard University Press, 1985.

Johnson, Barbara. *Défigurations du langage poétique.* Paris: Flammarion, 1979.

————. *A World of Difference.* Baltimore: Johns Hopkins University Press, 1987.

Jousse, Marcel. *L'anthropologie du geste.* 1969. Reprint, Paris: Gallimard, 1974.

Joyce, James. *The Critical Writings.* Edited by Ellsworth Mason and Richard Ellmann. With a foreword by Guy Davenport. Ithaca: Cornell University Press, 1989.

————. *Finnegans Wake.* 1939. Reprint, London: Faber & Faber, 1975.

————. *Poems and Shorter Writings.* 1939. Reprint, London: Faber & Faber, 1991.

————. *Stephen Hero.* Edited from the manuscript in the Harvard College Library by Theodore Spencer. 1944. Reprint, New York: New Directions, 1963.

————. *Ulysses.* Edited by Hans Walter Gabler. London: Penguin, 1986.

Kandinsky, Wassily. *Essays über Kunst und Künstler.* Bern: Benteli-Verlag, 1955.

Kaufmann, Michael. *Textual Bodies: Modernism, Postmodernism, and Print.* Lewisburg, Pa.: Bucknell University Press, 1994.

Kermode, Frank. *Romantic Image.* New York: Vintage Books, 1964.

Kern, Stephen. *The Culture of Time and Space, 1880–1918.* Cambridge: Harvard University Press, 1983.

Kirby, Michael. *A Formalist Theatre.* Philadelphia: University of Pennsylvania Press, 1987.

Kivy, Peter. *Sound and Semblance: Reflections on Musical Representation.* Princeton: Princeton University Press, 1984.

Klages, Ludwig. *Grundlegung der Wissenschaft vom Ausdruck.* Bonn: H. Bouvier, 1950.

Klein, Richard. *Solidarität mit Metaphysik? Ein Versuch über die musikphiloso-phische Problematik der Wagner-Kritik Theodor W. Adornos.* Würzburg: Königshausen & Neumann, 1991.

Knowlson, James. "Beckett as Director: The Manuscript Production Note-books and Critical Interpretation." In *Modernism in European Drama: Ibsen, Strindberg, Pirandello, Beckett,* edited by Christopher Innes and Frederick J. Marker, 212–27. Toronto: University of Toronto Press, 1998.

———. *Damned to Fame: The Life of Samuel Beckett.* New York: Simon & Schuster, 1996.

Kott, Jan. *Theatre Notebook, 1947–1967.* Translated by Boleslaw Taborski. New York: Doubleday, 1968.

Kristeva, Julia. Σημειωτικη: *Recherches pour une sémanalyse.* Paris: Editions du Seuil, 1969.

———. *La révolution du langage poétique: L'avant-garde à la fin du XIXe siècle: Lautréamont et Mallarmé.* Paris: Editions du Seuil, 1974.

Lacoue-Labarthe, Philippe. *Musica ficta (figures de Wagner).* Paris: Christian Bourgois Editeur, 1991.

Langhan, Janine D. *Hegel and Mallarmé.* Lanham, Md.: University Press of America, 1986.

Lawrence, D. H. *Sea and Sardinia.* 1921. Reprint, London: Olive Press, 1989.

Le Brun, Charles. *L'expression des passions et autres conférences.* Edited by Julien Philipe. Paris: Editions Dédale Maisonneuve et Larose, 1994.

Lefebvre, Henri. *Critique de la vie quotidienne.* Paris: L'Arche, 1958.

Lehmann, Hans-Thies. *Postdramatisches Theater.* Frankfurt am Main: Verlag der Autoren, 1999.

Levin, David J., ed. *Opera through Other Eyes.* Stanford: Stanford University Press, 1993.

Levin, David L. *Richard Wagner, Fritz Lang, and the Nibelungen: The Dramaturgy of Disavowal.* Princeton: Princeton University Press, 1998.

Levin, Jonathan. *The Poetics of Transition: Emerson, Pragmatism, and American Literary Modernism.* Durham: Duke University Press, 1999.

Lewis, Wyndham. *Time and Western Man.* Edited with an afterword and notes by Paul Edwards. Santa Rosa, Calif.: Black Sparrow, 1993.

Lindenberger, Herbert. *Opera: The Extravagant Art.* Ithaca: Cornell University Press, 1984.

———. *Opera in History: From Monteverdi to Cage.* Stanford: Stanford University Press, 1998.

Litvak, Joseph. *Caught in the Act: Theatricality in the Nineteenth-Century English Novel.* Berkeley: University of California Press, 1992.

Lukács, Georg. *Entwicklungsgeschichte des modernen Dramas.* Vol. 15 of *Georg Lukács Werke.* 1911. Reprint, Darmstadt: Luchterhand, 1981.

———. *Wider den mißverstandenen Realismus.* Hamburg: Claasen, 1958.

Lyons, Charles R. "Beckett's Fundamental Theatre: The Plays from *Not I* to

What Where." In *Beckett's Later Fiction and Drama: Texts for Company,* edited by James Acheson and Kateryna Arthur, 80–97. London: Macmillan, 1987.

Madau, Jean Pol. "Langue, mythe, musique: Rousseau, Nietzsche, Mallarmé, Levi-Strauss." In *Littérature et musique,* edited by Raphael Celis, 75–110. Brussels: Facultés Univ. Saint-Louis, 1982.

Mallarmé, Stéphane. *Correspondance.* Compiled and annotated by Henri Mondor and Lloyd James Austin. 11 vols. Paris: Gallimard, 1959–85.

———. *Igitur, Divagations, Un coup de dés.* Introduction by D'Yves Bonnefoy. Paris: Gallimard, 1976.

———. *Les interviews de Mallarmé.* Presented and annotated by Dieter Schwarz. Neuchâtel: Editions Ides et Calendres, 1995.

———. *Les noces d'Hérodiade, Mystère.* Edited by Gardner Davies. Paris: Gallimard, 1959.

———. *Oeuvres complètes.* Edited by Bertrand Marchal. Vol. 1. Paris: Gallimard, 1998.

———. *Poésies: Anecdotes ou poèmes, pages diveses.* Edited by Daniel Leuwers. Paris: Librairie Générale Française, 1977.

Mann, Thomas. "Versuch über das Theater." In *Reden und Aufsätze I,* 74–113. Oldenburg: Fischer, 1965.

Marinetti, F. T. *Teoria e invenzione futurista.* Milan: Arnoldo Mondadori, 1968.

Marranca, Bonnie. "Performance/Art/Theatre." In *Theatrewritings,* 143–46. New York: Performing Arts Journal, 1984. Originally published as "Soho's Bourgeois Gentilhomme: Douglas Davis" in *Live* 6–7 (1982).

———. *Theater of Images.* Baltimore: Johns Hopkins University Press, 1977.

Mauss, Marcel. "Essay sur le don." In *Sociologie et anthropologie.* Paris: Presses Universitaires de France, 1960.

McCarthy, Patrick. "Non-Dramatic Illusion in 'Circe.'" in *Joyce and Paris: 1902 . . . 1920–1940 . . . 1975: Papers from the Fifth International James Joyce Symposium 1975,* edited by J. Aubert and M. Jolas, 23–26. Paris: Editions du C.N.R.S., 1979.

McKenzie, Jon. *Perform or Else: From Discipline to Performance.* London: Routledge, 2001.

McMillan, Dougald, and Martha Fehsenfeld. *Beckett in the Theatre: The Author as Practical Playwright and Director.* London: J. Calder; New York: Riverrun, 1988.

McMulligan, Anna. "Samuel Beckett as Director: The Art of Mastering Failure." In *The Cambridge Companion to Beckett,* edited by John Phillin, 196–208. Cambridge: Cambridge University Press, 1994.

Meisel, Martin. *Realizations: Narrative, Pictorial, and Theatrical Arts in Nineteenth-Century England.* Princeton: Princeton University Press, 1983.

Meltzer, Anabelle Henkin. *Dada and Surrealist Performance.* Baltimore: Johns Hopkins University Press, 1976.

Meltzer, Françoise. *Salome and the Dance of Writing: Portraits of Mimesis in Literature*. Chicago: University of Chicago Press, 1987.

Mendelson, Edward. "Encyclopedic Narrative: From Dante to Pynchon." *Modern Language Notes* 91 (1976): 1267–75.

Mésavage, Mathilda. "Écriture, danse, et mondes imaginaires." *L'Esprit Créateur* 34, no. 3 (1994): 64–70.

Milesi, Lauren. "Vico . . . Jousse: Joyce . . . Langue." *La Révue des Lettres Modernes: Histoire des Idées et des Littératures,* 1988, 834–39.

Mondor, Henri. *La vie de Mallarmé*. Paris: Gallimard, 1941.

Moretti, Franco. *Modern Epic: The World-System from Goethe to García Márquez*. Translated by Quintin Hoare. London: Verso, 1996.

Morris, Desmond, Peter Collett, Peter Marsh, and Marie O'Shaughnessy. *Gestures, Their Origins and Distribution*. New York: Stein & Day, 1979.

Müller, Heiner. *Mauser*. Berlin: Rotbuch, 1997.

Nabokov, Vladimir. *Lectures on Literature*. Edited by Fredson Bowers. Introduction by John Updike. San Diego: Harcourt Brace Jovanovich, 1982.

Nietzsche, Friedrich. *Die Geburt der Tragödie aus dem Geiste der Musik*. 1872. Reprint, Stuttgart: Kröner, 1976.

———. *Richard Wagner in Bayreuth, Der Fall Wagner, Nietzsche contra Wagner*. Stuttgart: Reclam, 1991.

———. *Unzeitgemäße Betrachtungen*. 1876. Reprint, Frankfurt am Main: Insel, 1981.

Nussbaum, Martha. *The Fragility of Goodness: Luck and Ethics in Greek Tragedy and Philosophy*. Cambridge: Cambridge University Press, 1986.

O'Casey, Shivaun. *Women in Beckett: Performance and Critical Perspectives*. Edited by Linda Ben-Zvi. Urbana: University of Illinois Press, 1990.

Oppel, Frances Nesbitt. *Mask and Tragedy: Yeats and Nietzsche, 1902–10*. Charlottesville: University Press of Virginia, 1987.

Oppenheim, Lois, ed. *Directing Beckett*. Ann Arbor: University of Michigan Press, 1994.

Pavis, Patrice. *Languages of the Stage: Essays in the Semiology of the Theatre*. New York: Performing Arts Journal, 1982.

Perloff, Marjorie. *The Futurist Moment: Avant-Garde, Avant Guerre, and the Language of Rupture*. Chicago: University of Chicago Press, 1986.

———. *The Poetics of Indeterminacy: Rimbaud to Cage*. Princeton: Princeton University Press, 1981.

———. *Radical Artifice: Writing Poetry in the Age of Media*. Chicago: University of Chicago Press, 1991.

Peters, Julie Stone. *Congreve, the Drama, and the Printed Word*. Stanford: Stanford University Press, 1990.

———. *The Theatre of the Book, 1480–1880: Print, Text, and Performance in Europe*. Oxford: Oxford University Press, 2000.

Pfitzner, Hans Erich. *Werk und Wiedergabe.* Augsburg: Dr. Benno Filser, 1929.

Plato. *Plato's Republic.* Edited by Lewis Campbell and Benjamin Jowett. New York: Garland, 1987.

Platt, L. H. "Ulysses 15 and the Irish Literary Theatre." In *Reading Joyce's "Circe,"* edited by Andrew Gibson, 33–62. Amsterdam: Rodopi, 1994.

Pound, Ezra, and Ernest Fenollosa. *The Classic Nôh Theatre of Japan.* 1917. New York: New Directions Paperback, 1959.

Pountney, Rosemary. *Theatre of Shadows: Samuel Beckett's Drama, 1956–76.* Gerrards Cross, Buckinghamshire: Smythe, 1988.

Pretzsch, Paul, ed. *Cosima Wagner und Houston Stewart Chamberlain im Briefwechsel 1888–1908.* Leipzig: Reclam, 1934.

Puchner, Martin. "Polyphonous Gestures: Wagnerian Modernism from Mallarmé to Stravinsky." *Criticism* 41 (winter 1999): 25–40.

Qamber, Akhtar. *Yeats and the Noh: With Two Plays for Dancers by Yeats and Two Noh Plays.* New York: Weatherhill, 1974.

Quigley, Austin E. *The Modern Stage and Other Worlds.* New York: Methuen, 1985.

Rabaté, Michel. *James Joyce: Authorized Reader.* Baltimore: Johns Hopkins University Press, 1991.

Rampley, Mathew. *Nietzsche, Aesthetics, and Modernity.* Cambridge: Cambridge University Press, 2000.

Ratzinger, Joseph, and John Auer. *Dogmatic Theology: A General Doctrine of the Sacraments and the Mystery of the Eucharist.* Translated by Erasmo Leiva-Merikakis. Washington, D.C.: Catholic University of America Press, 1995.

Reinelt, Janelle G. *After Brecht: British Epic Theater.* Ann Arbor: University of Michigan Press, 1994.

Reinelt, Janelle G., and Joseph R. Roach, eds. *Critical Theory and Performance.* Ann Arbor: University of Michigan Press, 1992.

Richardson, Alan. *A Mental Theater: Poetic Drama and Consciousness in the Romantic Age.* University Park: Pennsylvania State University Press, 1988.

Roach, Joseph R. *The Player's Passion: Studies in the Science of Acting.* Ann Arbor: University of Michigan Press, 1993.

Robinson, Marc. *The Other American Drama.* Cambridge: Cambridge University Press, 1994.

Roche, Anthony. *Contemporary Irish Drama: From Beckett to McGuinness.* New York: St. Martin's, 1995.

Rousseau, Jean-Jacques. *Lettre à M. d'Alembert sur son article Genève.* Paris: Flammarion, 1967.

Ruddick, Lisa. *Reading Gertrude Stein: Body, Text, Gnosis.* Ithaca: Cornell University Press, 1990.

Ryan, Bestry Alayne. *Gertrude Stein's Theatre of the Absolute.* Ann Arbor, Mich.: UMI Research Press, 1980.

Safford, Lisa Bixensteine. "Mallarmé's Influence on Degas's Aesthetics of Dance in His Late Period." *Nineteenth-Century French Studies* 21 (spring–summer 1993): 419–33.

Said, Edward. *Musical Elaborations.* New York: Columbia University Press, 1991.

Sartre, Jean Paul. *Mallarmé: La lucidité et sa face d'ombre.* Paris: Gallimard, 1986.

Savran, David. *Breaking the Rules: The Wooster Group.* New York: Theatre Communications Group, 1988.

Schadewaldt, Wolfgang. *Die griechische Tragödie.* Frankfurt am Main: Suhrkamp, 1991.

Schechner, Richard. *Performance Theory.* London: Routledge, 1988.

Scheppard, Richard. *Modernism–Dada–Postmodernism.* Evanston: Northwestern University Press, 2000.

Scherer, Jacques. *Le "Livre" de Mallarmé: Premières recherches sur des documents inédits.* Preface by Henri Mondor. Paris: Gallimard, 1957.

Scheunemann, Dietrich. "Montage in Theater and Film: Observations on Eisenstein and Brecht." In *Avant-Garde: Interdisciplinary and International Review,* edited by Jan van der Eng and Willem Weststeijn, 109–36. Amsterdam: Rodopi, 1991.

Schmidt, Jean-Claude. "Ethics of Gesture." In *Fragments for a History of the Human Body, I–III,* edited by Michel Feher, Ramona Naddaff, and Nadia Tazi, 128–47. New York: Zone Books, 1989.

Schneider, Alan. "'Any Way You Like, Alan': Working with Beckett." *Theatre Quarterly* 5 (September–November 1975).

Scolnicov, Hanna, and Peter Holland, eds. *Reading Plays: Interpretation and Reception.* Cambridge: Cambridge University Press, 1991.

Searle, John. "The Logical Status of Fictional Discourse." *New Literary History* 6 (1975): 319–32.

Sedgwick, Eve Kosofsky. *Epistemology of the Closet.* Berkeley: University of California Press, 1990.

Segel, Harold B. *Body Ascendant: Modernism and the Physical Imperative.* Baltimore: Johns Hopkins University Press, 1998.

———. *Turn-of-the-Century Cabaret: Paris, Barcelona, Berlin, Munich, Vienna, Cracow, Moscow, St. Petersburg, Zürich.* New York: Columbia University Press, 1987.

———. *Twentieth-Century Russian Drama: From Gorky to the Present.* New York: Columbia University Press, 1979.

Seidel, Michael. *Epic Geography: James Joyce's Ulysses.* Princeton: Princeton University Press, 1976.

Sekine, Masura. "Yeats and the Noh." In *Irish Writers and the Theatre,* edited by Sekine Masura. Gerrards Cross, Buckinghamshire: Smythe, 1986.

Sekine, Masaru, and Christopher Murray. *Yeats and the Noh: A Comparative Study.* Gerrards Cross, Buckinghamshire: Smythe, 1990.

Sennett, Richard. *The Fall of Public Man.* New York: Knopf, 1977.

Shaw, Bernard. *The Perfect Wagnerite: A Commentary on the Nibelung's Ring.* New York: Dover, 1967.

Shaw, Mary Lewis. "Concrete and Abstract Poetry: The World as Text and the Text as World." *Visible Language* 23 (winter 1989): 29–43.

———. *Performance in the Texts of Mallarmé: The Passage from Art to Ritual.* University Park: Pennsylvania State University Press, 1993.

Simpson, Michael. *Closet Performances: Political Exhibition and Prohibition in the Dramas of Byron and Shelley.* Stanford: Stanford University Press, 1998.

Smith, Paul J., and Nic. Van der Toorn. "Le discours Didascalique dans *En Attendant Godot* et *Pas.*" In *Samuel Beckett Today/Aujourd'hui,* edited by Marius Buning, Sjef Houppermans, and Danièle de Ruyter. Amsterdam: Rodopi, 1992.

Sontag, Susan. "Film and Theatre." *TDR: Tulane Drama Review* 11, no. 1 (1966): 24–37.

States, Bert O. *The Pleasures of the Play.* Ithaca: Cornell University Press, 1994.

Stegmann, Vera. "An Opera for Three Pennies, a Violin for Ten Francs." In *Brecht Unbound,* edited by James K. Lyon and Hans-Peter Breuer. Newark: University of Delaware Press, 1995.

Stein, Gertrude. *Everybody's Autobiography.* New York: Vintage Books, 1973.

———. *Four Saints in Three Acts.* Elite Recordings 1982. Compact sound disk.

———. *Geography and Plays.* Edited by Cyrena N. Pondron. Madison: University of Wisconsin Press, 1993.

———. *How to Write.* 1931. Reprint, Los Angeles: Sun & Moon Press, 1995.

———. *Last Operas and Plays.* Edited by Carl van Vechten. 1949. Reprint, with an introduction by Bonnie Marranca, Baltimore: Johns Hopkins University Press, 1995.

Steinweg, Reiner. *Das Lehrstück: Brechts Theorie einer Politisch-Ästhetischen Erziehung.* Stuttgart: Metzlerische Verlagsbuchhandlung, 1972.

———. *Lehrstück und episches Theater: Brechts Theorie und die theaterpädagogische Praxis.* Frankfurt am Main: Brandes & Apsel, 1995.

Stephens, John Russel. *The Profession of the Playwright: British Theatre, 1800–1900.* Cambridge: Cambridge University Press, 1992.

Stravinsky, Igor. *Poetics of Music in the Form of Six Lessons.* 1942. Reprint, Cambridge: Harvard University Press, 1970.

Suchy, Patricia A. "When Words Collide: The Stage Direction as Utterance." *Journal of Dramatic Theory and Criticism* 6 (fall 1991): 69–82.

Symons, Arthur. *Poems.* 2 vols. London: Martin Secker, 1924.

———. *Studies in the Seven Arts.* Edited by Jan Fletcher and John Stokes. New York: Garland, 1984.

Szondi, Peter. *Das lyrische Drama des Fin de Siècle.* Frankfurt am Main: Suhrkamp, 1975.

———. *Theorie des modernen Dramas (1889–1950).* Frankfurt am Main: Suhrkamp, 1963.

Tafuri, Manfredo. *The Sphere and the Labyrinth: Avant-Gardes and Architecture from Piranesi to the 1970s.* Translated by Pellegrino d'Acierno and Robert Connolly. Cambridge: MIT Press, 1990.

Taylor, Richard. *The Drama of W. B. Yeats: Irish Myth and the Japanese No.* New Haven: Yale University Press, 1976.

Theweleit, Klaus. *Heiner Müller: Traumtext.* Frankfurt am Main: Stroemfeld, 1996.

———. *Virgil Thomson.* New York: Knopf, 1966.

———. *A Virgil Thomson Reader.* With an introduction by John Rockwell. Boston: Houghton Mifflin, 1981.

Todorov, Tzvetan. *Theories of the Symbol.* Translated by Catherine Porter. Ithaca: Cornell University Press, 1982.

Tommasini, Anthony. *Virgil Thomson's Musical Portraits.* New York: Pendragon, 1986.

Ubersfeld, Anne. *Lire le théâtre I.* 1977. Reprint, Paris: Belin, 1996.

———. *Lire le téâtre II: L'école du spectateur.* 1981. Reprint, Paris: Belin, 1996.

Vendler, Helen Hennessy. *Yeats's Vision and the Later Plays.* Cambridge: Harvard University Press, 1963.

Wagner, Richard. *Gesammelte Schriften und Dichtungen.* 10 vols. Leipzig: Verlag von Fritzsch, 1871–73.

———. *Oper und Drama.* 1852. Reprint, Stuttgart: Reclam, 1984.

———. *Siegfried.* London: Ernst Eulenburg, 1980.

Wagner, Valeria. *Bound to Act: Models for Action, Dramas of Inaction.* Stanford: Stanford University Press, 1999.

Wales, Katie. "'Bloom Passes through Several Walls': The Stage Directions in 'Circe.'" In *Reading Joyce's "Circe,"* edited by Andrew Gibson, 241–78. Amsterdam: Rodopi, 1994.

Watson, Steven. *Prepare for Saints: Gertrude Stein, Virgil Thomson, and the Mainstreaming of American Modernism.* New York: Random House, 1998.

Watt, Ian. *The Rise of the Novel: Studies in Defoe, Richardson, and Fielding.* Berkeley: University of California Press, 1957.

Webb, Barbara. "The Centrality of Race to the Modernist Aesthetics of Gertrude Stein's *Four Saints in Three Acts.*" *Modernism/Modernity* 7 (September 2000): 447–69.

Weill, Kurt. *Musik und Theater: Gesammelte Schriften.* Leipzig: Henschelverlag Kunst und Gesellschaft, 1990.

Weiner, Marc A. "Reading the Ideal." *New German Critique* 69 (1996): 53–83.

———. *Richard Wagner and the Anti-Semitic Imagination.* Lincoln: University of Nebraska Press, 1995.

Weir, Lorraine. "Choreography of Gesture: Marcel Jousse and Finnegans Wake." *James Joyce Quarterly* 14 (1977): 131–325.

Werner, Hans-Georg. "Gestische Lyrik: Zum Zusammenhang von Wirkungsabsicht und literarischer Technik in Gedichten Bertolt Brechts." *Germanica Wratislaviensia* 22 (1975): 5–27.

Williams, Raymond. *The Politics of Modernism: Against the New Conformists.* Edited with an introduction by Tony Pinkney. London: Verso, 1989.

Wilson, Edmund. *Axel's Castle: A Study in the Imaginative Literature of 1870–1930.* New York: Charles Scribner's Sons, 1931.

Winters, Yvor. *The Poetry of W. B. Yeats.* Denver: A. Swallow, 1960.

Wirth, Andrej. "Gertrude Stein und ihre Kritik der dramatischen Vernunft." In *LiLi: Zeitschrift für Literaturwissenschaft und Linguistik* 12, no. 46 (1982): 64–74.

Wöhrle, Dieter. *Bertolt Brechts medienästhetische Versuche.* Cologne: Prometh, 1988.

Worth, Katherine. *The Irish Drama of Europe from Yeats to Beckett.* Atlantic Highlands, N.J.: Humanities Press, 1978.

———. "The Space and the Sound in Beckett's Theatre." In *Beckett: The Shape Changer,* edited by Katharine Worth, 183–218. London: Routledge & Kegan Paul, 1975.

Worthen, William B. *The Idea of the Actor: Drama and the Ethics of Performance.* Princeton: Princeton University Press, 1984.

———. *Modern Drama and the Rhetoric of the Theater.* Berkeley: University of California Press, 1992.

Worton, Michael. "*Waiting for Godot* and *Endgame:* Theatre as Text." In *The Cambridge Companion to Beckett,* edited by John Philling, 67–87. Cambridge: Cambridge University Press, 1994.

Yeats, William Butler. *The Autobiography of William Butler Yeats.* 1924. Reprint, New York: Macmillan, 1965.

———. *The Collected Plays of W. B. Yeats.* New York: Macmillan, 1953.

———. *The Collected Poems.* Edited by Richard J. Finneran. Rev. 2d ed. New York: Scribner, 1996.

———. *Explorations.* New York: Macmillan, 1962.

———. *The Variorum Edition of the Plays of W. B. Yeats.* Edited by Russel K. Alspach. New York: Macmillan, 1966.

Zenn, Fritz. "'Circe' as Harking Back in Provective Arrangement." In *Reading Joyce's "Circe,"* edited by Andrew Gibson, 63–92. Amsterdam: Rodopi, 1994.

Zizek, Slavoj. *The Sublime Object of Ideology.* New York: Verso, 1989.

Index